MW01129353

The Complete Book of the
GREAT MUSICIANS

JOHN BULL, 1580

The Complete Book of the

GREAT MUSICIANS

A Course in Appreciation
for Young Readers

by

Percy A. Scholes

YESTERDAY'S CLASSICS

ITHACA, NEW YORK

This edition, first published in 2021 by Yesterday's Classics, an imprint of Yesterday's Classics, LLC, is an unabridged republication of the text originally published by Oxford University Press in 1923. For the complete listing of the books that are published by Yesterday's Classics, please visit www.yesterdaysclassics. com. Yesterday's Classics is the publishing arm of Gateway to the Classics which presents the complete text of hundreds of classic books for children at www. gatewaytotheclassics.com.

ISBN: 978-1-63334-141-8

Yesterday's Classics, LLC
PO Box 339
Ithaca, NY 14851

INTRODUCTION

The Book of the Great Musicians, designed for the children on lines calculated to interest them, is an addition to the most important branch of musical education. Its very simplicity is its highest recommendation; it invites the children's confidence and stimulates their curiosity; it makes the whole thing rather like a game in which an individual child or a whole class may find a great deal of pleasure. It combines in a happy way the basic facts of music (such as melody, harmony, structure) with the living examples in composition and the personal qualities of history.

In the hands of an imaginative teacher an Appreciation Class becomes a fascinating employment, and in its form of three separate small volumes this book is perfectly suited to become the basis of work for such a class. But there are many music pupils who have no opportunity of attending an Appreciation Class, and whose musical instruction is, perforce, given in the form of individual Piano or Violin lessons. To these pupils the reading of *The Book of the Great Musicians*, with an occasional friendly hint or suggestion from teacher or parent, will be a powerful stimulus and tend to remove the whole subject of music from the region of mere 'lesson' and 'practice'.

One suggestion that should hardly be necessary is that this attractive book, with its lavish illustrations, is obviously designed to be put into the hands of the young musician. A mere reading and retelling of its contents by the teacher cannot possibly convey the vivid impressions that go with actual possession and personal reading of the book itself.

H. P. ALLEN

The First Book of the
GREAT MUSICIANS

*A Course in Appreciation
for Young Readers*

by

Percy A. Scholes

YESTERDAY'S CLASSICS

ITHACA, NEW YORK

TO THE READER

If you want to play a good game at cricket or football or tennis you have to *learn* how the game is played, and to *practise* it. When you have learnt and practised, then you get the enjoyment.

And, in the same way, if you want to listen properly to lots of the very best music you have to *learn* about it and then to *practise* listening. And, here again, when you have learnt and practised you get the enjoyment.

But learning about a game, and practising it, are really quite good fun in themselves.

And I hope you will find that learning about music, and practising listening to it, are also quite good fun in themselves.

If you don't get some fun out of this book as you study it, and then, when you have studied it, get greater enjoyment out of listening to music, you will greatly disappoint—

The Author

CONTENTS OF BOOK I

CHAPTER I

THE COUNTRY PEOPLE AS COMPOSERS

A Chapter on Folk Music

THIS is a book about the Great Composers—by which we generally mean men of musical genius, who have had a long training in music, and learnt how to make beautiful songs and long fine pieces for piano, or orchestra, or chorus. But these are not the only composers.

It is not so difficult to compose little tunes as people think, and if you keep your ears open you will often find people composing without knowing they are doing it. For instance, if a boy has to call 'evening paper' over and over again in the street, night after night, you will find that he turns it into a little four-note song. Notice this and try to write down his song next time you hear it. Little children of two years old croon to themselves tiny tunes they have made up without knowing it. It would surprise their mothers if you told them their babies were composers—but they are!

And in all countries the simple country people, who

1

have had no musical training, have yet made up very charming music—songs or dance tunes, or tunes for playing games. Music such as this we call FOLK MUSIC.

A Folk Tune is never very long or difficult, and it is only a *'Melody'* (that is, it is only a single line of notes, without any accompaniment). But, in their simple style, the Folk Tunes are very beautiful, and no composer can make anything better than the best of them.

Just in the same way you will find that the country people in every land have Folk Tales and often Folk Plays—so they are not only composers, but authors and playwrights too.

Work Music, Play Music, and Religious Music

Some of the Folk Tunes are a part of children's games which have come down for centuries. Others are a help in work, such as rowing songs (to help the rowers to keep time with their oars), songs to be sung while milking, and so on. Others, again, are part of the religion—Folk Carols to sing at Christmas from house to house, and songs and dances belonging to far-off times, before Christianity, when people thought they had to sing and dance to welcome the Sun God when he reappeared in spring; such pagan dances and songs as these latter still go on in some places, though people have forgotten their full meaning. Then, of course, there are love songs, hunting songs, and drinking songs, and songs about pirates and highwaymen, songs about going to the wars, and sea songs. There are songs on all manner of subjects in fact, for everything that interested the country people was put into songs.

How Nations Express Their Feelings in Music

You cannot imagine a sad baby making up happy little tunes, can you? Or a happy baby making sad ones? And so with nations—their general character comes out in their songs. And every nation gets into its own particular way of making its tunes, so as to express its various feelings. English tunes are generally different from Scottish tunes, Irish from Welsh, and so forth. You can generally tell one of the negro songs from the Southern States when you hear it, and nobody who has heard much Folk Music of various nations is likely to hear a Norwegian song and think it an Italian or French one.

Collecting Tunes—A Useful Hobby

The trouble is that the country people are now hearing so many of the town-made tunes, that come to them in cheap music books or as gramophone records, that they are quickly forgetting their own old country songs. So some musicians have made a hobby of collecting the Folk Tunes before they get lost. They go out with note-book and pencil, and get the older folks to sing them the tunes that were sung in the villages when they were boys and girls, and where the old Folk Dances are still used they manage to see these, and to copy down the music of the fiddler and the steps of the dance. So much of the Folk Music is being saved (only just in time!), and some of it is now printed and taught in schools, so that it may be handed down by the children to coming generations.

In America, where so many races mingle, you can collect Folk Music of all nations. In the Southern Appalachian mountains, where the people are descended from British settlers of long ago and have not mingled much with other people because the mountains cut them off, the Folk Songs are still much the same as you find in England and Scotland. You can collect lots of Irish tunes in other parts of America, and Russian, and German, and Hungarian, and Italian tunes. In addition there are, of course, negro tunes (partly descended from African melodies) and American Indian tunes.

How Folk Songs Have Influenced Composers

In all the countries the skilled and trained composers have at times used Folk Songs as parts of their larger pieces. How they do this you will learn later in the book. And the 'Form' or shape of the Folk Tunes has shown composers how to form or shape their big piano and orchestral pieces. It will help us in our study of the big works of the great composers if we can come to understand the little tunes of the people.

The thing to do is to play or sing a Folk Tune and then find out how it is made up. For instance, if we take this little North of England song and examine it we shall learn a good deal.

BARBARA ALLEN

Here you see is a tune that falls into two parts, balancing one another, so to speak. We might call it a 'two-bit tune' (inventing a useful word).

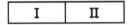

Now we will take another tune; this time it happens to be a Welsh one.

ALL THRO' THE NIGHT

There you see is a strain (I) which comes at the beginning and the end of the song, and in between, for the sake of variety, another strain (II). We might call that a 'three-bit-tune', or (if you like) a 'sandwich tune'. There are lots of tunes we can call by that name. You see what it means—don't you?

QUESTIONS

*(To See Whether You Remember
the Chapter and Understand It)*

1. If somebody said to you *'Can you tell me what is meant by the words "Folk Music"?'* what would you reply?

2. What do we mean by a 'melody'?

3. Mention some of the different subjects of the songs sung by the country-folk.

4. What should we mean if we said 'a nation's heart is seen in its songs'?

5. Which do you think is the most useful hobby: (1) collecting foreign stamps, (2) collecting bird's eggs, or (3) collecting Folk Tunes, and why do you think so? (Do not be afraid of saying what *you* really think.)

6. Say two ways in which skilled composers have got help from the music of simple folk.

THINGS TO DO

(For School and Home)

1. Play, or get somebody to play for you, a lot of Folk Tunes from some song book, and find out how each tune is made. You will find a great many of them are either in the two bits (I-II) or the three bits (I-II-I). This exercise is important: it will teach you how to listen.

2. Get into your head as many good Folk Tunes as you can, so that you will always have something jolly to sing or whistle. This will help to make you musical. Some of the country people in England know as many as 300 or 400 old tunes. How many can *you* learn and remember?

3. Play or listen to a good many Scottish tunes, and see if you can find out from them what sort of people the Scots people are. Then do the same with the tunes of the English, Irish, Welsh, or any other nation.

4. Get somebody to teach you a Folk Dance, or, if you cannot do this, make up your own little dance to one of the Folk Tunes in a song book.

5. Find a really interesting Folk Song that tells a story and then get some friends to act it with you, whilst some one sings the song. Dressing up will help to make this enjoyable.

6. Find a good FOLK tune with a marching or dancing swing; let one play it on the piano whilst the others put in a note here and there on glasses tapped with spoons, and any other domestic orchestral instruments of the kind. Some can also play the tune on combs with paper. (Glasses can be made to sound particular notes by putting more or less water in them.)

7. Discover any other ways of getting some fun out of Folk Tunes and learning a lot of them.

BRITONS AND BRETONS

The Story of a Thousand-year-old Song

In 1758 a British force landed in France—at St. Cast, in Brittany. A Breton regiment was marching to meet it when all at once it stopped—*the British soldiers were singing one of its own Breton national songs!* The Bretons, carried away by their feelings, joined in the refrain. The officers on each side told their men to fire—and the words of command were found to be in the same language. Instead of firing at each other, the two forces threw down their weapons and became friends.

How was this? The British regiment was Welsh, and the Welsh are descendants of the ancient Britons— driven into the mountains of Wales by the Saxons in the sixth century, at the same time as the ancestors of the Bretons were driven across the sea into Brittany.

After more than a thousand years, the descendants of these two bodies of the old British nation met, and found they knew the same language and the same songs. Differences had crept into the language and into the songs, of course, but the two regiments could talk together without much difficulty, and join in a chorus together.

This shows how people cling to their national songs. This one is now known in Brittany as *Emgann Sant-Kast* (The Battle of St. Cast) and is still popular in Wales as *Captain Morgan's March*. It can be found in some song books.

8

CHAPTER II

ENGLISH MUSIC IN THE DAYS OF DRAKE AND SHAKESPEARE

A CHAPTER ON THE BEGINNING OF MODERN MUSIC

An Explorer and His Music

When Francis Drake set out on his expedition round the world in 1577, tiny though his ship was, he yet found room in it for *musicians.* You would imagine that he would use all his little space for sailors and soldiers; but it was not so, and at meal-times he always had the musicians play before him. A Spanish admiral whom he took prisoner and whose diary has lately been printed says 'the Dragon' (for that was what the Spaniards called Drake) 'always dined and supped to the music of viols'.

The music of Drake and his men always interested the natives wherever they went. When the ship approached one island the king came off in a canoe to meet them, with six grave old counsellors with him.

9

The ship's boat was towing at the stern and the king made signs asking that the band whose music he heard might get into the boat; then he fastened his canoe to the boat and was towed along in that way, and (says Drake's chaplain, who wrote the story of the voyage) for an hour the king was 'in musical paradise'.

Drake's crew were great singers, and when they went on shore in another place, and built a fort to stay in for a time, the natives used to come to hear them sing their psalms and hymns at the time of prayers. 'Yea, they took such pleasure in our singing of Psalms, that whensoever they resorted to us, their first request was commonly this, Gnaah, by which they entreated that we should sing.'

If you read the chaplain's book, *The World Encompassed,* you will find many other little stories that will show you how musical were Drake and his seamen, or, if you prefer a modern tale book about Drake, Kingsley's *Westward Ho!* will tell you much the same.

So much for an Elizabethan explorer. Now for an actor and author.

A Dramatist and His Music

In these days the Stratford boy William Shakespeare was in London and had become a famous writer of plays. He must have been very fond of music, for we find he brings it into almost everything he writes. When he wants to make his audience believe in fairies (as in

A Midsummer-Night's Dream) he has music—pretty little fairy songs. And when he wants to make people realize how horrible witches are (as in *Macbeth*) he has grim witch songs. His mad people (like *King Lear*) sing little, disordered snatches of song in a mad sort of way. His drunken people sing bits of songs in a riotous way. His people in love sing sentimental songs.

When Shakespeare wants to represent a vision of any sort (as when Queen Katharine is about to die, in *Henry VIII*) he prepares the feelings of his audience by music. Whenever a marvellous cure is to be performed (as in *King Lear* and other plays) he has music. When there is fighting he has trumpets and drums, and when there is a funeral procession he has a Dead March.

There is much more music in Shakespeare than this, but enough has been said to show you how musical was that writer of plays and how musical must have been the audience for whom he wrote the plays. Because of course he wrote what he knew people would like.

A Queen and Her Music

Once when an ambassador from Queen Mary of Scotland came to the court of Queen Elizabeth of England, one of the courtiers took him into a room and hid him behind the arras so that he might hear the Queen play the VIRGINALS (a sort of keyboard instrument, something like a small piano)[1]. The courtier told him to be very quiet as the Queen would be angry

[1] The Virginals was a small harpsichord.

11

if she knew. But the Scotsman pulled the arras aside, and the Queen saw him. She seemed very angry with him for taking such a liberty, so he fell on his knees and begged to be forgiven. Then the Queen asked him—'Which is the better player, the Queen of Scotland or the Queen of England?' and of course he had to say 'The Queen of England'. As he did so he saw, of course, that his being taken to hear the Queen had really been at her command, so that she could ask this question.

So queens played in those days and were proud of their playing.

Everybody Musical Then

In those days everybody seems to have been musical. The common people sang their Folk Songs and their Rounds and Catches. The rich people and courtiers sang a sort of part-song called a MADRIGAL, and if you went out to supper it was taken as a matter of course that when the madrigal books were brought out you could sing your part at sight.

There were many musical instruments such as the Virginals (mentioned above), small Organs in churches, Viols (big and little instruments of the violin kind to play together in sets), Recorders (a kind of flute, big and little, also playing together in sets), Lutes (something like mandolines), and Hautboys, Trumpets, and Drums, for military and other purposes.

Choral Music

The choral singing was very famous then. It was so made that every voice or part (Treble, Alto, Tenor, and Bass) had a beautiful melody to sing, and yet all these beautiful melodies put together made a beautiful piece of music. There were lovely Anthems in the churches, made in this way.

The ROUNDS and CATCHES mentioned above were pieces where all the three or four voices sang the same melody, but beginning one after another, and the melody had to be carefully made so as to fit with itself when sung in this way. *You* can sing Catches; they are very good fun. A Round and a Catch are almost the same thing. We might say that when a Round has funny words we call it a Catch. *Three Blind Mice* is an Elizabethan catch.

Keyboard Music

The English composers led the world at that time in writing for the Virginals. They showed how to write music that was not just like the choral music, but was really suited for fingers on a keyboard. All the piano music of the great composers may be said to have sprung from the English virginal music of the sixteenth century. The Elizabethan composers laid the foundation, and Bach and Beethoven and Chopin and others have built upon it.

Form in Instrumental Music

When discussing Folk Songs we learnt a little about Form. In Queen Elizabeth's day composers were trying to find out good 'forms' for instrumental music.

One form they found was the VARIATIONS form. They would take some jolly tune (perhaps a popular Folk Tune), and write it out simply; then they would write it again with elaborations, and then again with furthur elaborations, and so on to the end. All the great composers down to our own day have been fond of the Variations form, and it was the English Elizabethan composers who invented it.

Another form was made by writing two little pieces in the style of the dances of the day and playing them one after the other, to make a longer piece. Generally one was a slow, stately dance called a Pavane, and the other a quick, nimble dance, called a Galliard.

The Fame of English Musicians

In these days English musicians were famous all over Europe, and were often sent for by the princes and kings of various countries to be attached to their courts. One called John Dowland became the King of Denmark's lute player and composer, and his music was printed in many European cities. Another, with the truly English name of John Bull, became organist of Antwerp Cathedral. A very famous composer of choral and virginal music in these days was William Byrd, and another was Orlando Gibbons. Try to remember the names of these men and to hear some of their music.

QUESTIONS

*(To See Whether You Remember
the Chapter and Understand It)*

1. What do you know of Drake and his music?

2. What do you know of Shakespeare and his music?

3. Tell a story about Queen Elizabeth and music.

4. What were the virginals like?

5. What were the viols?

6. What is the difference between a lute and a flute?

7. Mention a kind of flute common in the sixteenth century.

8. What is a Madrigal?

9. What is a Round?

10. What is a Catch? Do you know one?

11. How did English composers lay the foundation of modern piano music (two ways, please!)?

12. Describe 'Variations'.

13. Describe a form which consisted of dance tunes.

14. Mention four great English musicians of Shakespeare's day.

THINGS TO DO

1. Get two of your friends to learn this Catch with you. (It is quite easy.) Sir Toby, Sir Andrew, and the Clown sing it in *Twelfth Night*.

QUARRELLING CATCH

At first practise it, all singing the same notes, as though it were an ordinary song. Count the rests carefully and sing firmly.

Then sing it this way—first singer begins and when *he* gets to the mark ✶ second singer begins, and when *he* gets to ✶ third singer begins. Now all three are singing, but each treading on the tail of the one before, so to speak.

When the leader has sung the Catch about five times through he gives a sign and all stop together, or better, as this is a quarrelling Catch, after going through three or four times, shaking fists at each other, you can fall to fighting and so stop.

2. Then (for a change) practise this quieter Round of Shakespeare's day. Here some occasional soft singing will be in place. Try various ways of arranging soft and loud passages, with *crescendos* and *diminuendos* and settle on the way that sounds best.

CHURCH-GOING CATCH

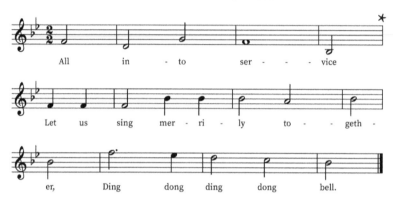

3. Now practise *Three Blind Mice* in the same way.

4. Play this Elizabethan hymn tune on the piano:

18

Glory to thee, my God, this night
For all the blessings of the light;
Keep me, O keep me, King of kings,
Beneath thy own almighty wings.

Forgive me, Lord, for thy dear Son,
The ill that I this day have done,
That with the world, myself, and thee,
I, ere I sleep, at peace may be.

You see that this tune has parts for four voices—Treble and Alto (on the top stave), and Tenor and Bass (on the bottom stave). Play or sing the Tenor by itself. Have you discovered anything?

Now perform the tune in this way. Get a friend to play it on the piano. You sing the Treble and get some grown-up male person to sing the Tenor.

This tune is called *Tallis's Canon*. Tallis was a great composer in Queen Elizabeth's reign. A CANON (as you have now discovered) is a piece in which one voice sings the same as another, but a few beats after it. We say that these two voices are 'singing in Canon'. In your Catches *all* the voices were 'singing in Canon'.

5. Go through any Shakespeare play that you know and find any allusions to music. Where Shakespeare means music to be performed in the play, see if you can find out why he does so.

6. If possible, get some grown-up or other good pianist to play you a piece in Variations form belonging to the Elizabethan times, for example:

John Bull's *The King's Hunting Jig*
Orlando Gibbons's *The Queen's Command*
Giles Farnaby's *Pawle's Wharfe*

Get them played several times and listen carefully, so as to find out how the tune is changed in each of the Variations.

7. In the same way get some one to play some of the other Elizabethan Virginals music. Giles Farnaby's is perhaps most likely to please you—especially when you get used to it (of course it is in a different style from the music of to-day, so may take a little getting used to).

He has one little piece called *Giles Farnaby's Dreame* (what sort of a dream was it that suggested this piece to him?) and another called *His Rest,* where you can feel him falling asleep. You can find bits of canon in *His Rest:* try to hear these as the piece is played.

Then there is a bright little piece called *Giles Farnaby's Conceit* ('conceit' in those days simply meant a bright idea), and another called *His Humour* ('humour' then meant character or temperament).

So in his music Farnaby used often to picture himself. Judging by these pictures, what sort of a man do you think he was? Listen to them carefully several times, and then make up your mind.

DIAGRAMS

1. TALLIS'S CANON

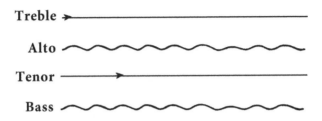

Treble
Alto
Tenor
Bass

The straight lines show the two parts that are written in Canon. The wavy lines show the parts which just go on their ordinary way, not in Canon (we call these 'free parts'). The arrow points show where the melody begins.

2. A ROUND IN THREE PARTS

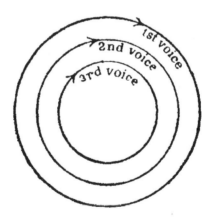

1st voice
2nd voice
3rd voice

It is a very good plan to make diagrams of the pieces you sing and play and hear, because it helps you to grasp how they are made, and so to understand and enjoy them, better.

CHAPTER III

HENRY PURCELL

THE GREATEST BRITISH COMPOSER

1658-1695

On a certain Tuesday afternoon in the month of February, 1660, four men sat before the fire in a Coffee House in Westminster. One was called Pepys, another Locke, another was a Captain Taylor, and the last was a Mr. Purcell.

There they sat chatting, and if you think for a few minutes of what you have read in your history books as occurring at that time you will be able to guess what it was they were discussing so eagerly as they sipped their coffee. What happened at the beginning of the year 1660? Why! *the King came back again!*

That is what excited them so much. The Long Parliament had been recalled and it had been decided to ask Charles to return.

'Look!' said Pepys suddenly, pointing at the window, and turning round they saw the glare of bonfires all along the river banks. The city was soon ablaze with

HENRY PURCELL

flames. 'Listen!' said Captain Taylor, and as they did so they heard bells beginning to ring: the bells of St. Clement's, and the bells of St. Martin's, and the bells of Old Bailey, and the bells of Shoreditch, the bells of Stepney, the bells of Old Bow, and, deep below them all, the big booming bells of Westminster Abbey and Old St. Paul's—soon they were all clanging and jangling together.

How They Sang Songs for Joy

Then some more friends came into the room, and they all began to sing. Locke and Purcell, who were both musicians, sang some Italian and Spanish songs, and Pepys struck up a tune too. And by and by Mr. Locke pulled out of his pocket a fine piece of music he had made as soon as he heard that the King was likely to come in again. It was a 'Canon' for eight voices, with Latin words, *Domine salvum fac Regem.*

So Locke taught them the tune and they all sat round the fire in their high-backed chairs, and one after another, at a sign from the composer, they began to sing the words *Domine salvum,* until they were all singing merrily together.

When Pepys got home that night he took down a little book in which he was accustomed to write his diary, and wrote his account of the day's doings, and how he had gone to the Coffee House, and seen the fires and heard the bells. *'It was a most pleasant sight,'* he wrote, *'to see the city from one end to the other with a glory about it, so bright was the light of the bonfires, and so thick round the city, and the bells rang everywhere.'*

Why Mr. Purcell Rejoiced

Now when Mr. Purcell got home (he had not far to go, for he lived in Westminster) you may be sure he told his good wife all about his doings, and it is certain that they both remembered one special reason for rejoicing that the King was coming back.

You see Mr. Purcell was a musician—one of the best musicians in London. Now, whilst the Puritans were in power there had been no Church Music. Mr. Purcell had earned money by singing in the Opera[2] and at private houses, and by teaching young ladies to play the harpsichord[3] or teaching men to sing. But with the King would come back the old Church ways, and that meant anthems and choirs and organs. The Puritans liked music—but not in church. The only music they allowed in church was plain psalm-singing by all the congregation—no organs and no choirs. Mr. Purcell loved anthems and other Church music, and knew that it was very likely that now his fine voice would earn him a good position in some choir. Besides he had a little baby son, and he may have had a fancy that he would in a few years make him a choirboy, and so get him a good musical training.

This chapter is really about the baby son, for he became the greatest British composer. But first it must be said that when the King came back and the music began again in Westminster Abbey, Mr. Purcell was chosen to be a member of the choir, as well as master of the choirboys and copyist of the music. (In those days there was little music printed: most of it had to be copied by hand.) And the King made him a member of

[2] An Opera is a play set to music.

[3] A harpsichord is a keyboard instrument that has quills to pluck the strings.

the Chapel Royal choir too, so he was now very happy.

Henry Purcell Becomes an Orphan

It was a sad thing that the little boy, Henry Purcell, was soon left an orphan. For the father died when the child was only about six years old. However, the father's brother, little Purcell's Uncle Tom, also a good musician, was very kind and adopted him, treating him as his own son.

Purcell Becomes a Choir Boy

In the same year that Purcell's father died his uncle got him admitted as a choirboy in the Chapel Royal. So every Sunday, with the other boys and men, he sang before the King. In Purcell's day they had not only the organ, but also four-and-twenty fiddlers, for the King loved the sound of stringed instruments, and as soon as he had returned had set up a band like that which he had heard at the Court of France.

So for nine or ten years young Henry sang in the King's choir, and in his leisure time practised the harpsichord and organ, and, no doubt, the violin also. And besides all that he soon began to compose. When he was twelve he was chosen, as the cleverest of the choirboys, to write a piece of music as a birthday present for the King. It was called *The Address of the Children of the Chapel Royal to the King on His Majesty's Birthday, A.D. 1670.*

Purcell's Voice Breaks

Purcell's voice broke when he was fifteen or sixteen, but they kept him on at the chapel for a time, perhaps making use of him for some odd jobs, such as teaching the younger boys. Then the Westminster Abbey authorities said they would make him a music-copyist (as his father had been twelve years before). And by and by some of the theatre managers heard what a good composer he was, and asked him to write music for their plays. So he soon began to be quite busy.

Organist of the Abbey and the Chapel Royal

Purcell was now becoming famous, and when he was twenty-two a wonderful thing happened. Dr. Blow, the organist of Westminster Abbey, seeing how clever Purcell was, offered to resign so that Purcell might take his place.

Purcell must have been grateful to Dr. Blow, for now, as Abbey organist, he had a big enough income to marry a girl of whom he had become very fond. So in a little house in Westminster Purcell settled down. Then two years later the King made him organist of the Chapel Royal. So now he held two great positions and had become the most important musical man in England, and you may be sure that his young wife was very proud of him.

Purcell's Compositions

All this time Purcell was very busy composing. He composed a great deal of church music—Anthems and Services for Westminster Abbey and the Chapel Royal. Some of the Anthems are very solemn, and those, I believe, were for Westminster Abbey. And others were quite gay; probably these were for the Chapel Royal, for Charles II loved jolly music, even in church.

For the Violin he wrote one piece—a wonderful Sonata—which was only discovered a few years ago.

Purcell also wrote a lot of lovely music for two Violins with one 'Cello and a Harpsichord. This music is very much neglected, which is a great pity.

Besides all this, Purcell wrote a good deal of music for the theatres, and when you hear a Purcell song, such as *Full Fathom Five,* or *Come if you dare,* or *Nymphs and Shepherds,* or *Come unto these Yellow Sands,* you are generally listening to one of Purcell's theatre pieces.

There are, too, some lovely sacred songs that singers to-day neglect frightfully—to their great disgrace.

Purcell's Kings and Queens

When Charles II died Purcell went on being royal organist, and so became a servant of James II. And when James II was turned out of the country, Purcell became organist to William and Mary. So he was royal organist in three reigns.

One of his tasks was to write 'Odes', or complimentary verses set to music, whenever anything happened in the Royal Family. For instance, when the King came back to London from his holidays, he would be welcomed with the performance of an Ode, for solo voices and chorus and orchestra. And Purcell would sit at the Harpsichord and lead the music.

He also had to play at two Coronations in Westminster Abbey, and at the funeral of Queen Mary.

Purcell's Death

It is a sad thing that the greatest British composer died when he was only thirty-seven years of age. Who knows what he might have done if he had lived twenty or thirty years longer?

The Form of Purcell's Music

If you take any little harpsichord piece of Purcell's and play it on the piano you will generally find that its form is like that of *Barbara Allen* and similar folk songs (p. 5). That is to say, it falls into two strains; in other words, it is a two-bit tune—or, to use the proper term, it is in BINARY FORM. You can find a sort of half-way house in the middle, where we have a CADENCE—that is, a sort of ear-resting place. Then the piece starts again, and we come to the end of the journey with another Cadence. Another word for Cadence is 'Close'.

It has already been said that the Elizabethan

Composers often strung two little pieces together to make one longer piece. Purcell went farther than this, and often strung three or four little pieces into one. Such a string of pieces we call a SUITE. Generally these little pieces were all in the style of the dances of the day, except the first piece, which was a PRELUDE, the word 'Prelude' simply meaning an opening piece.

Purcell for some reason does not seem to have cared much for the Air and Variations of which the Elizabethans were so fond. But he sometimes wrote what we might call a Bass with Variations, in which the same little bit of bass comes over and over again, with the tune above it changed every time. This we call a GROUND BASS, or simply GROUND. Some of his songs and some of his Harpsichord pieces are written in this way.

Some of Purcell's songs have a piece of RECITATIVE before them—that is, a piece of singing which does not make much of a tune, but imitates the way in which one would recite the words in a dramatic performance.

QUESTIONS

*(To See Whether You Remember
the Chapter and Understand It)*

1. How many historical events can you remember which will fix in your mind the time when Purcell lived? How old was Purcell when the Plague of London happened?—And the Fire?

2. How many facts can you remember about Purcell's family?

3. What sort of music do you think Cromwell liked in church? And what sort did Charles II like?

4. In what church was Purcell a choirboy? And in what churches was he organist?

5. How old was Purcell when he died?

6. Mention any instruments for which Purcell wrote music.

7. What is a Cadence? Give another name for it.

8. What is Binary Form?

9. What is a Suite?

10. What is a Prelude?

11. What is a Ground Bass?

12. What is a Recitative?

THINGS TO DO

1. Learn one of Purcell's songs (*Come if you dare!* and *Britons strike Home* are bold songs, and *Full Fathom Five* and *Come unto these Yellow Sands* are gentler songs. All are quite jolly and they cost very little if you get them in a school singing-class edition. *Full Fathom Five* and *Come unto these Yellow Sands* are settings of words in Shakespeare's *The Tempest*. You might turn up the play, if you like, and find out just how they come in.)

2. Get somebody to play a few of Purcell's Harpsichord pieces, and when you feel the middle Cadence has come, call out 'half-time'. Have each piece played several times and try to notice as much as possible how the piece is made. Some pieces are made almost entirely of one little group of four or five notes, over and over again, sometimes high and sometimes low. And in some pieces you can find bits of IMITATION— that is, one 'part' or 'voice' giving out a little bit of tune and another answering it. Most of the instrumental music by Purcell (like most of the Elizabethan music) is in 'voices' or separate little strands of melody woven together, almost as though (say) a Treble and Tenor and Bass were singing it.

3. If you are a pianist, practise some of Purcell's music for Harpsichord.

4. If you play the fiddle you can buy some little tunes of Purcell which have been arranged for that instrument, and practise them.

5. If you have a School Orchestra get it to play some of the Purcell tunes that have been arranged for stringed instruments.

6. You could make up a dance to some of the Purcell music. For instance, you could dance to the song *Come unto these Yellow Sands,* the words of which are about dancing on the beach.

7. Make a little play of Purcell and his wife giving a little party to celebrate the coronation of William and Mary and have some of his music performed as a part of the play.

CHAPTER IV

GEORGE FREDERICK HANDEL

1685-1759

How He Practised in the Garret

Handel's father was a doctor. He did not like music and would not let his children have music lessons.

But little George Frederick loved music so much that he could not do without it. So, somehow or other, he contrived to get either a clavichord or a small harpsichord into the garret, and there he taught himself to play. Or perhaps there was already an old clavichord or harpsichord among the lumber (in which case the little boy would surely have to tune it first, or get some one to do this for him).

He must have been about six years old when this happened.

There is a well-known picture which shows young George practising—and being caught in the act by his parents. History does not say whether he got a whipping, but if he did he cannot have minded it much, for he was far too determined to become a musician!

GEORGE FREDERICK HANDEL

How He Ran after the Coach

The doctor had an elder son who was servant to a great Duke, about forty miles away. One day the father set off on a visit to him.

Now the Duke had music in his palace, so George wanted to go too, to hear it. The father would not consent to take him. When the coach had gone some distance the father heard a voice calling, and looking out he saw little George Frederick running behind. It was now too late to turn back and take him home, so he was allowed to go after all.

How He Played to the Duke

George soon made friends with the Duke's musicians, and they were kind to him because they felt he was one of themselves.

One day, after service in the Chapel of the Palace, the Duke was going out when he heard the organ played in a way that surprised him. He stopped and asked who was playing, and they told him it was the little boy who was staying in the Palace. The musicians had put him on the organ stool to see what the Duke would think of his music.

The Duke was so pleased with George's playing that he told his father it would be a sin to make the boy a lawyer, as he had thought of doing, and made him promise to give him a good musical education.

How He Learnt Music

In Halle, the town in Saxony where the Handel family lived, there was a good musician called Zachau. He was organist of the Cathedral, and had a head stuffed full with every sort of musical knowledge—how to compose in various different forms, and how to play the harpsichord and the organ and the violin and the hautboy. Handel's father thought this would be the very man to make a good musician of his son. So it was agreed that Zachau should give George music lessons.

For three years the lessons went on, and every week George wrote for his master a MOTET (a sort of anthem). Everybody in Halle thought him wonderful, and so he was. He had great talent not only for composing on paper but also for IMPROVISING (that is, playing the organ or harpsichord and making up the music as he went along).

After a time Zachau said, 'I cannot teach that boy anything more,' so George's father sent him to Berlin.

Soon, however, the father died, and then George had to come back and begin to earn his living. When he was seventeen the people at one of the chief churches were glad to make so clever a youth their organist. He began to study at the University at the same time.

How He Began to Earn his Living

When Handel was eighteen he went to try his fortune in a larger place—Hamburg. There was an opera house there, and he became one of the violinists in the orchestra. Sometimes, too, when the conductor was away, he would take his place, sitting at the harpsichord and playing it to keep the band and singers together. (That was how conducting was done in those times. Nowadays we use a stick (or 'baton'), for the same purpose.)

Whilst at Hamburg, Handel wrote some operas which were very much liked.

A Visit to Italy

When Handel was twenty-one he decided to go to Italy, which was then a great country for music. In many of the cities they gave him a warm welcome, and he astonished the Italians both by his playing and by his composing.

Handel learnt a great deal from the Italians, for they have always been noted for two things—for writing effectively for the *voice*, and for making beautiful *tunes.*

Handel in London

From Italy Handel went home again to see his mother. Whilst in Germany he had a great honour; the Elector of Hanover made him his CAPELLMEISTER. (An Elector is a sort of King on a small scale, and a Capellmeister a sort of Conductor and Choirmaster on a large one.)

But Handel wanted to go to England, so the Elector gave him leave to do so.

When he arrived in London he wrote a fine opera called *Rinaldo*. This made a great stir, and he became famous. In *Rinaldo* there is a garden scene, and to make it look real they had live sparrows and let them fly about.

All the well-to-do people of London went to see *Rinaldo*, and they treated Handel so well that after going home to his duties for a time in Hanover he soon came back again.

How He Quarrelled with a King

The second time Handel came to London he stayed quite a long time, and the Elector was very cross at his Capellmeister's absence. Then, suddenly, the Elector was called to England himself. In the history books we now call him not Elector of Hanover, but George I of England.

This was serious for Handel, for it is not a happy thing to be in bad favour with the king of the country in which you live.

How the Quarrel Was Made Up

But some friends of Handel had a good idea. The Royal Family were going down the river in a barge, and it was arranged that as they came back there should be another barge behind, with a band of musicians. It was arranged that Handel should write the music, and the King was so pleased with it that he took him into favour again, and soon after promised to give him £200 a year for life, in addition to the pension Queen Anne had given him.

The music which ended Handel's trouble is called the *Water Music.*

Handel's Operas

Rich people in London in those days were very fond of Operas, and Handel wrote a great many of them. Some people thought another composer, an Italian called Buononcini wrote better operas than Handel, and soon there were two parties in London, each supporting the one composer and running down the other. The King was, of course, on Handel's side, but the Prince of Wales was against him.

It was a pity that people quarrelled so, because it led to some of them starting a new opera house, and then each of the opera houses spent so much money in trying to get better singers and scenery than the other that both failed. So, when Handel was fifty-two, in spite of all his famous doings, he became bankrupt.

Handel's Oratorios

It was really a good thing for the world that Handel failed in his opera work, because it made him try another plan—writing *Oratorios*. He said, 'I think, after all, sacred music is best suited for a man descending in the vale of years.'

That was how he came to write *Saul* (from which the great 'Dead March' comes), and *Judas Maccabaeus* (which is all about fighting), and *Israel in Egypt* (which is famous for its wonderful 'double choruses'—that is, choruses for two choirs singing at one time), and, greatest of all, *Messiah* (which is still often performed—at Christmas time especially). All these are Oratorios, that is, settings of sacred stories for solo singers and chorus and orchestra—in general style very much the same thing as Operas, except that they were merely to be sung and played, not acted.

How Handel Went Blind and Died

When Handel was about sixty he began to be ill. He went to Cheltenham to try if the waters would cure him, but he got slowly worse. Then, some years later, his eyesight failed (perhaps because he had done so much writing of music all his life). He had an operation for his eyesight, but it was no use, and in his last years he was quite blind.

He went bravely on, playing and conducting his music as usual, but one day, after conducting *The Messiah,* he became dizzy and faint. That was the beginning of his last illness, and on Saturday morning, April 14, 1759, he passed away, aged seventy-four.

QUESTIONS

*(To See Whether You Remember
the Chapter and Understand It)*

1. When was Handel born, and when did he die?

2. Tell any story that shows that he was very fond of music when a very small boy.

3. Did his father approve of his music? Tell any story showing how it came about that his father allowed him to have music lessons.

4. Who was his music teacher, and what did he learn?

5. What does 'Improvising' (or 'Improvisation') mean?

6. What is a Motet?

7. In what way did Handel begin to earn his living?

8. Why did Handel want to go to Italy? Did he learn anything there? Were the Italians kind to him?

9. What is a Capellmeister? To whom was Handel Capellmeister?

10. What did Handel do in London when he first went there? Mention an Opera he composed there.

11. How did Handel get into disgrace with George I, and how did he get out again?

12. What is an Oratorio?

13. How did Handel come to compose Oratorios?

14. Mention four of Handel's Oratorios.

15. What is a Double Chorus? Which Oratorio is famous for its Double Choruses?

16. What do you know about the ending of Handel's life?

THINGS TO DO

1. In some hymn-books you can find a hymn tune by Handel, which he wrote for the Methodists. It is called *Gopsal,* and its proper hymn (for which it was written) is *Rejoice, the Lord is King.* Play it and see what it is like.

2. Handel's *Water Music* can be got arranged for piano, and also arranged for School Orchestra. Try to get it or hear it, and find out how each piece is made.

3. Try to get somebody to sing you a solo from *Messiah.*

4. If you have a Singing Class or School Choir, get

your teacher to give you some solo or duet of Handel to practise as a choral piece. A good duet which will serve as a two-part chorus is *O Lovely Peace.* It is published in a form suitable for school choirs. After practising a piece like this look at the copy carefully and see how the piece is made. For instance, is it in Binary Form or Ternary Form—that is, is it a two-bit piece or a three-bit piece?

5. Play, or get somebody to play for you, the music of the Shepherds (the 'Pastoral Symphony') in *The Messiah.* Listen to this carefully and discover as much as you can about the way it is made up. It is said that in this piece Handel recalls his experiences in Rome, when he was there as a young man and the shepherds used to come into the city to play their bagpipes for money at Christmas time. Do you hear anything in the piece that reminds you of bagpipes?

6. Handel wrote a good many Suites for Harpsichord that make jolly music for piano to-day. The little pieces which are strung together to make a Suite of Handel are generally some of the following:

Prelude, an opening piece.

Allemande, a fairly serious kind of piece with four beats in a bar, in the style of a dance called Allemande, which was perhaps (as the name indicates) of German origin.

Courante, a bright, running sort of piece ('courant' is, as you know, French for 'running'), with three beats in the bar, imitating a lively dance of the name 'Courante'.

Sarabande, a rather solemn sort of piece, with three beats in the bar, imitating a stately Spanish dance of the same name.

Gigue, a piece in the style of a very lively dance, generally in what we call a 'compound time'—that is, with each beat divided into three smaller beats.

If you will look at these forms again you will see that after the Prelude comes a serious piece, followed by a lighter piece, followed by another serious piece, followed again by a lighter piece. So we get *variety.* Sometimes Handel gives the pieces in his Suites other names, but you always find this variety. Get somebody to play you a piece of each sort mentioned above and notice whether it corresponds in character with what you have just been told.

7. Now get somebody to play various pieces of Handel, several times each, whilst you listen carefully and find out how they are made up. Generally you will find there is a Cadence in the middle, as well as at the end, so that the piece falls into two parts—that is, it is in Binary Form. If you understand KEYS, notice in what key the beginning and end of the piece are, and in what key the middle Cadence. Often you will find that the whole piece is made out of one, two, or three tiny musical ideas used over and over again, sometimes high and sometimes low, sometimes in the right hand and sometimes in the left. Listen keenly, as the piece is played over and over again, until you feel you have found out all there is in it. This is the way to 'train your ears,' so as to become a good listener.

8. A very jolly piece indeed is the Air and Variations in the 5th Suite (this Air and Variations is often called *The Harmonious Blacksmith,* but Handel never gave it that name and there is no blacksmith about it). Play this (it is not very difficult) or get somebody else to play it. First have the Air played several times, so as to get it well into your head, and then have each Variation played several times to find out what Handel has done in each. Then have the whole set played straight through just for the fun of it.

This is the most popular of all Handel's Harpsichord pieces. Everybody loves it. But other pieces are just as fine, when you come to know them. Never be discouraged if you do not like a piece at first: there have been schoolfellows you did not care for at first, and afterwards, when you really knew them, they became your best friends.

9. Write and act a little play on some incident in Handel's life, bringing the performance of some of his music into it. There was a man who sold coals in London and held daily concerts at which Handel sometimes performed. Your teacher might look him up in Grove's *Dictionary of Music* or in the *Dictionary of National Biography,* and then tell you enough about him for you to give a little play called *The Coalman's Concert.* (His name was Thomas Britton.)

JOHN SEBASTIAN BACH

CHAPTER V

JOHN SEBASTIAN BACH

1685-1750

The Merry Miller and His Descendants

There was once in Germany a merry miller, whose name was Veit Bach. Besides being a miller he was also a musician, and whilst his mill was grinding away he would twang his zither, and, we may imagine, troll out a jolly song.

Now Veit had a son named Hans, who was a carpet weaver by trade, but, like his jovial old father, a musician as well. He played the violin, so, perhaps, the father and son played duets sometimes, for a zither and a violin would go pretty well together.

Hans, too, had a son, and he was called Christopher. He became chief musician to a great nobleman and had two boys, twins. They looked just alike, and, funnily enough, he called them both by the same first name, John—so they must have been very confusing when they were at school, especially if they were dressed alike. Their second names, however, were different. One was John Christopher, and the other John Ambrose. They were both good performers on the fiddle and played other instruments as well.

In his turn John Ambrose had two sons, and they were both great organ players and composers, but the younger was the cleverer, and he was called JOHN SEBASTIAN BACH. All this is told here in order to show you what a musical family the Bachs were.

The Orphan

When John Sebastian was only ten years old, his father and mother died, and he had to go to live with his elder brother. He could already play the violin, for his father had taught him to do that.

The brother sent him to school, to learn his ordinary lessons, and himself taught him to play the clavichord and harpsichord. But the boy could soon play all his music by heart, and then he wanted something more difficult.

Now the brother had a book of music of which he was very proud. It was all written by hand and had in it beautiful pieces by all the great composers of those days.

He never let little Sebastian play from this book. Perhaps he was jealous of him, and feared he would learn to play better than himself; or, perhaps, the little boy sometimes had dirty or sticky fingers, as boys in those days sometimes had.

At any rate John Christopher kept this wonderful book carefully locked up in a cupboard. But John

Sebastian made up his mind to learn the pieces in the book, so he managed to roll it up and pull it through the latticed door of the cupboard. At night he would do this, and then, by moonlight, set to work to copy all the beautiful pieces into a book of his own.

One night, however, his brother caught him, and then all his work was largely wasted, for his copy of the book was taken from him. It had taken six months to make. Still the labour was not altogether thrown away, for we may be sure that the copying had taught him a good deal about music and how it is composed.

Holiday Tramps

Soon after this, Bach went to school at a place called Lüneberg. There were good organists to be heard there, and he used to learn a good deal by listening to them. But at Hamburg, miles away, was a greater organist still, a famous old Dutchman, called Reinken.

When holidays came round, Bach used to put some food in his pocket, and all the money he had been able to save, and trudge off to hear the great organist.

One day he had been on one of these expeditions and was tramping back. His money was nearly spent, and when he came to an inn he did not dare go inside, but sat outside smelling the delicious things that were being cooked and wishing he could buy some of them.

Suddenly the window opened, and out at his feet fell two herrings' heads. He picked them up and inside each of them he found a silver coin. So he was able not only to satisfy his hunger, but actually to turn back again to Hamburg, to hear some more of the wonderful music.

Who was it who threw the money? He never found out, and now we shall never know.

The Young Organist

When he was eighteen years old, Bach became a violinist in the band of a Prince. After a few months, however, he left this band to become organist of a church at Arnstadt.

He soon got into trouble at the church where he played, because he went to Lubeck to hear the music there under the famous Danish organist, Buxtehude, and became so wrapped up in it that he stayed three months.

When he came back they found fault with him not only for his absence, but also because, when he accompanied the CHORALES (or hymn tunes) on the organ, he put such wonderful accompaniments to them that he disturbed the people in their singing.

His fame as an organist was, however, very great, and during the next few years, in his several organist's posts, he became recognized as the best organ player of the day.

He wrote most of his famous organ pieces at this time of his life.

The Prince's Chamber Music

When Bach was thirty-two he took service with a Prince, at Cöthen, as his Capellmeister. Here he did not have to play the organ, but to direct the chamber music for the court concerts. So this was a time when he composed no church music, but, instead of that, a great deal of beautiful music for other instruments than the organ.

The Prince loved music, and was so fond of Bach that he made him go with him on his long journeys.

Bach at Leipzig

When Bach was thirty-eight he made the last move of his life—to Leipzig. Here he was 'Cantor' at the Thomas School and Director of the Music in two churches. He had to teach singing and to give the younger boys in the school lessons in Latin. At the University he conducted the students' musical society. It was a very important position that he held.

A House of Music

Bach's house at Leipzig was overflowing with music. His wife sang and all his children were clever musicians. Then, too, he had a lot of pupils about the house. They came from far and near to learn from him.

Whenever any musicians came to Leipzig they always went to Bach's house to pay their respects to him.

Just as he wrote organ music in his earlier life (when he was mainly an organist), and other instrumental music in his middle life (when he was chief chamber musician to the Prince), so he now wrote beautiful church music such as Motets and Cantatas and Passion Music for the two churches with which he was connected. A CANTATA is something like an Oratorio. PASSION MUSIC is also like an Oratorio and tells the story of the last days of Christ.

The King Sends for Bach

When Bach was sixty-one years old he got an invitation from Frederick the Great to come to his court at Berlin. Bach's son was a musician at this court, and Bach was no doubt glad to have a chance of seeing him, as well as honoured by the King's request.

As soon as he got to the court, they told the King, who was playing the flute, but who put it down and announced to his courtiers: 'Gentlemen, old Bach is come!' He made him play, just as he was, and without giving him time to remove the dust of travel.

Whilst Bach was at the court, the King made him improvise a great deal, and also try all his organs and pianos. The piano was still a new instrument, and Bach preferred the harpsichord, or, still more, the clavichord.

Keyboard Instruments

Pianoforte, Harpsichord, and Clavichord all have keyboards, but

1. The **Pianoforte** has Hammers to strike the strings.

2. The **Harpsichord** had Quills to pluck them.[4]

3. The **Clavichord** had what are called 'Tangents', which cut off (as it were) the right length of string to make the note, and struck it at the same time.

4. The **Organ** has pipes, not strings.

Bach Goes Blind

Like Handel, Bach went blind in old age. All his life he had been so busy copying and playing music that he had strained his eyes.

Bach died at Leipzig in 1750, aged sixty-five years. He is often spoken of as the greatest musician who ever lived.

---

[4]The Virginals was a small Harpsichord.

QUESTIONS

*(To See Whether You Remember
the Chapter and Understand It)*

1. Handel belonged to an unmusical family. Did Bach? Tell anything you happen to remember about his father, uncle, grandfather, and great-grandfather.

2. What do you know about Bach's early life in his brother's house?

3. What was Bach's first post when he ceased to be a choirboy? And what was his next?

4. What is a Chorale? How did Bach's playing of the Chorales get him into trouble when he was a young man?

5. What were Bach's duties in his next important post?

6. What was his last post, and how long did he occupy it? (You can easily reckon.)

7. What sort of music did Bach write in his last post?

8. What is a Cantata? What is Passion Music?

9. Tell the story of the meeting of Frederick the Great and Bach.

10. What are the four keyboard instruments, and how is the sound produced in each?

11. What do you know of Bach's last years?

THINGS TO DO

1. Most hymn-tune books have some Chorales composed by Bach or else older ones *harmonized* by him (that is, the tune, or treble part, was old, but Bach wrote the alto, tenor, and bass parts to it). Look through a hymn-book for these and play them, so as to get a good idea of what a Chorale is like. Bach made a great deal of use of Chorales, using them a good deal in his Cantatas and Passion Music.

2. If you can, get hold of a copy of Bach's *Christmas Oratorio,* and get somebody to play the Pastoral Symphony out of that (the piece that begins Part II) and compare it with Handel's Pastoral Symphony in *Messiah.*

3. Now get somebody to play you a Suite of Bach's, just as they did a Suite of Handel's, so that you can compare the two styles. Notice again the *variety* in the pieces.

Then, as in the case of Handel, have an Allemande played separately and study how it is made, and do the same with a Courante, a Sarabande, and a Gigue—or several of each.

4. Besides the Allemande, Courante, Sarabande, and Gigue, Bach almost always adds some more pieces (generally just before the Gigue); some of these are as follows:

Bourrée, a lively old French dance with four beats in a bar, and every phrase beginning on the fourth beat of the bar.[5]

Gavotte, like the Bourrée, but with every phrase beginning on the third beat of a bar.

Menuet (or Minuet), a fairly stately, yet bright, dance with three beats in a bar.

Get somebody to play you one of each of these from Bach's Suites, and so get to know their style. Then have each played several times and study carefully how it is made up.

5. If possible, get somebody to play you a Violin piece of Bach, and then study how that is made. Always after studying a piece carefully have it played once more, just for fun.

6. Make up a little play on some incident in Bach's life, bringing in a performance of some of his music.

[5]Music is divided into 'phrases' which are something like the separate lines of a piece of poetry. In the folk-songs on page 5 you will see the phrases shown by the 'slurs', or curved lines, placed over the notes.

CHAPTER VI

'C-O-N-T-R-A-P-U-N-T-A-L'

A Big Word Explained

1.

THERE is a big, long, ugly word which is often used to describe such music as that of Bach and Handel. The word is C-O-N-T-R-A-P-U-N-T-A-L. Let us understand it.

2.

You know that there is (or used to be) a form of government called **Absolute Monarchy.** In countries that have this, one man governs and has his own way, and the rest just support him and do as they are told.

3.

Then there is the very opposite form of government called a **Republic.** Here all are supposed to take their share of the management of the country. As the Irishman said of America, 'Every man is as good as every other man, and sometimes better.'

4.

Now music also falls into two classes. In one class there is a beautiful tune in the top part, and all the other parts underneath simply support it with harmony.

Play the *Old Hundredth,* or almost any hymn tune, and you will find this to be the case. First play the top part (the tune) and then play in turn the Alto, Tenor, and Bass parts. You will find these underneath parts have little interest in themselves.

Now play the whole thing, with all its four parts, and you will find that the under parts, whilst (as we found) not of great interest in themselves, serve to support the top part and make it more interesting. We say that such a piece has a MELODY or tune (at the top) and that it has HARMONY (or chords) to support the tune. That is 'Absolute Monarchy' in Music.

5.

Now play just a few lines from a chorus of Handel's *Messiah.* You will generally find that every voice has a tune of its own, or else imitates the tune of one of the others. So here there is MELODY, and HARMONY too (for all the voices combine together to make chords). But in addition there is COUNTERPOINT (that is, tune in every part).

6.

Nearly all the music you have so far heard as illustrations of this book has been Contrapuntal.

You remember the Catches in Chapter 1. Those, of course, were Contrapuntal, because every voice that was singing had a real tune—the same tune, as it happened, in this case.

Then, the Elizabethan hymn tune on page 18 was Contrapuntal, for the Tenor had a real tune, which, in this case was the same as that of the Treble (the Alto and Bass parts were not very 'tuney' in this piece; try them over and you will find that they do little more than fill up the Harmony).

Nearly all the Keyboard Music of the Elizabethan composers and of Purcell and Bach and Handel was more or less Contrapuntal, and some of it was entirely so, that is, although meant to be played by fingers it was written in 'parts' or 'voices' almost as if intended to be sung, and each of the 'parts' or 'voices' had real tune in it. Some of the pieces, it is true, had passages in them that were merely 'harmonic', but, in that case, there soon came back again passages with Counterpoint in them.

A piece of 'contrapuntal' music is like a piece of beautiful tapestry. A number of threads are woven together to make the fabric. Each thread is beautiful in itself, and combined they make a beautiful whole.

7.

So now you know what is meant by saying 'The music of Bach and Handel is Contrapuntal.'

QUESTIONS

*(To See Whether You Remember
the Chapter and Understand It)*

1. If we say that a piece has a good 'Melody', what do we mean?

2. If we say it has good 'Harmony', what do we mean?

3. If we say it is 'in good Counterpoint', what do we mean?

SOMETHING TO DO

Most people can easily appreciate a piece with one good Melody, at the top.

And most people can also appreciate good Harmony. But if there is Counterpoint they very often lose it altogether, because their ears are not trained to hear two or three melodies going on at the same time. They can generally hear the top part (or 'voice'), but they miss the lower part or parts.

There is a game you can play, which will train you

to hear lower parts. It takes two to play it, but more can join.

We will suppose two are playing it. Each of them prepares at home six puzzles made like the following, with a well-known tune below and another specially made-up tune written above to disguise it. Each player then, in turn, plays one of his tunes (with its disguise, of course) and the other has to find out what it is. If he finds out the very first time the tune is played it counts 1; if he finds out the second time it is played it counts 2; if the third time it counts 3—and so on down to 6, if he finds it out the sixth time it is played. If he cannot find out the tune in six 'goes' it counts ten. The one who gets the smaller number of marks wins, of course. The game is called

'CAMOUFLAGED TUNES'

Well known to everybody—

Well known to Scotsmen—

Often heard in Church—

Another Church tune—

A Northern Song—

A Convivial Song—

(Top part to be played *staccato*.)

Before you look at the above tunes get somebody to play them carefully to you, and see how few marks you can get. Listen *hard* to the lower 'voice'.

You may think this a difficult game to play, because the 'camouflage' has to be made up before you begin. But it is in the rules of the game that you can use the piano to help you to find a camouflage. What you do first, of course, is to write down the tune itself; and you then try to find notes that will go with it to make a good camouflage. Most people can soon learn how to do this even if they have never had lessons in Harmony and Counterpoint.

Of course if you have not learnt to write music you cannot play this game, but in that case perhaps you can get your teacher to make up some 'Camouflages' and to play the game with the class.

Do not be discouraged if you find this game harder to play than you expected. Some people find it very hard to hear an underneath part until they get the 'knack' of it; others find it easy.

One way of making the game a little easier is to have the tune played an octave lower (leaving the camouflage in its old place). If the game is *still* too hard, make it a rule that the tune shall be played a little louder than the 'camouflage'.

CHAPTER VII

ALL ABOUT FUGUES AND HOW TO LISTEN TO THEM

BACH and Handel wrote many pieces which are called FUGUES. Some of these anybody can appreciate right away, because they have a jolly swing about them. But others are not so easy to understand, and so some people, feeling rather bewildered, make up their minds that to appreciate a Fugue is beyond *them*, and give up trying. But if you know how Fugues are made it is not, as a matter of fact, very hard to understand them, and once you do understand a good Fugue you get fonder and fonder of it, until, at last, hearing that Fugue (or playing it) becomes one of the great pleasures of your life. It is worth a little study and effort to add a new pleasure to life, and that is why this chapter is written.

Fugues Are in 'Voices'

The first thing to tell you about a Fugue is that it is entirely (or almost entirely) 'Contrapuntal'. It may be a Fugue for keyboard, yet at the beginning you will generally see the words 'In three voices', or 'In four voices', or 'In five voices', and so you see, although there may be no *real* voices it is written and performed as though it were actually to be sung by three or four or five people, or sets of people in a choir.

Of course some Fugues are meant really to be sung. Handel's *Messiah,* for instance, has Fugues for choir.

A Fugue Has a 'Subject'

A Fugue is largely made out of a little bit of tune which we call its 'subject'. The Subject of a Fugue is generally like the text of a sermon—nearly the whole thing is supposed to be made out of it.

Here are one or two of Bach's Fugue Subjects, which will give you an idea of what such things are like.

A rather gay Subject in the minor—

A quiet happy Subject in the major—

A fairly solemn Subject—

A really quite skittish and rather long Subject—

(Play these Subjects neatly and rhythmically, or get somebody to play them to you.)

How the Fugue Begins

The Fugue begins by one of the 'voices' giving out the Subject; then, whilst this 'voice' goes on with something else, another comes in with the Subject, so that now two 'voices' are going on together—one with the Subject, and one with 'something else'. Then a third voice comes in with the Subject, whilst the other two go on with 'something else', so that three are going on together—and so on until all the voices have had their turn. You will see that this part of a Fugue is something like the Rounds you sang in Chapter 1.

But there is one special thing you must be told about these voices and the Subject. The first voice brings in the Subject in the proper chief key of the piece, the second one brings it in in the key of five notes higher (or four notes lower),[6] the third brings it in in the old key again, and so on.

---

[6]This we call the 'Dominant' Key (i.e. the note that was 'Dominant' or *Soh* is now the new 'Tonic' or *Doh*).

The entries of the Subject that are in the *'other key'* we call ANSWER. We can make diagrams of this part of the Fugue (which we call its EXPOSITION) if you like. Here is a diagram of a Fugue in five 'voices' in Key C.

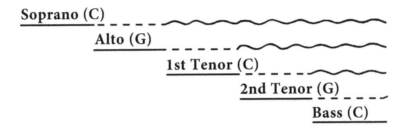

In this Fugue, as you see, the top voice came in first.

Now we will have a Fugue in Key E, with one of the middle voices beginning.

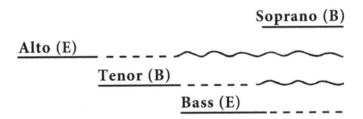

So that is all clear and easy to understand, is it not? And now the thing is to get somebody to play you the 'Expositions' of three or four Fugues, so that you can learn to listen for the Subject coming in in each voice in turn.

Sometimes the voice that has just sung the Subject (or Answer) goes on with another Subject, which we call a COUNTER-SUBJECT. The Subject and Counter-Subject together are, as you will no doubt realize, something like one of the tunes on pages 61-62 with its 'Camouflage'. In the diagrams above, the Subject is shown by a straight line, the Counter-Subject by a dotted line, and everything else by wavy lines. Look carefully again at those diagrams, please, and get them fixed in your mind's eye so firmly that they will always stay there.

Episodes—and Then More 'Entries'

You know what an 'episode' is in a story. The author leaves the main plot of the story for the moment, and goes on to tell you of a little incident that is not really part of the main plot, but still has something to do with it. A Fugue has episodes like that, and after the Exposition we usually have such an Episode. Generally you will find that this is made out of some little bit of the Subject or Counter-Subject, and it is interesting to listen keenly to the Episode and find out how it *is* made.

The first Episode takes us into some other key, and then comes in the Subject again, perhaps in one part, perhaps in two, or three, or all. We say that it 'enters' and call this an Entry.

Then follows a second Episode, and a further 'Entry' in still another key, and so on to the end of the Fugue, where the Subject comes back at last in its old key—the main key of the piece.

'Stretto'

Sometimes in one or more of the Entries the Subject comes in in several voices, one voice entering with the Subject before the other has finished with it. This we call a STRETTO. If we made a diagram of it, it would look like this

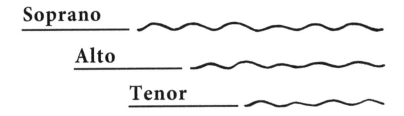

That, as you will see, is *very much* like a Catch or a Canon. The Subject 'overlaps'. The voices come in with it one after the other, treading on one another's tails.

Pedal

Sometimes, in an Organ piece, as you may have noticed, the player puts his foot on one of the low notes which are played by pedals, and keeps it held down and booming away whilst with his hands he plays the upper 'voices' of his music. This is also done in Piano Fugues (only here, of course, it is done with the little finger of the left hand), and it is also done in Choral Fugues (only here the low note is sung by the basses). But we always call such a note a PEDAL, whether it is on the

Organ or on the Piano, or sung by a Choir, or played by the bass instruments in an Orchestra. The effect is generally rather thrilling.

Preludes

Many of Bach's Fugues have a piece before them which we call a PRELUDE. Bach wrote two big books of Preludes and Fugues, each with a Prelude and Fugue in every major key (twelve, that is) and in every minor key (another twelve). Each book has thus twenty-four Preludes and Fugues, making in all, what we often call 'Bach's 48', or sometimes his *Well-tempered Clavier.*[7]

QUESTIONS

*(To See Whether You Remember
the Chapter and Understand It)*

1. What do we mean when we say 'That Fugue is in four voices'?

2. What is the 'Subject' of a Fugue?

3. What is the 'Answer'?

4. What is a 'Counter-Subject'?

5. Describe the 'Exposition' of a Fugue.

---

[7] 'Well-tempered' means tuned in the modern way instead of in a certain old-fashioned way, which only allowed you to play in a few particular keys because it sounds harsh in all the others. Clavier means keyboard.

6. Without looking at p. 67 make a diagram of an Exposition of an imaginary Fugue in four voices, with the Subject coming first in the bass.

7. Now do another one, in three voices, with the Subject coming in the middle voice.

8. What is an 'Episode'?

9. What is an 'Entry'?

10. What is a 'Stretto'?

11. What is a 'Pedal'?

12. What is 'Bach's 48'? What is its other name?

(If you can answer all those questions correctly you know a great deal about Fugues—far more than many grown-up musical people. Yet, you see, it is not really a difficult matter.)

THINGS TO DO

1. If you play the Piano, and are advanced enough to play a Fugue, get your teacher to give you one and then mark in pencil the Subject, Answer, Counter-Subject (if there is one), Episodes, and all the other features.

Then practise it carefully and play it to somebody, first playing all the different features separately and explaining them, and then playing the whole Fugue several times to see if they understand it. Then you will really be giving a little Lecture on 'How To Understand a Fugue'.

2. Get your Teacher or some pianist friend to play Fugues to you, seeing how much you can find out about them just by ear and without looking at the music. Can you answer these questions after hearing it twice or three times?

(a) How many voices has this Fugue?

(b) How many Entries has it after the Exposition?

(c) Has it any Stretto?

(d) Has it a Pedal?

3. If you know an organist ask him to play you a good Fugue on the organ. Tell him you prefer a merry one, if he has such a thing, but, if not, a solemn one will do. An organist often plays Fugues after the service, but generally the people are in such a hurry to get out that they only hear a bit of the Exposition.

4. If *Messiah* is going to be performed, go to hear it, but, before you go, get some good pianist to play you some of the choruses, and study how they are made. Also study the Fugue which forms part of the Overture.

5. There are just a few Fugues to be got on the Gramophone. By and by there will be more. If you have a Gramophone try to get a Fugue record (look right through the catalogue to find one) and then listen to it, over and over again, finding out all about it by very careful listening. (You can get the *Messiah* Overture as a record, for one.)

CHAPTER VIII

HAYDN

1732-1809

A Musical Family

Haydn was born in a place called Rohrau, in Austria. As his father was only a village wheelwright, there can hardly have been much money to spare for luxury. Nevertheless the family was a very happy one, and a great pleasure they had was plenty of music. The father had a tenor voice, and accompanied his own singing on the harp, two of the brothers must have been musical, for they became professional musicians when they grew up, and Joseph himself had a beautiful voice, and, besides, used to sit on the bench by the fire and pretend to play the violin like the village schoolmaster, but with two pieces of stick for the instrument and bow.

How Haydn Went to the Town

One day, whilst little Joseph was singing and pretending to play, there came in a relative, a musician in the town near by. He thought the little boy must have

JOSEPH HAYDN

music in him, and so begged the parents to let him take him away to be trained.

So Haydn became a choir-boy, and worked hard to make himself a good musician. He got 'more flogging than food', he used to say in after-life, when he looked back, but yet he felt grateful to his relative. 'Almighty God', he said, 'to whom I render thanks for all his unnumbered mercies, gave me such facility in music, that by the time I was six, I stood up like a man and sang masses in the church choir, and could play a little on the harpsichord and violin.'

A Cathedral Choir-Boy

There came to the town one day an important man—choirmaster of the great St. Stephen's Cathedral in Vienna. He heard Haydn sing, and, after putting him through an examination to see what he knew, he said he would take him to be a choir-boy in the Cathedral. So to Vienna little eight-year-old Joseph went. Here he learnt singing and harpsichord and violin playing from good masters.

What troubled Haydn was that they did not teach him to compose. He wanted to write music as well as to sing it and play it. However, as they did not teach him, he thought he would teach himself, so he got every piece of music-paper he could find, and covered it with notes. 'It must be all right if the paper is nice and full', he said. One day the Cathedral choirmaster found him trying to write a great piece of church music in twelve voices, and advised him to write in two first of all. But he never showed him how to do it, and the little boy had to struggle and find that out for himself.

By and by, Joseph's brother, Michael, became a chorister at the Cathedral, too. This was very nice for both of them, but at last Joseph's voice began to break, and then the choirmaster used to put his younger brother up to sing the solos before the Emperor and Empress, which was mortifying for poor Joseph.

Then the choirmaster began to want to get rid of Joseph, and waited for an opportunity. Now the choir-boys all had pigtails, and one day, Haydn, being in a mischievous mood, and having a new pair of scissors he wanted to try, snipped off the pigtail of one of the other boys. So the master gave him a good thrashing and turned him adrift.

The Hungry Haydn

Many great men have gone through a time of hunger, and so did Haydn now. He had a big boyish appetite, and no money to buy food. However, friends helped him a little, and he hired an attic, and got hold of an old worm-eaten harpsichord. There he sat, day after day, playing and studying the Sonatas of Emanuel Bach (son of the great Sebastian), and then trying to write others like them. He also practised the violin.

Fortunately, after a time he became known to a famous singing teacher called Porpora, and was invited to act as accompanist at the singing lessons. In this way he learned a great deal about the voice, and also met many famous musicians, who gave him advice—for Porpora knew them all.

All this time, and all his life, Haydn was a very hard worker, and that is one reason why he became so great.

Haydn Becomes 'Capellmeister'

Gradually Haydn's musicianship became known, and at last a great chance came to him, for a Count Morzin made him his chief musician. In return for his labours he had his board and lodging, and twenty pounds a year. This he thought was wealth, so he straightway got married.

The Count sometimes had a famous visitor, Prince Anton Esterhazy. By and by, when Count Morzin decided to give up his band, Prince Esterhazy engaged Haydn, and then he had to direct an orchestra and chorus, church music, concerts, and operas. That was a splendid thing for Haydn, because it gave him such an opportunity of gaining experience, and when he wrote a piece of music he could have it tried, see what it sounded like, and then sit down and write a better one. The time was largely spent on the Prince's country estate, and Haydn said, in after-life: 'I was cut off from the world, there was no one to confuse or torment me, and I was forced to become original.'

Haydn in England

English musical people had heard a great deal about Haydn, and had pressed him to come to England, but he could not do so. At last the Prince died and he was free. A London conductor, named Salomon, was in Germany when this occurred, and he at once set off to see Haydn. He persuaded him to come to London, and they started together. This was in 1790, when Haydn was fifty-eight years of age. It was on New Year's Day that Salomon and Haydn crossed from Calais to Dover. There were no steamboats then and it took nine hours.

When they got to London everybody flocked to welcome Haydn, and the University of Oxford invited him to go up to receive the degree of Mus. Doc. The Prince of Wales became a great friend of his, and used to play the violoncello whilst he played the harpsichord.

Haydn stayed in England eighteen months, and after some time in Austria, came back again in 1794. He wrote some splendid Symphonies for London Concerts. One of these he called the 'Surprise Symphony', because, in one movement, he lulls the audience almost to sleep by his quiet music, and then suddenly wakes them up with a loud chord.

The Last Concert

When Haydn was an old man of seventy-six they carried him in his arm-chair to hear a performance of his great Oratorio *The Creation*. They placed him there in the centre of the hall, amongst the greatest people of the land, and clapped and cheered until they were tired. Then the performance began and Haydn became very excited. When the concert was half over they thought it best to take him home, and as he went out at the door a famous musician of about forty years of age kissed him. This was his former pupil, Beethoven.

Haydn then turned round and held up his hands, as if blessing the people, and for the last time looked on an audience gathered to hear his music. Five days later he died.

QUESTIONS

*(To See Whether You Remember
the Chapter and Understand It)*

1. Was Haydn a Frenchman or an Italian or a German—or what was he?

2. Had he a long life or a short one? When was he born and when did he die?

3, What do you remember about his family?

4. What age was he when he began to earn his living by music?

5. Why was he turned out of his place? And what did he then do?

6. Think over all you have just read about his early life, and then say what you remember about his musical education. What did he learn, and how?

7. When Haydn obtained his important post as Capellmeister to the Prince, what were his duties?

8. Tell anything you remember about Haydn in England.

9. What Oratorio did Haydn write?

THINGS TO DO

1. Get somebody to play you music by Haydn, and listen carefully to find out how it is made up. They might play an air and variations from one of the Symphonies, or any slow movement from a Sonata or Symphony. Or they might play you or sing you something out of *The Creation*. (The longer movements of the Sonatas and Symphonies should be left until you have done Chapter X.) Besides finding out how the pieces are made, try to get an idea of Haydn's style, and the *flavour* of his music, so that if some day you hear somebody playing one of his pieces that you have never heard before you may be able to say, 'Oh, that must be a piece by Haydn!'

2. When Haydn was in England he admired the tune of 'God save the King'[8] so much that he decided to write a national anthem for his own country. So he wrote what is often called *Haydn's Hymn for the Emperor*, which will be found in almost any hymn-tune book under the name *Austria*. (During the war this was an enemy's national anthem, so we could not sing it, but you may like to play it now that the war is over. Haydn was a great friend of the British people.)

3. Make up and act a little play on one of the incidents of Haydn's life.

4. If you can play the piano, get some of Haydn's music arranged for piano duet and play it with a friend.

5. If you like dancing, get a Haydn Minuet (perhaps from one of the Symphonies) and make up a dance to it.

6. If you have a school band, get some of Haydn's music for it.

7. And if you have a school choir, ask for some Haydn music for that.

[8]American children sing this tune, the British National Anthem, to *My country 'tis of thee.*

CHAPTER IX

MOZART

1756-1791

Two Children on Tour

A little boy of six and his sister of eleven, with their father to take care of them, were making a concert tour. Both the children played the harpsichord beautifully, and some of the pieces they played were their own compositions. First they went to Munich, and played before the great Elector; then, as every one had praised their playing so much, they went to Vienna. On the way they had often to stop and give little performances to the rich and great people whose houses they passed, for their fame had gone before them.

When they came to a place called Ips, where there was a Franciscan monastery, the little boy sat down at the organ and played so well that the monks all left their dinner, and came into the choir to hear him.

In the Customs-House

The children played the violin, as well as the harpsichord, and the father, writing home to the mother,

MOZART, AGED 7, WITH HIS SISTER AND FATHER

told how music had been useful when they had to pass through the customs-house at Vienna. He said:

'Our business with the revenue officers was short, and from the principal search we were entirely absolved. For this we had to thank Mr. Woferl, who made friends with the *douanier,* showed him his clavier, and played him a minuet on his little violin.'

'Mr. Woferl' was the pet name for the little boy, Wolfgang Amadeus Mozart; as for 'douanier', you all know French, of course, so there is no need to tell you that this means customs officer. 'Clavier' is a word that would do for any sort of keyboard instrument, but here it means a harpsichord (perhaps a small one, such as the little party would be easily able to take about with them).

How They Appeared at Court

It was a great day for the father when he got a summons from the Emperor to bring his children to court. Woferl was too little, however, to feel what an honour this was, and when they got there, he sprang into the lap of the Empress, clasped her round the neck, and kissed her very heartily.

How Woferl Offered To Marry a Princess

Woferl was such a little boy that he could not be expected to behave like a courtier. He used to run and jump about the room, and once, when he fell on the slippery floor, the Princess Marie Antoinette helped him to get up, and he said to her: 'You are good, and I will marry you.'

The Princess was then a little girl, being only a year older than himself. As you know, she did *not* marry Mozart, but became Queen of France.

About thirty years after this little incident poor Marie Antoinette lost her life by the guillotine. When she was being tried her cruel accusers noticed that she sometimes moved her fingers as if playing the harpsichord. So we see that she was a musician too, and we can imagine that when she was going through that awful experience, she cheered herself by thinking she was playing some of her favourite pieces—quite possibly pieces by her old friend, Mozart.

In Court Dress

The stay at Vienna was very jolly for the children. The Emperor made them valuable gifts, and paid the father well. Marianne had given to her a grand court dress of white silk, which had belonged to one of the young Archduchesses, and Wolfgang received a violet-coloured suit, trimmed with gold braid, which had been made for a little Archduke. The father was very proud of his children, and had their picture painted, dressed in this splendid fashion.

This enjoyable visit came to an end through the little boy catching scarlet fever, for when he recovered it was thought best to return home to Salzburg.

Paris and London

Next year, however, they all set off on their travels once more. This time they went to Paris, where they had a great welcome, and then to London. You will remember that there were no trains or steamers in those days, so that the travelling had to be done by coach and sailing boat. The boat to Dover made them all very sick, but they soon got over this, and went on to London to see the King.

How the Children Played to George III

The King was astonished at Wolfgang's playing. This is what the father wrote home to the mother at Salzburg:

'The King placed before him pieces by Wagenseil, Bach, Abel, and Handel, all of which he played off. He played on the King's organ in such a manner that his hearers preferred him on the organ to the clavier. He then accompanied the Queen in an air, and a performer on the flute in a solo. At last he took up the bass part of one of Handel's airs that by chance lay in the way, and, upon the mere bass, performed a melody so beautiful that it astonished everybody.'

How the Father Fell Ill in England

Whilst they were in England the father fell danger-ously ill. They were obliged to be as still as mice, so as not to disturb the invalid, and, as Wolfgang could not play, he composed. He filled a manuscript book with his compositions, and this has lately been printed, and is very interesting indeed.

Mozart's first Symphony was written at this time. His sister sat by him as he wrote it, and he said: 'Remind me that I give the horns something good to do.'

When the father recovered the children gave many concerts, and the orchestra used to play the Symphonies that the young composer was now writing.

The Happy Boyhood Ended

And now we must pass on from those boyish days, and we shall be saddened to find that poor Mozart's happiness did not last. It really seems as though there are a great many people in the world who welcome a clever boy musician rather because he is a *boy* than for the sake of his *music*. When Mozart was a young man, he found that the great people who had treated him so kindly were no longer much interested in him. He went to Paris again, taking his mother with him. He had to take a poor little lodging, so small that there was no room even for a harpsichord. Wolfgang's old friend, Marie Antoinette, was now Queen of France, but he could not find any one who could take him to court and present him to her.

A Rude Duchess

Some one gave him an introduction to a great society lady, the Duchess of Chabot, who invited him to call. But when he did so, he was first allowed to stay for half an hour in an ice-cold waiting-room, and then to sit for an hour whilst the Duchess sat at a table with some gentlemen, drawing.

Then they asked him to play the piano, but went on all the time with their occupation, and when they praised his playing he knew that they were only giving him worthless compliments.

But the greatest misfortune in Paris was the death of his mother. After this he was quite alone in the great city, and very much he felt it.

Mozart and the Archbishop

After all these troubles we may be sure the young man was glad to get back home to Salzburg. Here his father obtained for him the position of Court Organist to the Archbishop.

The Archbishop was proud, and whilst he was glad to have a great musician like young Mozart in his employment, he did not treat him with respect. At meals the Court Organist had to sit with the valets and cooks. The pay he received was very small and was not given him promptly. Then his master would very rarely give him permission to play anywhere but in his own house.

At last poor Mozart could stand this life no longer, so he sent in his resignation. The Archbishop used rough and rude language to him, and the High Steward was very violent, and it is even said that he kicked Mozart out of doors.

The Operas

Happily, Mozart's luck was not always so bad as this, and it is pleasant to know that soon after he had left the Archbishop people began to realize what a wonderful composer of Operas they had in him. So Mozart had some very joyous experiences, as well as some sad ones, in his grown-up life. Mozart's Operas number about twenty: the best known are *Figaro, The Magic Flute,* and *Don Giovanni.*

Mozart's Death

It is sad to think that Mozart's last work was a Requiem, that is to say, a Mass for the Dead. He wrote this on his death-bed. When he died, his wife, who loved him dearly, was so overcome with grief that she could not go to the funeral, and when she was sufficiently recovered to visit the churchyard, nobody could tell her where her husband had been buried.

It seems a pitiful thing that this great man should have died at so early an age as thirty-five, and that the world should have taken so little interest in its loss of him that people did not even mark his grave.

QUESTIONS

*(To See Whether You Remember
the Chapter and Understand It)*

1. When was Mozart born and when did he die? How long was his life?

2. Tell all you remember about the childhood of Mozart and his sister. This should be quite a lot—experiences in Vienna, Paris, London, etc. If you are studying this Chapter in class with your friends, have a competition to see who can remember most.

3. Tell all you remember about his troubles when he became a young man.

4. What are the names of some of Mozart's most famous operas?

THINGS TO DO

1. If you play the piano, get your teacher to give you some music by Mozart. Some of the movements in the Sonatas are interesting, but others are now old-fashioned and sound soulless and thin: ask your teacher to give you the interesting pieces.

2. Get somebody to play you some of Mozart's shorter pieces and try to find how they are made up. In one of the Sonatas there is an Air with Variations that everybody likes, and there are also some Minuets that are quite jolly. (Keep the long movements of the Sonatas and Symphonies until you have read Chapter X.)

3. Make up and act a little play on some incident of Mozart's life.

4. Have one or two pieces of Mozart played and then one or two pieces of Haydn, and see if you can learn to distinguish the 'flavour' of one composer from that of the other. (I wonder if you can!)

5. If you have a Gramophone at home, get your parents to buy a record of the *Figaro* Overture (or any other Mozart piece), and listen to it carefully until you know it well, and understand just how it is made up.

CHAPTER X

SONATAS AND SYMPHONIES

HAYDN and Mozart wrote many Sonatas and Symphonies. So did Beethoven, of whom you will learn in the next chapter. So the time has now come to tell you what Sonatas and Symphonies are like, and then you can hear lots of them and understand them.

First it must be said that a Sonata and a Symphony are one and the same thing—except that a Sonata is for one instrument, or perhaps two, whereas a Symphony is for full Orchestra (you will find a chapter on the Orchestra later).

The Sonata a Sort of Suite

In the chapter about *Music in the Days of Drake and Shakespeare* we found that composers in those days often wrote a piece that consisted of two shorter pieces put together—two dance-tune pieces, a stately one and a lively one for contrast.

Then in the chapters about Purcell and Handel and Bach we found that these composers went further and strung a good many pieces together into what we call a Suite.

Well, a Sonata (or Symphony) is like a Suite in this—it consists of three or four shorter pieces strung together to make one long one, and these pieces are so arranged as to contrast with one another. We call these shorter pieces MOVEMENTS, and say 'that Sonata has three Movements', or 'I like the first movement of that Sonata', or 'I don't care for the last movement of such and such a Symphony'.

The First Movement

The first movement is usually the longest and most important of the Sonata or Symphony. Very often it is in a particular kind of form which we call 'Sonata Form', or (more sensibly) 'First Movement Form'. This form is made up in the following way.

First the composer takes a good tune that has come into his mind, or that he has invented, and then he takes another (in a different key, for contrast). Between these two tunes he puts a little passage, leading from the one to the other, which we call (quite sensibly this time) a BRIDGE PASSAGE. The two tunes we call FIRST SUBJECT and SECOND SUBJECT, but you will see they are not just little bits of *melody*, like Fugue Subjects, but real long tunes, with Melody, Harmony, and possibly, here and there, a bit of Counterpoint.

After the Second Subject is finished the composer generally adds a little tail-piece or CODA to round off that part of the movement. We call all this, so far, the EXPOSITION, or the ENUNCIATION, of the movement, because it 'exposes', or 'enunciates', the 'Subjects', or tunes, out of which the whole movement is to be made.

We can make a little diagram that will make the Enunciation quite clear—

ENUNCIATION OF A SONATA

I	Bridge	II	Coda

Very often the composer tells the player to repeat this Enunciation before he goes farther. The idea of this is to get the Subjects well into the listener's head, which is very important.

After the Enunciation comes a part of the Movement which we call the DEVELOPMENT. Here the composer takes a bit of one subject and works it up in various ways and then, perhaps, a bit of the other. And he 'modulates' a great deal—that is, he takes us through many different keys, and generally excites us a good deal by doing so. It is difficult to explain how the Development is made, because it may be done in so many different ways. When you come to listen carefully to a few Sonatas, you will get to understand this.

After the Development we come to the RECAPITU-LATION, which is simply a repetition of the Enunciation, but with both the Subjects in the same key this time. And perhaps the composer gives us a good long Coda to finish with. So a diagram of the whole movement would look like this (you will notice that in the movement imagined here it has been supposed that the composer has given a short Introduction before the First Subject enters).

FIRST MOVEMENT OF A SONATA

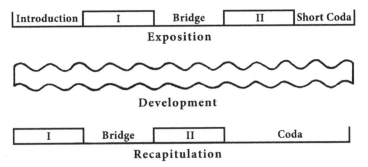

Now you understand 'Sonata Form' or 'First Movement Form', and the thing is to hear some movements that are in this form, and listen to them carefully. Sometimes second or third or last movements are in this same form and a great many Orchestral Overtures are in it, too.

The Middle Movements

One of the middle movements is pretty sure to be a slow, expressive one, and very likely the other will be a lively MINUET AND TRIO, or a SCHERZO.

You have already learnt what a Minuet is like (page 56). The Trio is simply another Minuet, so made as to contrast with the first. After the Trio the first Minuet is repeated, so together they make 'Ternary Form' (or a 'sandwich').

Minuet	Trio	Minuet

Scherzo means 'joke', and so the Scherzo is generally a very lively, jolly movement. Sometimes it is simply a very bright Minuet.

The Last Movement

The last movement of all is sometimes in First Movement form and sometimes in some other form. Often it is a RONDO, that is, a piece with a chief Subject that comes round and round again, perhaps like this—

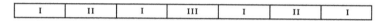

Here there is a chief Subject (I), followed by another Subject (II), with a third Subject in the middle (III, or possibly instead of III being a Subject it may be a sort of Development of the others).

Explaining Form on paper is very dull. What you really want is to hear lots of pieces and find out by using your ears how they are made. That is much more fun.

QUESTIONS

*(To See Whether You Remember
the Chapter and Understand It)*

1. What is the difference between a Sonata and a Symphony?

2. What is the difference between a Sonata and a Suite? (This is a question that is not answered in so many words in the chapter, but you can soon think of the answer if you try.)

3. What is the word by which we call the various shorter pieces that are put together to make up a Sonata or Symphony?

4. How many of these shorter pieces generally make up the longer piece?

5. Would this be a good plan for a Symphony or Sonata?—

>Long quick piece,
>Short lively piece,
>Merry piece,
>Very rapid piece.

6. Would you prefer this?—

>Slow expressive piece,
>Funeral March,
>Solemn piece.

7. There is one dance piece often found in the Sonata and Symphony. What is it? How is it made up and what is its 'form'?

8. Describe the form often used for the first piece in the Sonata or Symphony (generally called 'Sonata Form'). How many chief tunes (or 'Subjects') does it usually have, and how are these used? What do we call the first part of the piece? What do we call the middle part? And what do we call the last part?

9. Are the two subjects when they first appear in the same key—and if not, why not? Do they ever appear in the same key in any other part of the piece?

10. What do we call those little tail-pieces that round off a piece or a section of a piece?

11. What do we call a passage that is perhaps not very important in itself but leads from one Subject to another?

12. Can you mention any differences between a Fugue Subject and a Sonata Subject?

13. What is the name for the jolly, joking sort of piece that we sometimes find as one of the middle pieces of a Sonata or Symphony?

14. Describe a Rondo of any kind.

THINGS TO DO

1. Get somebody to play you just the opening bars of each movement of a good Sonata, so that you may note the contrast between the different Movements.

2. Next get them to play the whole Sonata through, so that you can get a general idea of the Movements.

3. Next pick out the Movement you like best and find out, by listening carefully, how it is made.

4. Then do the same with all the other Movements. The great thing to do first is to find out which are the Subjects and to learn these *thoroughly,* so that you know them again wherever they occur in the piece.

5. If you play the piano find somebody else who does so and practise with him or her one or more of Haydn's Symphonies as a duet. These, of course, are really for Orchestra, but they can be got 'arranged' for Piano Duet (or Piano Solo either). Mark in pencil where

the Subjects come, and study the form of the various Movements as much as you can.

6. If you have a Gramophone, get records of any Sonatas or Symphonies and listen to them over and over again, making up your mind as to which are the Subjects, and noticing where they reappear.

7. In the same way, get records of any Overtures by Mozart or Beethoven. These you will generally find are in 'Sonata Form', that is, they have only one Movement and it is like the First Movement of a Symphony.

8. If you have a Pianola get any of these pieces as Pianola rolls, and practise them well. You can pencil on the roll where the Subjects come, if you like and if you are clever enough to find out.

9. Try to go to some orchestral concerts to hear Symphonies and Overtures. (You can sometimes hear these on the pier at a seaside place in summer.)

CHAPTER XI

BEETHOVEN

1770-1827

How would you like to be dragged out of bed late at night so that you might have a music lesson? That was what poor little Beethoven had to put up with, and the thoughtless and unkind teacher was—*his own father.* Of course it was a good thing for little boy Beethoven that he had a parent who was a musician, but the sad part was that the father was a foolish man, and worse than that, a drunkard too. He was a singer in the choir of the Elector of Cologne, at Bonn on the Rhine.

The Young Organist

When Beethoven was twelve years old, there came to Bonn, where he lived, a young musician called Neefe. The Elector had appointed him court organist, and he soon made use of the boy, making him his assistant. Then, too, the court theatre gave the boy an opportunity of using his talents. In those days a theatre orchestra included a 'cembalist' (that is, a harpsichord player), and as Beethoven played the harpsichord and pianoforte very well, he was appointed to this important position.

BEETHOVEN

So I suppose he was now earning his living, and it was a good thing he was able to do so, for his father had by now become very drunken, and did little to support the family.

A Visit to Vienna

The city of Vienna has always been one of the greatest musical centres of the world, so Beethoven longed to go there. He was seventeen before this wish was realized, and he was not able to stay long, as they sent him word that his mother was dying, and he had to hurry back.

Whilst he was at Vienna, he made one very important friend—Mozart (then about thirty years old). The elder musician was so struck with the gifts of the younger one that he gave him some lessons, and no doubt these were very valuable to him. Later he had lessons from Haydn.

Some Good Friends

But it does not do for a young musician to study nothing but music. He ought, also, to become fond of reading, and to love poetry, and pictures, and all good things. And besides that, he needs sympathy, for it is as hard for any kind of artist (poet, painter, or musician) to develop without that as for a rose-tree to bloom in a cold climate.

So it was a very happy thing that Beethoven made

some good friends in Bonn, a family called von Breuning. He used to teach the children music, and the mother did all she could to help him with his general education, and to teach him good manners, and encourage him in every way.

Then there was a Count Waldstein, who became a good friend too, and in later years Beethoven dedicated to him the great piano piece which we call the 'Waldstein Sonata'.

Beethoven and the Aristocrats

By and by Beethoven went to Vienna again, and this time he settled there. Indeed he lived there for the rest of his life. The great aristocratic people at Vienna very much admired his playing and they put aside any prejudice they had against him on account of his humble birth. Beethoven himself always thought that, since he was a musician, he was as good as any one else; he thought (and rightly, too) that it is a greater thing to be born with genius, and to cultivate it perseveringly, than to be born 'with a silver spoon in one's mouth', as people say. So he never allowed any one to snub him, but always held his own.

Holidays

Beethoven loved nature, and when he took a holiday he would wander about the fields and woods, thoroughly happy. He wrote a Symphony called the

Pastoral Symphony, and in that you will find that he has actually put the songs of birds and the music of the brooklet.

Some people used to stare at Beethoven in the country, because he was so wild. He would rush about and wave his arms and shout his joy.

Sometimes he was easily offended by people, and sometimes he was bad tempered. But very often his health was the cause of this, and the troubles he had to go through.

How Beethoven Went Deaf

Have you ever realized that there are some fine works of Beethoven that you can enjoy, and that he himself was never able to hear? It is so!

Deafness began before he was thirty, and it got worse and worse all the time. It is almost as sad for a musician to become deaf as for a painter to become blind.

An Ungrateful Nephew

Then Beethoven had another great trouble. He adopted a nephew who proved very unsteady and was a great anxiety to him. The love seemed to be all on the uncle's side. He worked hard to earn money to give the boy a good education, and in the end got him a commission in the army. But nothing except disappointment came from all these efforts, and the young man's behaviour was a great trouble to Beethoven.

Whenever you read anything about Beethoven being rough in his manners, or bad tempered, remember three things. *Firstly,* He was a great genius, and such a man is often irritable, because his mind is so much occupied with great big thoughts straight from heaven that he cannot help being annoyed by tiny little earthly worries. *Secondly,* He was deaf, and this often makes people suspicious. *Thirdly,* He had the great trouble with his nephew of whom I have just spoken.

But he was a warm-hearted and generous man, and is worthy of our greatest admiration.

What Beethoven Wrote

Amongst the treasures Beethoven left for us are nine Symphonies (some of them *wonderful* works) and thirty-two piano Sonatas. Then there are some Sonatas for violin and piano, and Trios and Quartets, and a Septet, and some other pieces of the kind we call 'Chamber Music'.

One Opera exists, and one only; it is called *Fidelio.* Another name it went by was *Leonora,* and the three *Leonora* Overtures and the *Fidelio* Overture often heard at concerts, were all attempts to write an overture to the opera—one that should be really *just* the thing. They show how persevering the composer was, and how hard he found it to satisfy himself.

One of the very greatest of all his works is the Solemn Mass in D.

Beethoven adopted the same 'forms' as Haydn and Mozart (the Sonata, the Symphony, the String Quartet, and so on). But he put a greater depth of thought and of emotion into these forms. So his music, though not more beautiful than that of Haydn and Mozart, has more *meaning* in it and moves us more strongly.

QUESTIONS

*(To See Whether You Remember
the Chapter and Understand It)*

1. When was Beethoven born?

2. Where was Beethoven born? And where did he spend most of his life?

3. What do you know about his life as a boy?

4. Mention three of Beethoven's teachers.

5. What do you know of Beethoven's holidays?

6. What misfortunes did Beethoven have to endure?

7. When did Beethoven die?

8. Mention all the works of Beethoven you can remember.

THINGS TO DO

1. Get somebody to play you some of the shorter pieces of Beethoven, such as the Minuets and Trios, or the Scherzos from his Sonatas and Symphonies, and listen carefully to find out how they are made. Make diagrams of them.

2. If you have a school Orchestra, get the conductor to teach it something of Beethoven.

3. Get your Singing Class teacher or School Choir conductor to give you something of Beethoven's to sing.

4. If possible, get hold of some book with the plot of Beethoven's opera *Fidelio,* and read it.

5. Get some pianist to play some Haydn and Mozart pieces and then some Beethoven, and see if you can feel the difference of 'flavour'.

6. If you have a Gramophone at home, get your parents to buy records of one or two Beethoven orchestral pieces, and get to know these really well.

7. Act a bit of *Fidelio* with somebody putting in some of the music at the piano, here and there, if possible.

8. Or, Act some little scene from the life of Beethoven, bringing in some of his music if possible.

9. Get up a School BEETHOVEN CONCERT, with little explanations of all the pieces read before each is performed. These little explanations should be written after you have carefully studied how the pieces are made

up, and should be so written as to help the audience to understand the music. Before the programme begins (or, perhaps better, just after the first piece), let some one read a tiny life of Beethoven, lasting about five minutes—specially written for the purpose, of course. If you like, you can intersperse the Concert with anecdotes of Beethoven, or descriptions of some special features in his life and work, each read or told by a different person, so as to bring in as many of your fellow pupils as possible.

CHAPTER XII

WHAT IS AN ORCHESTRA?

WHEN next you see and hear an Orchestra, notice that it is a sort of small town, made up of just a few families.

The 'Scraper' Family

Members of the family—
    1st Violins.
    2nd Violins.
    Violas.
    Violoncellos. (Can you spell that word?)
    Double-basses.

If you like you can consider the gruff DOUBLE-BASS as the father, the sweet-voiced VIOLONCELLO as the mother, the VIOLA as the eldest boy, and the VIOLINS as twin girls. Notice that there is no difference between the First Violin and the Second Violin, as instruments. They have both Treble voices, but sing Treble and Alto as children often do at school. The Violas sing Tenor, the 'Cellos sing Bass, and the Double-basses sing—'double-bass'! So the stringed instruments are like a church choir or choral society, with its four voices, only they have a special party of giants, with deep voices, to sing a very low bass, underneath the other bass.

The Two 'Blower' Families

There are two families of 'blowers'—the 'Wood-Wind' and the 'Brass'.

Wood-Wind.	*Brass.*
Flute.	Horn.
Oboe.	Trumpet.
Clarinet.	Trombone.
Bassoon.	

1. The Wood-Wind Family

You all know a FLUTE when you see it. It is just a plain tube, blown through a hole in the side.

The OBOE has a reed, a *double* one (two little pieces of thin wood making a small mouthpiece). It has a sweet but rather piercing tone. A rather bigger Oboe is called COR ANGLAIS (a very silly name, for Cor means Horn and Anglais means English, and it is neither a horn nor English).

The CLARINET has a reed, too (a *single* one), as a part of its mouthpiece. Its tone is sweet and much smoother than that of the Oboe.

Get some one to show you the Oboe player and the Clarinet player; then watch them, and try to distinguish the tone of their instruments.

PICCOLO

FLUTE

OBOE

COR ANGLAIS, or ENGLISH HORN

BASSOON, or FAGOTTO

DOUBLE BASSOON, or CONTRAFAGOTTO

CLARINET in B flat

BASS CLARINET

The above Illustrations are not strictly proportionate in size

THE WOOD-WIND OF THE ORCHESTRA

The BASSOON is a sort of bass Oboe. It is too long for the player to blow it at the end, so there is a little tube coming down the side for him to put in his mouth.

2. The Brass Family

The HORN is the curly instrument. It can play lovely gentle tones or hard loud ones.

The TRUMPET you all know, so why waste space telling you about it? (In some bands they have Cornets instead of Trumpets; they are much shorter, so you cannot mistake them.)

The TROMBONE. When the Shah of Persia came to England they took him to hear an orchestra. He said he enjoyed two things: 'The piece the band played before the man came and waved the stick (you know what that was) and the magicians who swallowed brass rods and pulled them up again.' These magicians were the Trombonists, so now you know what a Trombone is like. You have all seen their little conjuring trick!

The 'Banger' Family

The chief bangers are two very gentle members of the family, though they can be fierce sometimes. We call them KETTLEDRUMS. They can be tuned to particular notes, and it is good fun to see the man doing this in the middle of a piece.

Two rowdy members of the family are the BIG

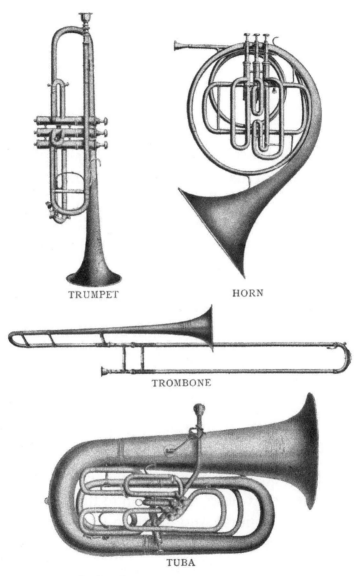

TRUMPET   HORN

TROMBONE

TUBA

The above Illustrations are not strictly proportionate in size

THE BRASS OF THE ORCHESTRA

Drum (or Side Drum) and the brass Cymbals. Then there is a charming but rather brainless member who generally appears in public when merrymaking is going on—the Triangle.

Warning

If you know any players in orchestras, don't tell them that we called them 'Scrapers', 'Blowers', and 'Bangers'. They would not like it, and it is no good hurting their feelings. But that is all they really are, isn't it? Only of course they scrape, blow, and bang very artistically.

QUESTIONS

(To See Whether You Remember the Chapter and Understand It)

1. What are the four families of the Orchestra?

2. What are the members of each of these four families?

3. In the Strings, which instrument corresponds to the Trebles in a Choir? And which to the Altos? And which to the Tenors? And which to the Basses? And when you have answered those questions say whether there is any other string instrument left to be mentioned, and tell anything you can as to *its* business in life.

4. What is the difference between a Flute and an Oboe?

5. What is the difference between an Oboe and a Clarinet?

6. What is the difference between an Oboe and a Bassoon?

7. Mention the chief three Brass instruments.

8. What are the various 'Bangers' of the Orchestra called?

THINGS TO DO

1. The first 'thing to do' is to go and hear an Orchestra and to 'spot' the various instruments, so that you will know them again whenever you see them and will also know whereabouts their players usually sit in the orchestra.

2. Be there in good time and listen to the tuning-up, so as to learn what each instrument sounds like. Then keep your eye on any particular instrument and watch for its coming in, so that you may listen to its tone again.

3. Notice what the sound is like when Strings alone are playing.

4. And notice what the sound is like when Brass instruments alone are playing.

5. And, also, what the sound is like when the Wood-Winds alone are playing.

6. Keep a special eye for about a quarter of an hour on the Oboe and Clarinet, so as to catch them playing any bits of Solo, and thus learn the difference in tones so that you can tell them in future with your eyes shut.

7. If you have a Gramophone and some orchestral records, try to discover, by listening carefully, what instruments are playing at different places in the records.

NOTE

It is a good thing at the first three or four concerts to sit very near the front, so as to be able to watch the players. After a time, when you know where all the players sit and what all the instruments sound like, you can sit farther away.

In the second volume of this book there will be given a great deal more information about Orchestras, but what is given in this volume is enough to make orchestral concerts very enjoyable if you only study it carefully and go to as many concerts as possible.

If you see a man playing a Flute or Cornet or other instrument in the street, stop and listen to him and notice what the instrument sounds like (often, as you will notice, the high notes sound very different from the low notes, so that if he were playing in an orchestra and you were not near him you would think the high passages and the low ones came from two different instruments).

CHAPTER XIII

ROBERT SCHUMANN

1810-1856

A School Band

In the town academy at Zwickau in Saxony, in the year 1823, or thereabouts, there might have been seen a group of boys enjoying themselves in music after school hours. The leader of the group, young Robert Schumann, sits at the piano, and around him are grouped two violinists, two flute players, two clarinet players, and two horn players—quite a nice little band for a school, though strangely lacking in the stringed instruments, the place of which the leader has to supply on the piano so far as he can.

A great deal of happiness the boys get out of their band, and the leader looks very pleased as they play some music he has written specially for them.

Portraits in Music

This is not the first school at which Robert has been famous for his music. At the school for younger boys, to which he went previously, he used to make great fun by playing portraits of his schoolfellows.

How can one 'play a portrait'? Well, of course, no composer, however clever, can make up a piece that will show you what a person looks like, but it is possible to give a sort of portrait of a person's character or, shall we say, temperament?

For instance, if a boy is a merry, mischievous boy, it will be possible to give some idea of this by playing merry, mischievous-sounding music. And if a boy is a solemn boy, one can play solemn music, and so forth.

That is, no doubt, what young Robert Schumann, as a boy of ten, used to do, and he was considered to be very clever indeed at it.

Schumann the Book-Lover

There is one thing about Schumann's early life that is very important, for it seems to have influenced him as long as he lived. That thing is this—*He was brought up amongst books.*

His father was a bookseller and an author too, and so, seeing books all around him, Robert grew up a book-lover. He was especially fond of poetry and of books of a romantic kind. All this affected his music in after years, for as a composer he often pictured in music (so to speak) the characters and feelings of the people he read about, just as, when a boy, he had done the same with those of his schoolfellows. And all his

ROBERT SCHUMANN

music was very 'romantic', if you know what that means. You shall have a chapter later to explain the word.

It was a sad thing for Robert that his father died when he himself was only fifteen years old. The father had encouraged him not only to read books but also to study music, but the mother wished him to be a lawyer.

They Try To Make Him a Lawyer

By and by Robert was sent to study law at the University of Leipzig. But it was really precious little law he studied there, for he came to know a very clever piano teacher called Wieck, and spent his time having piano lessons and practising.

Wieck had a little daughter named Clara, who was only half Robert's age (for she was nine and he was eighteen). She was already a very clever pianist and used to play in public with great success.

Besides practising the piano, Robert began to compose, and at last it became so clear that nature had intended him to be a musician that he was allowed to give up working at law.

'More Haste, Less Speed'

The trouble was that he wanted to become a great pianist too quickly, and so he used some piece of apparatus that he thought would improve his right hand. But instead of this, it injured the hand, and he realized that he could now never become a really fine player.

This was, after all, a blessing in disguise, because it made him give himself to composition. Now if Schumann had been merely a great pianist, we to-day would have had no pleasure out of him (though our grandfathers might have done). But as he became a composer, he has given pleasure to a great many people who were born long after he died, and will give pleasure to boys and girls and men and women for long years after we, too, are dead and done for.

How Schumann Edited a Paper

In those days, as now, there were a great many people who liked frivolous, silly music, and did not appreciate music that was really beautiful. Now Schumann, having been brought up amongst books and writers, had the idea of starting a musical paper to help people to like good music. He had a little band of friends who assisted him, and their paper did a great deal of good.

Schumann used to write a great many fine articles in this paper, and whenever a brilliant young musician appeared, he did all he could, by writing about him in the paper, to encourage him and to get people to pay attention to his music.

How Schumann Fought for a Wife

As Clara Wieck grew older she and Robert Schumann realized that they were meant for each other. But old Wieck would not hear of it, as Robert was not rich, nor was he famous.

So there was a lawsuit about it, and Robert made the father come into court and state his reasons for refusing his consent. When the court heard the reasons they said these were not good ones, and told Wieck that he must allow Clara to marry Robert.

So Clara and Robert were married, and happy ever afterwards—that is until a great sorrow came, of which you shall hear something in a moment.

On his marriage Schumann suddenly took to writing songs, as if to express his feelings. For a year he wrote song after song, and most of his beautiful songs were written at this time.

The Sadness of Schumann's Life

The sad thing about Schumann's life was its ending, for he went out of his mind, and at length he had to be put in an asylum.

His nature had for some time seemed a little queer, and he often did things that struck people as odd. For instance he was very silent, and at a restaurant at Dresden he would sit night after night at a particular table, with his back to the people, just thinking quietly or working out his music in his mind.

That sort of thing did not matter much, and people only took it as one of the strange ways that genius often has. But when he became really mad every one felt very sorry, and when he died in the asylum in 1856 (aged only 46) there was great regret.

His widow gave up the rest of her life to playing the piano all over Europe to get money for her children and to make her husband's wonderful compositions known. She lived for forty years after the death of her husband.

QUESTIONS

*(To See Whether You Remember
the Chapter and Understand It)*

1. When and where was Schumann born, and when did he die?

2. What do you know about his music-making at school?

3. What was his father's profession, and what influence had this on him and on his music?

4. For what profession was he educated?

5. Who taught him the piano when he should have been studying law?

6. Say all you know (which should be a great deal) about this piano teacher's daughter.

7. What accident did Schumann have in trying to become a great pianist?

8. And what do you remember of his writing about music?

9. Tell something about his marriage.

10. And about his death.

THINGS TO DO

1. If you are a pianist get Schumann's *Album for the Young,* and learn some of the pieces in it. (If you are a pretty fair sight-reader you can play them without much 'learning'.) Then study how they are made and make little diagrams of some of them. Look at their titles and see if you think the music expresses the idea of the title. If you cannot play yourself, get one of your friends to play them to you, and, by listening carefully, learn all you can about them.

2. Get somebody to play you some of Schumann's bigger and harder pieces, and study them in the same way.

3. Write a little life of Schumann and paste it in your copy of the *Album for the Young* or any other music of his you possess.

4. Make and act a little play about Schumann.

5. If you have a Gramophone at home get your parents to buy some Schumann records: if you have a Pianola get them to buy some Schumann rolls—of pieces that would be too hard for you to play by hand.

CHAPTER XIV

CHOPIN

1810-1849

WHEN you hear Chopin's music you must remember that its composer was half a Pole and half a Frenchman. For his father was a Frenchman and his mother a Pole.

Now the French have always been noted for writing beautifully graceful and neat music, and the Poles are very fond of wild dances, and besides this have been so much oppressed that in their music you often find something very sad or very fierce. And one or other of these various qualities, French and Polish, you generally find in the lovely piano pieces Chopin wrote.

A Boy Pianist

When little Frederic was only nine years old he had become quite well known as a clever pianist. The rich Polish noblemen used to send for him to perform at their houses, and one day he had an invitation to take part in a great public concert.

FREDERIC CHOPIN

This was the first time Frederic had performed before a large audience, and there was great excitement in the Chopin household. The little boy was dressed with great care. He stood on a chair and his mother put his best clothes on him.

There was one thing which he had never worn before, and he was very proud of it. His mother was not able to go to the concert, and when he came back she asked him, 'Well, what did the people like best?' And instead of naming one of his piano pieces the little chap exclaimed, 'Oh, Mother, every one was looking at *my collar!*'

At this concert Frederic played a PIANOFORTE CONCERTO. This, as you probably know, is a piece in which the solo instrument, the piano, has the chief part, but a full orchestra plays too. Sometimes the piano plays alone, and sometimes the orchestra, and sometimes they both play together. To play a Piano Concerto well is a great feat.

How Frederic Tamed Rough People

At that time Warsaw was ruled by the Russian Grand Duke Constantine, and he was said by everybody there to be a very violent and brutal man. But when Frederic played to him, as he often did, the Grand Duke was always as kind and gentle as possible.

But there are some people even harder to tame than Grand Dukes, and these are—*schoolboys!* Now

Frederic's father had a school, and one day, when he was out, the master left in charge could not keep order.

Whilst the uproar was at its height Frederic came in and begged the boys to be quiet whilst he played them a story on the piano. Then they kept as still as mice, and the young pianist put out the lights and began to play. As he did so he told them what the music meant. It was all about robbers, who tried to get into a house with ladders, but were frightened by a noise and ran away. They came to a dark wood and lay down to sleep.

When the story got to this point Frederic played more softly until not only the robbers, but his hearers too, dropped off, one by one, to sleep.

Then he stopped playing and crept quietly out of the room to fetch his mother and sisters, so that they should have a good laugh at the sleepers. They brought lights into the room and then Frederic struck a loud chord on the piano to waken the boys.

You can imagine they all had some fun out of this incident. Is this tale true? What do you think? Can boys be lulled to sleep as easily as that?

How He Played to the Emperor of Russia, and Then Began To See the World

When Frederic was fourteen the Emperor of Russia came to Warsaw. Probably the people of Warsaw were proud of their young pianist, for he was asked to play before the Emperor.

All this time Frederic had hardly been outside his native city, and it was not until he was nineteen that he began to see the world. It chanced that a professor of natural history was going to Berlin, to attend a great congress of naturalists. So it was arranged that Frederic should go with him, and that whilst the professor was attending his lectures and meetings the youth should go to concerts and the opera, and also make the acquaintance of the musicians of Berlin.

Mendelssohn, who was the same age as Chopin, and who then lived in Berlin, was present at the Congress, but Chopin did not like to introduce himself to him, because Mendelssohn had already become famous, whereas he himself was almost unknown outside his home city.

The Pianist at the Inn

In those days travelling was, of course, done by coach, and when the professor and the young pianist came to a certain little town they stopped to change horses.

In the inn parlour Chopin found a grand piano, so he began to play. The landlord and the landlady and their daughters were delighted, and so were all the coach passengers. For some time the coach could not start, for the people would not get into it. When at last Chopin stopped playing the landlady and her daughter came to the coach after him, bringing lovely cakes to eat on the way, and wine to refresh him on the dusty road.

A Concert at Vienna

It was now time for Frederic to be making himself known as a musician wider afield, so his father urged him to go to Vienna and give a concert there. He was then twenty.

Most of the people who heard him were delighted, but a few of the Viennese thought that he played too quietly. They were fond of loud noise. It is a good thing that Chopin did not listen to them, for his natural style, both as player and composer, was a graceful, quiet style. Sometimes his music has to be played loudly and brightly, but much of it is meant for gentle, expressive playing, and none of it is rowdy.

From Vienna Chopin went on to other capitals, such as Prague and Dresden, so now he was really seeing the world, and the world was hearing him. But for some time Vienna was his centre, to which he returned after his journeys, and where he spent many months. You will remember that this was the city where Haydn, Mozart, Beethoven, and many other composers had spent a large part of their lives. It has always been one of the most music-loving cities of the world.

How Chopin's Compositions Became Famous

Some of the people at Vienna thought Chopin was a very fine pianist but not much of a composer, but gradually it became recognized that he was great in both ways.

When he composed some variations for the piano, which were published, Schumann, who, as you may remember, edited a musical paper, was so delighted with them that he wrote an article in which were the words, *Hats off, gentlemen—a Genius!*

And one day when Chopin was in the Imperial Library at Vienna, he was astonished to see a book of music there with the name 'Chopin' on it. He said to himself, 'I have never heard of any other musician named Chopin, so perhaps there is a mistake somewhere.'

However, he took up the volume, and looked inside, and lo and behold! it was all in his own handwriting. The publisher of his variations had realized that the composer would one day become famous, and, after printing the variations, had sent the manuscript to be carefully kept for ever in the Emperor's library.

So Chopin had a great surprise, and he wrote home to tell his mother and father about it, and the letter can still be read.

Life in Paris

When Chopin was twenty-two he decided to go to Paris. There he made friends with many of the chief musicians, but he found life very expensive, and almost decided to emigrate to America. But one day in the street he met Prince Radziwill, who had been good to him when he was a boy, so he told the Prince about the American project.

The Prince said nothing to dissuade him, but persuaded him to come that evening to a party at the house of the great rich Baron Rothschild. There he was, of course, asked to play, and all the people present admired his playing so much that he realized that the tide had turned and success was at hand. So he never went to America after all, but stayed in Paris and grew more and more famous.

Chopin and the Poles

Whenever a poor Pole was in Paris, Chopin, who now began to make lots of money, was ready to help him. Once he had arranged to go with his friend the musician, Hiller, to the Lower Rhine Musical Festival, which Mendelssohn was to conduct. But when the time came he had given all his money to some of the poor Poles who had fled to Paris for refuge, and he had to tell Hiller to go alone.

But Hiller would not consent, and then a thought struck Chopin. He took up the manuscript of his beautiful E flat Waltz, ran off with it to a publisher's, and came back with 500 francs. So the two friends were able to go together after all. At the Festival Chopin became great friends with Mendelssohn.

Chopin as a Teacher

Chopin had a great many pupils amongst the Parisians. The chief thing that he taught them was to play with a beautiful light touch.

As you know, there are some pianists who have done lots of scales and exercises and made their fingers very strong, but who cannot play lightly. It is good for these people to practise Chopin's compositions, because these need to be played with a light touch, or they are spoilt.

Chopin in Britain

All the latter part of his life poor Chopin had bad health. He was consumptive. Once he went to London especially to consult some famous doctor. He did not want people to know he was there, so he called himself Mr. Fritz. But some ladies who persuaded him to play to them guessed who it must be.

Then, in 1848, when he was thirty-nine years old, he went again. He used to be very fond of Broadwood's pianos and used to go to their shop in London to practise. But he was now so weak that, to save him exertion, some one in the shop would lift him up like a child and carry him up to the piano room.

After playing the piano a good deal at parties at some of the big houses in London, he went to

Manchester, and then to Edinburgh and Glasgow. The Scottish people, who are very hospitable, almost killed him with kindness. This visit to Britain was altogether too tiring, and poor Chopin went home exhausted.

The Death of Chopin

At last, at the age of only 40, poor Chopin was found to be dying. One of the last things he asked for was music. He begged a Polish Countess, who had come to visit him, to sing and play, and she did so, much to his comfort. Then, a day or two later, he passed away.

Chopin's Music

If you are old enough to play Chopin's music you have perhaps already found out that he did not write many Sonatas or other long pieces with several 'movements'. He preferred to write shorter pieces such as Nocturnes, Preludes, Studies, Impromptus, Ballades, Waltzes, Mazurkas, and Polonaises.

All Chopin's best music was for piano. You see this was the instrument he loved and played so beautifully, and he understood perhaps better than any one who has ever lived how to write music that should sound well on it.

QUESTIONS

*(To See Whether You Remember
the Chapter and Understand It)*

1. What was Chopin's nationality?

2. What effect would you expect this to have on his music?

3. Tell anything you remember about the concert he played at when nine years old?

4. What is a Pianoforte Concerto?

5. Tell a story about Chopin playing to his schoolfellows.

6. Tell a story about his playing in an inn.

7. What can you remember about Chopin's life in Vienna?

8. Why did he nearly go to America, and why did he decide not to go after all?

9. What do you remember about his doings in Paris?

10. And what do you remember about his life in Britain?

11. And what do you know about Chopin's style of piano playing?

12. How did he die? And how old was he? Can you remember any other composers who died rather young?

13. What sort of music did Chopin write?

THINGS TO DO

(For School and Home)

1. Get somebody to play you one or two of the Nocturnes, and find out how they are made.

(a) What sort of work has Chopin given the right hand to do, for the most part?

(b) And what sort of work has he given the left hand?

(c) What is the 'form' of the piece? Try to make a diagram of it.

(d) When you have found out the form and made the diagram, find out the chief keys (if you understand keys) and put these in the diagram.

(e) Then see if you can find out how Chopin keeps up your interest in the piece by variety in the character of the tunes (or 'subjects') he uses, and in their keys.

(f) When you have done all this, have the piece played again and listen to it carefully to notice all these details.

(g) And finally have it played once more, without troubling much to listen to the details, but just enjoying the beauty of the piece.

2. Get some one to play you one or two of each of the following kinds of pieces by Chopin:

(i) **Polonaise.** As the name indicates this is a piece written in the style of a Polish national dance. It has ___[9] beats in a bar.

(ii) **Mazurka.** This is another Polish national dance with ___ [9] beats in a bar (slower than a Valse but quicker than a Polonaise).

(iii) **Valse** (or Waltz). Another piece in the style of a dance. It has ___[9] beats in a bar.

3. Get somebody to play you Chopin's Berceuse. As you know, 'Berceuse' is French for Cradle Song or Lullaby. Do you think this would be a good piece for rocking a baby to sleep? How is it made? Find out all about it by listening carefully, and then make a diagram of it. Last of all have it played again just for pleasure.

4. If possible get somebody to play you one of the Ballades and any other suitable Chopin pieces, in the same way.

5. If you have any of Chopin's music, write a little *Life of Chopin* and paste it in the beginning of the music.

6. Make up and act a little play on some incident in Chopin's life.

7. Prepare and give a little lecture on Chopin to your friends, playing, or getting some friends (young or grown-up) to play some Chopin music to illustrate it.

8. If you have a Pianola at home get your parents to buy some rolls of Chopin pieces—some of those that would be too hard for you to play by hand. Remember, however, that to get a good effect with fine music on the Pianola you will need to practise it a bit.

[9]Listen and find out how many, and then fill up this blank for yourself.

CHAPTER XV

WHAT IS 'ROMANTIC MUSIC'?

A Simple Explanation

Suppose we were going through a picture gallery. We should find there were two kinds of pictures.

One kind would make us say, 'Oh, how beautiful!' We should realize that the pictures of that kind were made up by painting beautiful things, and painting them in a beautiful way. And we should get a great deal of *pleasure* from looking at them.

But we should find another kind of picture, which might, or might not, be as beautiful as the first kind, but which would make us *feel* deeply, so that we might stand in front of it and as we looked become very happy and excited, or very sad, or very awestruck, or very sympathetic.

There might, for instance, be a picture of Lord Kitchener about to go on board the 'Hampshire'. And if the artist were a very clever one we should find he had put into the great War Minister's face such strength of character and determination, that we ourselves should feel braver as we looked at it.

Or there might be a picture of a Sailor Boy leaving his poor old mother to go to sea, and then we should be made to feel sorrowful as we thought of the mother's sorrow, and her fears that she might never see her boy again.

Or there might be a great Battle Scene, which would stir our blood, and make us wish to fight for our country, or a picture of a Stormy Day that would make us imagine we were battling with the wind and rain, or a lovely Sunset picture that would make us feel full of awesome delight, as we do when a summer's evening ends with coloured clouds that seem to be curtains hanging before the doors of heaven.

Now the first set of pictures we might call 'Beauty Pictures', and the second sort 'Imagination Pictures'. Some of the 'Beauty Pictures' would stir the imagination a little, but their first object would be beauty, and all of the other pictures would be beautiful, more or less, but their first object would be to stir our imagination. And this second set we might call 'ROMANTIC'.

And, just in the same way, there is 'Beauty Music' and 'Imagination (or Romantic) Music'.

'Beauty Music'

Now play over on the piano (or get some one else to play for you) a few little bits of music, the openings of three or four pieces.

Here is the beginning of one of Bach's *Inventions:*

INVENTION, BY BACH

Look at that little scrap of music carefully. It is all made out of a jolly little tune which climbs up and then runs down, given first to one hand and then to the other. If you examine the music you will see how neatly Bach has fitted things in, and the whole piece is made up just as beautifully and neatly, as you will see if you get a copy of it.

Now this piece, played in a lively way, is a quite beautiful one, and we enjoy hearing it. But it does not stir our *imagination* much.

Here is the opening of another piece, the Rondo, from one of Mozart's Piano Sonatas.

RONDO, BY MOZART

In this case there is a graceful tune and a simple accompaniment—but no great *imagination*.

'Imagination Music'

Now we come to something very different. Play these bars, if your hands are big enough. They are from the opening of Beethoven's *Pathetic Sonata*.

SONATA, BY BEETHOVEN

Do you not at once feel that in this Sonata Beethoven is going to stir our feelings? This is music of quite another kind from what we have just been playing. It makes us feel solemn and awestruck. It is a piece of 'Imagination Music' or (to use the proper word) 'Romantic Music'.

Here is another Imaginative piece, of a very different kind. Play this several times and see what you think of it.

'ARLEQUIN', BY SCHUMANN

Schumann calls this piece *Harlequin,* and we feel as soon as we hear it that he has set out to make us feel we are in the midst of a gay party of revellers. Again, we have a piece of 'Romantic Music'.

And here, to close with, is a Mazurka, by Chopin.

MAZURKA, BY CHOPIN

As in the Mozart piece given above, there is a beautiful tune in the right hand and a simple accompaniment in the left. But this time the tune is not only beautiful; it is full of tender feeling. So here again is a piece of 'Romantic Music'.

The 'Romantic Composers'

Schumann and Chopin are what are called 'Romantic Composers'. And the 'Romantic School',[10] as we call the composers who write this kind of music, grew up chiefly during the first half of last century (between 1800 and 1850). Some of the chief 'Romantic' composers are Weber, Schubert, Schumann, Chopin, Mendelssohn, and Sterndale Bennett. But much of Beethoven's music is Romantic, too (perhaps most of it, in fact), and Bach and Mozart sometimes wrote romantically, as you will find when you grow older.

'Romantic' Literature

I need not tell you that, just as there are Romantic pictures and music, so there is Romantic literature. Indeed, the word really belongs to literature, though we have borrowed it for music. Any poem or tale, or description, that sets your imagination working hard, and fills you with a sense of wonder, or awe, or

[10]This doesn't mean a real School like yours, but just a *set* of Composers who wrote in something the same way as one another. We speak of a 'school of composers' just as we speak of a 'school of fishes'.

excitement, is Romantic. Scott's novels are 'Romances', and Shakespeare's *Midsummer-Night's Dream* and *Tempest* are very Romantic plays.

Beware!

Some people when they grow older lose the spirit of Romance, and settle down into matter-of-fact business men or anxious housewives. That is a great pity, and must not be allowed to happen to you. If the author of this book should meet you when you are *quite* old (say thirty or forty), he hopes that he will find that a beautiful country lane, or an imaginative picture, or a piece of Schumann's music, or a fairy tale, or a moving story of real life can still make you feel the thrill of *Romance.* Never let the hard blows of the world knock that out of you!

QUESTIONS

*(To See Whether You Remember
the Chapter and Understand It)*

1. Can you describe the two sorts of pictures—and the two sorts of music?

2. Who are the chief Romantic Composers'?

3. About when did they live?

THINGS TO DO

1. Get somebody to play over to you a good lot of pieces (or parts of pieces) by Bach, Mozart, Beethoven, Schumann, Chopin, and the other composers mentioned in this book, and see which you think could be described as Romantic.

2. Then have them played again and see what *emotion* you think the composer has been expressing in each.

EDWARD GRIEG

CHAPTER XVI

GRIEG AND HIS NORWEGIAN MUSIC

1843-1907

A LITTLE Norwegian boy of five stood before his mother's piano. The lid was open and he was looking at the keys from which his mother got such wonderful sounds every day. He thought he too would like to make music.

So, as he stood there, he timidly put down a note. That sounded all right, but what he liked, when his mother played, was the sound of several notes played together, so he tried to find another to go with the first one and this is what he found:

That he thought was lovely, and he played it quite a lot for the pleasure of hearing it:

Then he began to wonder whether he could find a third note to go with these two, and, by and by, he discovered this:

Then he began to get excited. Could he find a fourth? He tried:

but that would not do (try it yourself and see). So then he tried:

and that made him very happy. His eyes sparkled with joy. He had found four notes that sounded beautiful when they were played together.

Now he became really ambitious. He wanted to find still another note, to make five altogether. His little fingers felt about on the keys and he got this chord:

Years after, when Edward Grieg was a very famous man, he was asked what was the first success of his life. And, in reply, he did not tell of the first piece of music of his that was ever published, or the first concert at which he played, but of finding that simple chord (which we call the 'chord of the ninth') when he was a little boy of five. That childish discovery had given him as much pleasure as anything he ever did in his life.

A great deal of the charm of modern music lies in what we call 'harmony' (that is, as you know, putting notes together so that they sound beautiful with one another), and Grieg, when he was a man was to become famous for his lovely 'harmonies'. So it is not surprising to learn that he had an 'instinct' for 'harmony', even when he was only a little chap of five.

The First Music Lessons

Now as we all know (only we don't like to talk about it), some children (though of course not many) are—*lazy!* But it is a consolation to know that even the laziest children sometimes grow out of their laziness and become useful people in the world, and that even great men were often lazy little boys.

So it was with Grieg. When his mother, who was a good player, began to give him piano lessons, a year later than the incident I have just related, he was at first delighted, but when he found that it meant *Practice*—then he felt sad. You see a good deal of what we have to practise, if we want to become good pianists, has not much music in it. We soon get tired of this little tune, don't we?—

And even this longer tune—

is not very exciting!

But Grieg's mother said that he must practise these tunes, and other tunes no better, or he would never become a good player, and instead of letting him sit down at the piano making up little tunes of his own and finding fresh chords, she kept him at the drudgery.

Grieg liked to *dream,* and his mother wanted him to *do.* So there was sometimes trouble. But the mother's will was stronger than the child's, and so little Edward began to make progress.

School Days

When he went to school it was the same thing. He did not at all like the hard work. Here is a little tale he tells of an arithmetic lesson.

The teacher said there should be some little reward for the first to get a sum right.

Now Grieg had a brilliant idea. He thought ' "0" means nothing; if I leave out all the noughts, it will save time in reckoning and make no difference to the answer'. So, as he added, or multiplied, or divided, whenever there came a nought he just left it out. That, he thought, was a short cut to success. But he didn't get the prize!

When he made a mistake in the English lesson Grieg's master made great sport about it, because Grieg's father was the British Consul at Bergen. And then the boy went red and felt ashamed of himself, and very unhappy.

The boys were unjust, too. I do not know whether you have ever noticed it, but children at school are often very cruel. One day, in the reading lesson, they came to the word 'Requiem', and the master asked if any of them knew what great composer had written a piece of church music with that name. Grieg answered

'Mozart', and as he was the only one who knew, the other boys were jealous and started calling him 'Mozak', and shouting it after him in the streets. That, as you will admit, was both foolish and unfair.

The Singing Class

In the singing class Grieg could always do well. One day the master asked them about the scales and their sharps and flats, and Grieg was the only one who knew them. Now the singing master was a nice, kind man (as, of course, all music-teachers are!) and he gave Grieg such warm praise that it encouraged him for weeks after, and made him feel a little more self-confident.

A Piece of Good Luck

For a time Grieg was not very well, and had to stay away from school. He thought he was going to make a holiday of it, but his father did not mean him to be idle and kept him at work. In particular he made him learn by heart the history of the French king, Louis XIV. This was a bitter task, but it had to be done, and the father was not satisfied until every word in the chapter was known.

One day when Grieg had returned to school, the teacher said he would examine the boys in history. Here is Grieg's own description of what happened:

'The teacher sat as usual, and balanced himself on one leg of his chair, while he turned over the leaves backwards and forwards, considering where he could catch me best. A long and painful silence. At last he came out with: "Tell me something about Louis XIV." It poured out as from a barrel with the bung out. Unceasingly flowed the stream of my speech. Not a word was left out. It was all as if nailed to my memory. The teacher was dumb with astonishment. He tried not to believe his ears; but the facts had spoken. There was nothing more to bring against me.

'Once more a turning over of the leaves, once more a wriggle on the leg of the chair. The sweat of anxiety burst from my forehead. It was impossible that for the second time I should be more lucky than wise. But my good star did not forsake me. "Can you tell me what Admirals were on the Black Sea under Catherine II?" With a loud voice I answered, "Admirals Greigh and Elphinstone."

'Those names had been welded into my consciousness ever since my father had told me that our family arms, which bore a ship, denoted that our original ancestor was, in all probability, the Scotch Admiral Greigh. The teacher clapped the book to. "Quite right; for that you will get a 'one' and a star."

'I was as proud as a Field-Marshal after a victory. I almost think that was the greatest success of my school life. All the greater shame to me that its real meaning was so small!'

Grieg's First Musical Composition

The next incident related shows that Grieg's lucky star was not perpetually shining. One day he brought to school a music-book on which he had written in large letters:

VARIATIONS ON A GERMAN MELODY,

BY EDWARD GRIEG. OPUS 1.

This he showed to a schoolfellow, who, however, took so lively an interest in the composition as to attract the teacher's attention. This personage insisted on knowing what was the matter, and at last was told, 'Grieg has composed something.'

'The teacher came to me, looked at the music-book, and said in a peculiar, ironical tone: "So the lad is musical, the lad composes. Remarkable!" Then he opened the door into the next class-room, fetched the teacher in from there, and said to him: "Here is something to look at. This little urchin is a composer!"

'Both teachers turned over the pages of the music-book with interest. Every one stood up in both classes. I felt sure of a grand success. But that is what one should never feel too quickly. For the other teacher had no sooner gone away than my master suddenly changed his tactics, seized me by the hair till my eyes were black, and said gruffly: "Another time he will bring the German Dictionary with him, as is proper, and leave this stupid stuff at home." Alas to be so near the summit of fortune, and then, all at once, to see oneself plunged into the depths! How often that has happened to me in later life! And I have always been driven to remember the first time.'

The Friendly Lieutenant

Opposite the school there lived a young lieutenant who was fond of music, and a good pianist. Grieg came to know him, and used to take his attempts at composition to show him.

The kind lieutenant, unlike the harsh schoolmaster, was always interested, and used to ask Grieg to make him copies of everything. All Grieg's life through he remembered this lieutenant, and felt grateful to him for his encouragement, and when, step by step, his friend rose to be a general, he felt very pleased indeed.

The Story of Ole Bull, and Grieg's Going to Leipzig

There was at that time a very famous Norwegian violinist called Ole Bull. He was a very adventurous man and went all over the world playing his violin to big audiences everywhere. Especially he loved to play the old Norwegian folk-tunes. Grieg had often heard his father and mother talk of this wonderful man. One summer's day, when he was nearly fifteen, he saw a rider on a fine Arab horse dashing up the road from

Bergen. When he reached the Griegs' gate, he stopped and jumped off. It was the celebrated Ole Bull, and he had come to visit them.

First he told them jokes and wonderful tales of his adventures in America. Then he made Grieg go to the piano, and, when he had heard him play some of his own boyish compositions, he became serious, and talked quietly to the parents.

Then he came over to Grieg and said, 'It is all arranged. You are to go to Leipzig and become a musician.'

That was a great day for Grieg!

So across the North Sea to Hamburg went young Edward. And very lonely he felt when at last he was deposited in a boarding-house at Leipzig, with no one around him who could speak a word of his native Norwegian.

Grieg and the Peasants

As the readers of this book are young people, this chapter is chiefly about Grieg's younger days. But it is necessary to tell just a few very important things about him when he grew up.

One thing you ought to know is that Grieg was a very patriotic Norwegian. He loved his native country, and though he was trained in music largely in Germany, he tried to write real *Norwegian Music*.

You already know that country people, who have

never had music lessons, nevertheless possess beautiful songs that are handed down from generation to generation. Grieg was very fond of the Folk-Songs of Norway, and used to love to hear the peasants singing them. And, whenever he could, he would get the country fiddlers to play him some of their jolly Folk-Dance music.

What Grieg Wrote

Grieg wrote a great deal of music for the piano—far more than most people know, for nearly every pianist plays the same few pieces instead of getting to know all of them.

Then he wrote a very fine Piano Concerto. He also wrote a lot of music for a lovely play by the Norwegian writer, Ibsen. This play is called *Peer Gynt*. Some of the music for *Peer Gynt* he also arranged in such a way that orchestras could play it as concert music, and it is in two 'Suites' or sets of pieces, called the *'Peer Gynt' Suites*. You can get these for piano solo or duet if you like, and very beautiful they are.

Many charming songs are amongst Grieg's works. His wife (who was also his cousin, by the way) was a beautiful singer, and sometimes the pair would go to England (of which country they were very fond), and Mrs. Grieg would give Song Recitals of her husband's songs, with the composer as accompanist.

There are also three sonatas for Piano and Violin and one for Piano and 'Cello. Altogether Grieg left us a lot of charming music, and all young musicians should look forward to playing more and more of it as they grow older.

QUESTIONS

*(To See Whether You Remember
the Chapter and Understand It)*

1. When was Grieg born? When did he die?

2. Tell the story of his first experiment in harmony.

3. Did he like his music lessons? Do you like yours?

4. Tell any tales you remember about his school-work—arithmetic, history, singing class, and so on.

5. Tell about the teacher who discouraged his composing and the soldier who cheered him.

6. Who was Ole Bull, and what did he do for Grieg?

7. What was Grieg's nationality, and how did this affect his music?

8. Mention any music Grieg wrote.

THINGS TO DO

1. If you are a pianist ask your teacher for some of the Grieg pieces such as you can play (perhaps one or two of the *Lyrical Pieces*).

2. If you are a pretty good player get the *Peer Gynt* suite, arranged for Piano Solo or Duet, or some of the other music so arranged, and practise it.

3. If you have a Gramophone or a Pianola get your parents to buy some Grieg records or rolls: there are plenty of good ones.

(Whatever you do, mind you study how the pieces you play on Piano or Gramophone, or by the Pianola, are made, and notice as much as you can about them.)

4. If you are a pretty good pianist get Grieg's *Four Norwegian Dances* (Op. 35) for Piano Duet, and play them with a friend. They are *very* jolly music.

5. Get somebody to play to you as much Grieg music as possible, and study how it is made. Make diagrams of it. Notice any Norwegian peculiarities. You can soon find out what they are, for they will strike you as quite different from anything you have heard in the English, German, Austrian, Polish, and French music previously studied.

6. If you have some of Grieg's music, write a little *Life of Grieg* and paste it at the beginning.

7. Make a little play of Grieg and act it with your friends.

CHAPTER XVII

EDWARD ELGAR

Born 1857

You know, I suppose, that Elgar was born into a very musical family. His father was an organist and music-seller in Worcester. If you go to that city you can still see the shop where Elgar's father lived and did his business and where Elgar himself was born. The name Elgar is still there over the shop window.

Elgar's First Music Lesson

Living amongst music as he did, little Edward soon began to think he would like to be a music maker. He was only five years old and, of course, did not understand things very well, but he noticed that when people played or sang they had a piece of paper before them with lines ruled on it, and black marks for the notes. So he got a piece of paper and ruled some lines and began to compose a grand piece.

It was a bright warm spring day, so he went outside to do his work, and sat down at the side of the house. He thought he was writing something very fine indeed

SIR EDWARD ELGAR

and sat there absorbed in his work, lost to everything going on around him.

Now whilst little Elgar, the musician, was composing his music, a house-painter was at work near him. The painter saw the little boy sitting there below, and wondered what he was doing so intently. By and by he came down his ladder and looked over the child's shoulder. 'Why!' he exclaimed, 'your music has only got four lines to each stave. Music always has five lines!'

That was the first music lesson Elgar had.

A Musical Home

As has been said, music was all around Elgar when he was a little boy. On Sundays he heard his father play the organ at St. George's Roman Catholic Church, and during the week people were coming into the shop all day to buy songs and piano pieces, and, of course, talking to his father about the music they wanted to buy. Nearly all the conversation, as the family sat at meals, was about music. Music seemed the most natural thing in life to that family—just as natural as eating and drinking.

Now that is a very important thing to remember. As you have read the lives of various great musicians in this book you must have noticed that most of them were brought up in a musical 'atmosphere'—they 'breathed' music, so to speak. Many of them had musical homes, where they heard music from their earliest years. Others became choir boys, and so were brought up amongst music. Of course there are some exceptions to this (as, for instance, Handel), but generally it was so. And certainly in Elgar's case we owe a great deal to the fact that the household in which he was born and in which he lived was a musical one.

A Great Event

But though little Edward Elgar lived amongst music and took an interest in it, and learnt a great deal about it almost without knowing he was doing so, it was one particular event which occurred that really roused him. He has told the present writer all about it, and here it is.

One day, as he was looking at some of the music in his father's shop, he came across Beethoven's First Symphony. (Beethoven wrote nine symphonies, as you already know.)

Now the First Symphony is, naturally, the simplest of all the nine. But it has a Scherzo that when it was written must have astonished people very much by its rapid modulations.

And as Elgar looked at the first page of this Scherzo, he suddenly felt on fire with excitement. He had never seen such a piece before, and rushed off with the book under his arm to study it in quietness. With six children about it, a house is rather noisy, as some of you may have experienced, but Elgar found a quiet place outside, and there he stayed reading this marvellous music through, over and over again, and taking in its harmonies and modulations.

If you look carefully at the page of music given, you will find it begins in key C, but 'modulates' by the time it gets to the double bar into key G. Then comes a modulation into E♭, followed by one into C minor. A♭ follows, and before long it is in D♭. As those of you who know something of the theory of music will agree, it has now travelled a very long way in a very short time. These modulations are very 'romantic'. When the piece is well played they make you feel quite excited. You will see that Beethoven inspired Elgar, and perhaps in future times it will be recorded that Elgar inspired you or some other boy or girl. For music is like measles in one way: it is 'catching'!

The Instruments Elgar Played

Now that Elgar had become really 'keen' about music he began to teach himself to play all the instruments on which he could lay hands. He became a pianist, and in later years had a good reputation about Worcester as an accompanist. He played the organ, too, and was able to take his father's place at the church, when necessary. The violoncello and the double-bass he also played pretty well, and when the orchestral society gave a symphony by Mozart or Haydn, he would play one of these instruments.

Then, too, Elgar learnt to play the bassoon, and with four friends made up a quintet.

Elgar as Violinist

But Elgar's chief instrument was the violin. He worked hard at this and became a very good player. And for years to come he was known not as a composer but as a violinist.

One of the finest works Elgar has ever written is a Violin Concerto. If ever you have a chance be sure to hear this. When you do so you will realize that it is a work that could never have been written by any composer who had not been a violinist. All the powers of the violin are used in it, and it is perhaps the most difficult violin piece ever written.

Studies in Theory

Besides studying these various instruments, Elgar worked at the theory of music. You must remember that his success is not due merely to his being born with musical 'genius', and brought up in a musical 'atmosphere', but also to his having lots of perseverance. He really *tried.*

When he was talking to the present writer about his early life he showed him a parcel of his early studies that had just been found at Worcester and sent to him. There was sheet after sheet of music paper, with the exercises he had worked, and the attempts at composition he had made. You see a great composer has to *work,* just as you have to do. If a boy wants to be a good pianist he has to toil at his exercises and scales, and if he wants to be a composer he has to struggle with his harmony and counterpoint.

From Mozart to Elgar

It is rather interesting to know that Elgar is a sort of musical descendant of Mozart. Mozart had a friend and pupil called Michael Kelly—an Irishman. And Kelly had a pupil called Sutton (a Dover man), and Elgar's father learnt music from Sutton, and Elgar naturally learnt a good deal of music from his father. Thus we may see that, in a musical way, Elgar is a great-great-grandson of Mozart, which is an interesting little fact to remember—and one of which he is proud.

Elgar's Works

The list of Elgar's works is a very long one. Besides a great many shorter pieces, such as songs and part-songs, and violin solos, it includes the oratorios, *The Dream of Gerontius, The Apostles* and *The Kingdom,* the fine *Enigma Variations* for Orchestra, two Symphonies, a Violin Concerto, a 'Cello Concerto, and some Chamber music.[11]

---

[11]By 'Chamber Music' we mean such music as String Quartets and other pieces for two or more instruments, such as are meant rather for people to play together in a room (or chamber) than for public performers to play in great concert halls.

QUESTIONS

*(To See Whether You Remember
the Chapter and Understand It)*

1. When and where was Elgar born?

2. Tell anything you remember about his home.

3. What piece of music really woke Elgar up to the wonders of music, and how did it do this?

4. What instruments did Elgar learn to play? Which was the chief one?

5. Give the names of any pieces of Elgar.

THINGS TO DO

1. Get somebody to play you one of the *Pomp and Circumstance* Marches, or get it played on the Gramophone. Listen to it carefully and find out how a military march is made (these marches were written specially for the British Army). Make a diagram.

2. If you have a Gramophone get your parents to buy one or two of the Elgar songs—particularly those from the children's play, *The Starlight Express.*

3. Play or get somebody to play, or perform on the Gramophone, *The Wild Bear, The Tame Bear,* and the other pieces from *The Wand of Youth* suite. Find out how these pieces are made and make diagrams of

them. Also discuss with your friends what is the idea of each piece as suggested to you by its title, and consider whether this idea is successfully carried out.

4. Elgar wrote music to accompany a wonderful poem by a Belgian poet, all about the German invasion of Belgium. It is called *Carillon,* and has bell music in it. You can get this on two Gramophone records, and the orchestral effects come out very well. If possible get records of this, and after hearing it once or twice, so as to get hold of the poem and its general ideas, begin to study how the music is made. (A piano version of the music can also be had, but the Gramophone records are really better, because they give you the Reciter and the Orchestra.) As you have had a chapter on the Orchestra you can study the instruments with these records. The brass instruments come out especially well.

5. If you have any of Elgar's music write a little *Life of Elgar* and paste it in.

6. Make up and act a little play about Elgar as a boy.

7. Play or get somebody to play you the piece which 'awakened' Elgar, and try to find out what it was that stirred him so much.

CHAPTER XVIII

MACDOWELL—THE AMERICAN COMPOSER

1861-1908

THIS is the only chapter in the book about an American composer. Why is that? Well, the fact is that America has not yet had a great many really big composers, though she may soon have more. How does that come about? Why should Russia and France and Germany and Austria and Italy and Britain have long lists of great composers, and America only a short list— and that without many names of world-wide fame?

A New Country

The reason is a simple one. America is still a *new country*. Of course we know that Europeans settled in America long since. The Pilgrim Fathers landed from their little 'Mayflower' boat in 1620, and that is three hundred years ago. But, in the history of a country, three hundred years is a very short time.

EDWARD MACDOWELL

Just think for a moment of those Pilgrim Fathers landing at the place they called Plymouth Rock, on the rough Atlantic coast. What a desert place they found! At first they were so busy in trying to get food and to make shelter for themselves that we may be sure they thought little about music. They had to grow crops and kill wild animals, defend themselves against the fiercer Indian tribes and make friends with the more kindly ones—and all this gave them enough to do!

The Music of the Pilgrim Fathers

Of course even busy people have some music, and so had these Pilgrim Fathers. They had no orchestras, nor string quartets, nor harpsichords, nor organs, but in their simple Sabbath worship they had the singing of Psalms to some of the old tunes they had learnt in England.

These brave men and women had with them some copies of a book of psalm-tunes which had been printed for them in Amsterdam at the time they were taking refuge in Holland, before they came to America, and they had other psalm-books which had been printed in England for use in church services there.

By and by, only twenty years after they landed, they even printed a psalm-book of their own, generally called to-day *The Bay Psalm-Book*. This was a very famous book, so much so that in England and Scotland also people printed and sold copies of it. Thus the Pilgrims were giving back to the old country they had come from some of the old tunes they had brought with them from it.

So the Puritans who went to America loved psalm music: tunes like the 'Old Hundredth', for instance, they sang heartily. But it was not to be expected that their music should get much beyond this for some time. It is generally understood that no organ was ever seen in America until 1741, one hundred and twenty-one years after the Pilgrims landed. And as for music out of church they cannot have had a great deal.

No Orchestras nor Organs in America in Those Days

You see that while music is a *necessity,* it is also a *luxury.* Everywhere in the world people have music. If people are to have such things as great organs and orchestras and sonatas and symphonies they must live in towns and cities, and must be rich enough to pay for the music they enjoy.

If you went to Central Africa to-day you could sing songs and hymns there, and get others to join you, but you could not get up an Orchestra, could you? And so you could never perform a Symphony. And you could not find amongst your companions a composer to write beautiful Piano Sonatas, because all your companions would be busy growing crops and shooting lions and building bungalows. Very likely you would have to wait fifty years before you could have any *elaborate* music, and it might be two or three hundred years before the settlement you had founded could produce a great composer.

Music in America To-day

So it was with America. But as the country became dotted with towns, more and more music was heard, and now in America you will hear fine big organs, well played by famous American organists, and piano recitals by American pianists, and orchestral concerts given by magnificent orchestras in such cities as New York, Boston, and Chicago. And nowadays there are quite a lot of American composers, though, as has been said, few really *great* ones as yet. By great, we mean, of course, in the sense that Byrd and Bach and Beethoven are great.

The Greatest American Composer

Most people think that the greatest composer America has yet produced is Edward Macdowell. Perhaps you will think that must be a Scottish name, and so it is, for Macdowell had Scots blood in him.

There have been other fine American composers during the last sixty years, but Macdowell has given us the greatest amount of fine music, and if you are a musician you ought to know something about him and, still more, know some of his music. Most of it is of such a kind that young folks can easily understand it, and some of it you will really love as soon as you hear it.

Macdowell's Boyhood

It will not take long to tell about Macdowell's life, for it had no great adventures.

He was born in New York (what date—do you remember?). As he was so fond of music his parents allowed him to have lessons from the best pianists to be found there.

When he was fifteen the boy came to Europe to continue his studies. First he went to Paris and studied in the Conservatoire there. Then he went to Wiesbaden, in Germany, and worked hard under some of the most famous teachers of piano and composition, especially one called Raff (whose *Cavatina* some of you have heard).

He Becomes a Teacher and University Professor

After this he began teaching—though of course, like all great men, he continued learning until the end of his life. He became the chief piano teacher at the Conservatoire at Darmstadt, and also taught in other German cities. He was very fond of England and Scotland, and often visited them.

When he was twenty-seven Macdowell returned to America. He went to Boston and became well known as a fine pianist and teacher of piano. Then the great Columbia University, in New York, invited him to become its Professor of Music, and unfortunately he said he would go.

Why 'unfortunately'? Well, you see, Providence had meant him to be a Pianist and a Composer—*not* a Professor, and the work of preparing lectures and teaching classes was not good for him. He had lots of worries, and this prevented him from composing as much as he ought to have done. So it is a pity he ever went to the University.

After nine years at Columbia he gave up his post and then, sad to say, his brain gave way.

Now it is a sorrowful thing when a clever man dies, but perhaps it is even more sorrowful to see him still living but without his full reason. However, Macdowell's weakness was a rather beautiful sort of weakness, for he did not become mad but simply, as it were, a child again. He would sit in his chair for hours and play with gold pieces, or quietly amuse himself in some other way.

Mrs. Macdowell

Do you remember that in the Grieg chapter you were told about Mrs. Grieg, and in the Schumann chapter about Mrs. Schumann? Grieg was very happy in his wife, because she was a musician and a great help and comfort to him, and just the same was the case with Schumann.

So it was also with Macdowell. He married one of his pupils, and she was able to appreciate his musical gifts and help him in his work, and, after his death, to carry on his work by playing his compositions everywhere up and down America.

Macdowell's Music

Macdowell invented a new term to describe his works. He called it 'Suggestive' music.

You know that there is a great deal of beautiful music that we love to hear because it is beautiful, but that does not suggest any particular thoughts to us. But there is other music which is also beautiful and which reminds us of brooklets or mountains, or fairies, or fighting—as the case may be. Perhaps the composer had one of these things in his mind when he wrote the piece; and when you hear the piece the same thought probably comes to you. That is what Macdowell meant by 'Suggestive Music'. It is a sort of Romantic Music.

If you look at the titles of Macdowell's piano pieces you will see such titles as *Elfin Dance,* or *March Wind,* or *To a Wild Rose,* or *Will o' the Wisp,* or *From a Deserted Farm,* or 'MDCXX'.

All these show that when Macdowell wrote music he was not merely trying to write down beautiful sounds, but also trying to put into the sounds some of the charming thoughts that were always passing through his mind. He was a very *imaginative* man, and another name for his music would be 'Imaginative Music'. You can call it that if you like.

By the way, what does that title 'MDCXX' mean? Isn't that a strange title for a piece—just a date and nothing else? What date is it? If you do not remember, look through the earlier part of this chapter and see if anything there reminds you. Then get some one to play you this piece and see what 'suggestion' it makes to you. Use your imagination as you hear it, and you will enjoy it all the more.

QUESTIONS

*(To See Whether You Remember
the Chapter and Understand It)*

1. What do you think is the reason that there have not yet been a great many *big* American composers?

2. When did the Pilgrim Fathers land, and what sort of music did they have?

3. Why do we not find great composers in new countries?

4. When was Macdowell born and where?

5. Where did he study piano-playing?

6. And where did he teach the piano?

7. When he returned to America where did he settle first—and where next?

8. Tell anything you remember about his death.

9. Do you remember anything about Mrs. Macdowell?

10. How did Macdowell describe his music, and what did he mean by this description?

THINGS TO DO

1. If possible get somebody to play you Macdowell's piece called *MDCXX* (in the *Sea Pieces*) and see what impression it gives you. Can you feel the sea? Do you get any impression in any part of it of the Puritan psalm-singing? Do you think the composer has succeeded in giving a picture of Puritan courage and sincerity?

After thinking about these things study how the piece is made and make a diagram if you can (it is a rather hard piece to make a diagram of, perhaps). Then try to find out how Macdowell got the effect of the sea into his music.

2. Get somebody to play you other pieces by Macdowell and study them in the same way. There are lots of short pieces which are very beautiful and each of them 'suggests' something. Ask yourself what it suggests and then study how it is made up and how the 'suggestion' is conveyed. I do not think that there is any composer mentioned in this book whose pieces you will like better than those of Macdowell. Many of them are just the thing for young listeners. You would, for instance, like the rather humorous pieces, called *Marionettes,* the *Woodland Sketches,* the various *Sea Pieces,* the *Fireside Tales* (especially 'Brer Rabbit'), and some of the *New England Idyls.*

The Second Book of the
GREAT MUSICIANS

*A Further Course in Appreciation
for Young Readers*

by

Percy A. Scholes

YESTERDAY'S CLASSICS

ITHACA, NEW YORK

TO THE READER

HERE is a Second Book of the Great Musicians—for those who have already read the first one. As whilst they have been reading it they have been growing older and cleverer, I have not used such simple language this time as I did before, and I have made the chapters rather longer and fuller. I want to offer a word of thanks to Mr. Emery Walker, as well as to Mr. F. Page of the Oxford University Press, who have taken a great deal of trouble to help me to find suitable pictures to illustrate this book, and to Mr. W. R. Anderson, Editor of the monthly journal, *The Music Teacher,* who has read the proofs for me. A Third Book of the Great Musicians is in preparation and will complete the series.

The Author

CONTENTS OF BOOK II

SCHUBERT

CHAPTER I

SCHUBERT

1797-1828

A School Band Practice

THE school orchestra was practising. The oboe and flute and bassoon and horn and kettle-drum were vigorously playing their parts or counting their rests, and the string players were fiddling away. One of the big boys was the leading Violin. It was a musical school, and this boy had been there a long time and could play beautifully. What were they playing? Well, for a guess, one of Haydn's symphonies. This school was in Vienna, and Haydn and Beethoven both lived in Vienna at that very time, and their music was popular with the Viennese; so we will suppose that the band was playing a Haydn symphony, since a Beethoven symphony is, as a rule, too difficult for a school orchestra. By and by came a break in the playing, as one movement of the symphony ended and before the next began, and the big boy, the leader (Spaun was his name), turned round to see who it could be who was playing behind him, with such firm rhythm and in such good tune.

1

There he saw a little new boy, a round-faced, curly-headed fellow, with spectacles. His name was Franz Schubert, but already he had a nickname—'The Miller', because when he came to be examined for entrance to the school he wore a light coat. Spaun nodded at him with approval, and then the playing began again. But when the practice was over he learnt more about 'The Miller', and in a few days he had become one of his truest friends.

School Joys and Troubles

Franz needed friends. His father was poor, and the school life, though happy in many ways, was in others a hard one. At the time Franz was admitted to this school he had ten or eleven brothers and sisters, and as years went by more came into the world, so that in the end there were seventeen children in the family. Now the father, though a hard-working man, did not earn a great deal of money. So when, to his great joy, he managed to get his clever son Franz into the school I have been speaking of, which was the Emperor's choir school, and trained the boys for the court chapel, he could not supply him with those little luxuries that boys at a boarding-school seem to expect, and it is quite certain, for instance, that Franz had no 'tuck box'. 'Tuck box' indeed! Why, he had not even enough plain wholesome food, as you may find from a letter he wrote some time after this to his elder brother, Ferdinand, who was his favourite brother and always, through his whole life, very good to him. This is what he wrote:

My dear Brother,

I have been thinking over my life here, and I find it's really not a bad one, on the whole, but there are some ways in which it could be improved. You know how much one enjoys a roll or an apple now and again, and all the more when one has to wait eight-and-a-half hours between dinner and supper! All the money Father gave me, which wasn't much, has gone long ago, so what am I to do? This is what I've been thinking—Can't you let me have a shilling or two a month? . . . .

You see, in those days, neither schoolmasters nor Emperors had any idea of making schoolboys comfortable. They had a notion that if you gave them plenty to eat and well-warmed rooms to work in (the rooms at this school had no fires in winter) the boys would be 'spoiled'. All the same, if you or I were an Emperor we would treat our choir-boys better, wouldn't we? and risk 'spoiling' them!

The Young Composer

Besides food and warmth there was something else of which young Franz felt the lack. He was already a composer, and composition was as necessary to his life as games are to yours. And he couldn't get music-paper. Here was a chance for the big boy, Spaun, to help him, and help him he did, so that Franz just poured out music—songs and piano pieces, and string quartets, and church anthems, all of which his school friends

3

were willing and eager to try over as fast as they were written. It was really a splendid school for Franz, in that way, at any rate; there was plenty of music going on. But one thing he missed badly, and really suffered from all his life—though they taught the boys to sing and play, and had a rehearsal of the orchestra every day, nobody ever taught them to compose. So Franz had just to pick up composition as best he could, which was a pity, for even a born composer needs teaching, just as a born cricketer is all the better for some good coaching.

Holidays

You see that Franz lived in music, when at school, and so he did, too, at home, for when there came a holiday time, and he hurried home, he got to work at once with his father and brothers, playing away at string quartets. Franz played the Viola on these occasions, his father the 'Cello, and two brothers the first and second Violins. This family string quartet became well-known in the neighbourhood, and by and by was enlarged to a little band, by taking in other players, so that Haydn's symphonies could be played (with a bit of special arrangement); then neighbours liked to drop in and hear the music, and the room at home became too small, and so another and larger one was taken, and after that a still larger, and then the little band of musicians was increased to a full orchestra. All this time Franz went on playing the Viola, and also composing. In his last year at school he composed a symphony for the school orchestra, and later he wrote some symphonies for the home orchestra too.

Earning a Living

When Franz left school there was the question of what to do with him. He was determined to be a composer, but to earn a living by composing was even more difficult in those days than in these. So he decided to be a schoolmaster. His father was the master of a parish school in Vienna, and Franz joined him and taught the lowest class. I think he hated the work, and what he really liked was to slam the school door at the end of the day and get home to his composing, or else to run off to see his old friends at the Choir School and join them in their music-making, or take them some new music he had just written. About this time he began to have a few lessons in composition. There was in Vienna a musician named Salieri, the Emperor's chief musician (or 'Capellmeister'). He had helped Beethoven, in his earlier days, by advice and lessons, and now he helped Schubert in the same way, for he saw that the youth was a genius and was well worth helping.

How Schubert Wrote and Performed a Mass

One great event about this time (he was now seventeen) was Schubert's composition of a Mass for one of the churches. He conducted it himself, his brother played the organ, a celebrated violinist, called Mayseder, came and led the violins, and the performance went off very well and made quite a stir. To commemorate the occasion his father, who was delighted to see his son doing such great things, spent a good deal of his hardly-earned money and gave him a piano. (Harpsichords, of which you have read in the previous volume, were now fast going out, and pianos were becoming quite common.)

Schubert's Friendships

There is one thing you cannot help noticing when you read Schubert's life—the number of friends he made and the splendid way these stuck to him. You have just read how Spaun helped him, when he was a schoolboy, and now you will hear how a young man called Schober did the same. This Schober had come across some of Schubert's songs—in manuscript, for nothing of Schubert's was yet printed. He was so much struck with these that he called to see the young composer, and when he found that he was wasting his days in an occupation for which he was not fitted, he said to him 'Come and live with me, and I'll look after you.' The father was willing, so off the youth went, and now he could compose to his heart's content, instead of correcting short division sums or giving spelling lessons. Other friends gathered round him too, and tried to help him. One thing they felt really should be done was to print some of the lovely songs he had written. But they could not persuade any publisher to look at the work of an unknown youth, so in the end Schubert had to go on composing year after year and living one hardly knows how (for he could not stay very long with his friend Schober, as Schober had to take in a brother). And when he was twenty-five nothing was yet in print, so that his beautiful music, instead of being at the service of all the world, was known only to a few keen musicians in his own native city.

Now the father of one of Schubert's old friends of his school-days had a large house, and used to give fine concerts there of Schubert's music, so as to make it known, and the plan was hit upon of printing one of the best of the songs, having it sung at a concert, and then offering it for sale to the audience. The first song to be printed was the one which is now perhaps most famous—*The Erl King*. This was sung by one of Schubert's friends, who had a fine voice and a dramatic way of singing, and at once the people in the audience bought one hundred copies. This provided enough money to print another song, for the next concert, and so on! One reason why publishers would not undertake to bring out such a song as this was the difficulty of the piano part, which in *The Erl King* goes very fast and gives a wonderful feeling of a horseman galloping through a dark night and a ghostly enemy following swiftly after. You can get the song as a Gramophone record, and you will notice at once that it is quite as much a piano piece as a song. After hearing it you will be astonished to learn that Schubert wrote it in one afternoon.

Schubert's Songs

Schubert, from a boy upwards, took to song writing like a duck to water, and to instrumental writing (we may say) like a man to water. That is to say, song writing seemed natural to him, but instrumental writing he had to learn, as swimming has to be learnt. He wrote a lot of most beautiful instrumental works, but sometimes you feel (especially in a long piece) that he was not quite so much the complete master of this sort of composing as of the other.

If he got hold of a book of poems and opened it, at once he would seize on some verses, read them once or twice through, and see in a flash what was the best way to set them so as to bring out all the meaning and the feeling of the poet's words. Then he would sit down and write the music straight away.

There is a most lovely setting by him of Shakespeare's song, *Hark, hark, the lark.* It came about in this way. Schubert was walking in the country and saw a friend sitting at a table in an inn garden. He joined him, and took up the book he had been reading. It opened at *Cymbeline,* at the poem which Cloten's musicians perform to Imogen, to wake her sweetly in the morning—*Hark, hark, the lark.* 'Oh!' said Schubert, 'I have thought of such a lovely tune for that! What a pity I haven't some music-paper here!' The friend took up the bill of fare and drew some music lines on it with his pencil, and Schubert at once wrote that beautiful song that has now gone all through the world and is loved in every civilized country. (This song also you can get as a Gramophone record.) So quickly did Schubert write his songs that once or twice he actually forgot them again. On one occasion one of his friends put before him on the piano a manuscript song in the friend's own

SCHUBERT

writing. Schubert played it through and said, 'That's not bad! Who composed it?' 'Why,' said the friend, 'you yourself did, and you gave it me a fortnight ago, but as it was too high for me I wrote it out afresh in another key.'

Altogether Schubert composed in his lifetime over 600 songs. As you have learnt, the publishers would at first not look at them. Later the tide turned, and the publishers became more willing. But they rarely gave him more than a few shillings for a song, and in spite of his genius he remained ever a poor man.

Instrumental Music

If you have not yet made acquaintance with Schubert's Piano Music (such as his *Impromptus,* and his *Moments Musicaux,* for instance), let us hope you may soon do so. Then there is some beautiful Chamber Music, and there are some Symphonies, of which two are most heard—the great C major Symphony and the one in B minor, of which only two movements exist, and which is therefore always called *The Unfinished Symphony.*

Schubert's Death

Like this symphony, Schubert's life itself was 'Unfinished'. If you will look back at the heading of this chapter, and see the dates there, you will realize that he only lived thirty-one years. It will strike you, too, that he died the year after Beethoven. For years Beethoven and Schubert had lived in the same city of Vienna, but

9

Beethoven was known to everyone, was admired, and had wealthy friends, whereas Schubert was known and loved only by a small circle of people, generally not so high in the social scale as those with whom Beethoven associated. So Beethoven knew nothing of Schubert and Schubert loved Beethoven at a distance. Then one day a friend took Schubert to visit Beethoven, but the younger man was so bashful that when the elder one asked him a question, instead of answering it on the writing-tablet held out to him (you remember, Beethoven was deaf), he caught up his hat and rushed to the door and bolted! Later he got more courage, and as for Beethoven, when he was shown some of the songs, he said, emphatically, 'Truly, Schubert has the divine gift in him!'

When Beethoven was dying Schubert visited him, and at the funeral he was one of the torch-bearers. On the way home he and the two friends who were with him stopped at an inn, and solemnly drank to the memory of the great man. Then they drank another solemn toast to the first of them who should follow him. This, as it turned out, was Schubert himself, who, weakly for many years, fell ill and died, lovingly cared for in the house of that elder brother, Ferdinand, who had been so kind to him from his boyhood. On his death-bed he was cheered by reading *The Last of the Mohicans* and other novels by the American novelist Fenimore Cooper, and a few days before he died he wrote to a friend asking him to lend him more books by the same author. He had begged to be buried near Beethoven, and his wish was fulfilled. In music he left over 1,000 compositions; in money— £2 10*s*. The stone placed over him has these words:

Music has here entombed a rich treasure—

But still fairer hopes.

QUESTIONS

*(To See Whether You Remember
the Chapter and Understand It)*

1. What was Schubert's nationality?

2. In what city did he spend his life?

3. What other great composers lived there in those days?

4. What was Schubert's father?

5. To what school was Schubert sent?

6. What instrument did he play in the family quartet?

7. How did he earn a living when he left school?

8. Was Schubert in your opinion a surly sort of fellow or a pleasant sort? Why do you think so?

9. Was he a slow, laborious composer, or a quick one? Can you remember any circumstances that will illustrate your answer?

10. Mention two or three of his songs and tell anything about how they were composed, or performed, or published.

11. Mention one or two Symphonies.

12. How old was Schubert when he died? Did he die poor or rich?

13. Tell anything you remember about Schubert's meetings with Beethoven.

14. Which of the two died first—Schubert or Beethoven?

THINGS TO DO

(For School and Home)

1. Get somebody to play you some of Schubert's music. Listen to it carefully and see if you really like it, and which pieces you like best, and why. Write down your opinion.

2. Next day get the same performer to play the pieces again, without your looking over them, and see if you can remember the name of each piece. Then look at what you wrote down yesterday and see if you still like the same pieces best.

3. If there are any parts you don't like, or seem not to understand, get the player to do them again, and look over the music so as to see how these parts are made up. Then listen again and see if you now understand better.

4. If you have a Pianola, Piano-player or Player-piano, get your parents to buy or borrow some Schubert rolls, and practise these yourself.

5. If you can play the Piano pretty well, ask your

teacher if there is any Schubert piece suitable for you.

6. If you know a Singer, get him or her to sing you some Schubert songs. Before each is sung, read the words through and understand them. Then listen to the song the first time just for its music, and the second time to see how the song-part and the piano-part express or set off the words. Then listen a third time just for the pleasure of it.

7. If you have a Gramophone, get hold of some Schubert song records, and of the records of *The Unfinished Symphony*. In listening to the Symphony, see if you can find places that illustrate what Schumann said about the Wind Instruments in Schubert's orchestration—'They chat with one another like human beings'.

8. If you have any of Schubert's music, write a preface to it, giving briefly the chief facts about the composer's life, and paste it on the back of the title-page.

9. Make up a little play about Schubert, write it out and act it with your companions.

10. Prepare a little lecture on Schubert, and give it, with musical illustrations by yourself and friends or by the Pianola or Gramophone.

JOHN FIELD

CHAPTER II

THE INVENTOR OF THE NOCTURNE

JOHN FIELD

1782-1837

What is a Nocturne?

Before you begin to read this chapter play one of Chopin's Nocturnes, or get some one to play one to you. And as you play or hear it try to notice what it is like—what it is that makes a Nocturne a Nocturne, and not (say) a Minuet or a March.

The word 'Nocturne' means, of course, just a Night Piece—the sort of dreamy, tender music that might come into a composer's head as he stood looking over the fields or the sea on a starlight or moonlight night. But, besides suggesting this feeling, Chopin's Nocturnes, you will find, have also got other characteristics in common. Look, for instance, at the favourite one in E flat. You will notice that in the right hand we have a beautiful melody, that *floats*, as it were, on spreading waves of harmony in the left hand, which are made to sound on by the use of the sustaining pedal. Almost all the Chopin Nocturnes are like that, though the left-hand part is not in some of the Nocturnes so wave-like as in this Nocturne, whilst in others it is more so. This way of treating the two hands is really one of the 'distinguishing marks' of a Nocturne. If you were to make up a bit of slow melody, put to it a left-hand accompaniment of the sort described, and then play it to any one who knew anything about piano music, they would say at once, 'Why, that must be the beginning of some Nocturne.'

Who First Composed Such Pieces?

Now most people think the Chopin Nocturne style was invented by Chopin, but this was not so. An Irishman invented Chopin's Nocturnes for him, which, being a sort of 'bull', is just what an Irishman would do. This Irishman was John Field, and he was writing Nocturnes before Chopin was put into trousers. At one time everybody played his music, but now hardly anybody does so, and thus what he did for music is in danger of being forgotten.

Where and When Field was Born

Field was born in Dublin in 1782—that is to say, whilst Haydn was in his prime (how old was he?) and Beethoven a boy (and how old was *he*?). And he died in

1837, the year Queen Victoria came to the throne, when Schubert and Beethoven had been dead respectively nine and ten years, and Chopin and Schumann and Mendelssohn were all young men of twenty-seven or twenty-eight. That fixes him in his chronological place in your mind, I hope.

The Young Pianist

Field's father and grandfather lived together in Dublin and kept a sort of little school of music. The grandfather was an Organist and Pianist and the father played the fiddle in a theatre orchestra, and taught it to as many pupils as he could get. These two elder musicians gave the younger one (for Field had early taken to piano playing) many a good thrashing, thinking perhaps that they could whip music into him through the skin, instead of making him take it up gradually with the mind. Once the boy ran away from home to escape the whippings he got there, but he seems to have gone back again pretty soon.

At that time there was in Dublin a famous Italian pianist named Giordani (pronounce that 'Gee-or-daa-nee', saying the first two syllables quickly, which is as near as I can get to it in English spelling). To this man was young Field sent for lessons, and he got on so well that when he was nine his master made him appear at concerts, describing him on the bills as 'the much admired Master Field, a youth of eight years of age'. I am sorry to tell you that nearly all these youngsters who appear before the public are made out to be younger than they really are. When I visited Beethoven's birthplace at Bonn, I saw there a printed bill of his father's announcing the appearance at a concert on March 26, 1778, of his little son of 'six years'. You, who have read the account of Beethoven in my first volume, and know in what year he was born, can see what a shocking lie *that* was!

Field in London

When Field was eleven, his father left Dublin for Bath, and later went to London, where he became a member of the orchestra at the Haymarket Theatre. And in London the boy became pupil to a celebrated pianist of the day, that Clementi whose sonatinas you may know, and who was then the finest player in London. In 1794 young Field (this time 'aged ten') appeared in public, and old Haydn, who was in London just then, was in the audience and predicted that the boy would become a great musician.

Now Clementi was not only a player of pianos but also a maker of them, and he made Field spend a great deal of time in his piano shop, playing brilliant passages to customers, and showing off the instruments. Then when Clementi went abroad for the purposes of giving recitals and of selling pianos he took Field with him. When they got to St. Petersburg (which we now call Petrograd) Clementi opened a show-room for the pianos, and poor Field (aged nineteen, yet, as the great musician Spohr tells us, 'in an Eton suit which he had much outgrown') was kept at work displaying the qualities of the instruments.

When Clementi left Petrograd, Field remained behind, and a certain general took him in as his guest and introduced him into society. Soon he became very well known as a concert player, and had crowds of aristocratic pupils. Indeed he became so popular that he was spoilt, becoming lazy and frivolous. One of his pupils was Glinka, who became the founder of modern Russian music.

Field's Compositions

So long did Field live in Russia, and so connected with that country in people's minds did he become, that often he is spoken of in books as 'Russian Field'. He did a great deal of composition, and in 1814 composed his first Nocturnes. He also wrote Piano Sonatas and Concertos. The Concertos were for years very much played, and Schumann, in his time, praised them highly, but we never hear them now. Later, Field left Petrograd and lived in Moscow, and sometimes he travelled on recital tours. He played in London, and in Paris, and Florence, and Venice, and elsewhere, and the best judges of music were astonished at his playing, which was very simple and unaffected in style, and very neat and finished.

SECOND BOOK OF THE GREAT MUSICIANS

Field's Death

In Naples Field fell ill, and spent nine months in a hospital. A Russian nobleman found him there, and took him away with him. Gradually he was able to travel back to Russia with the nobleman, but there he fell ill again and died. The city of Moscow, recognizing what a great man he was, gave him a public funeral. His life was not a short one (fifty-five years), but probably it would have been longer and happier if he had not been so sternly treated as a boy at home, and then overworked in youth by Clementi. The result of this harshness seems to have been that when he got away from restraints, and was made much of in Russia, he 'lost his head' and became careless of his health and intemperate.

The Two Nocturne Writers

If possible get your teacher or some friend to play you not only the Chopin Nocturne I have mentioned (the one in E flat, Op. 9, No. 2), but also a certain one by Field in the same key (No. 1).

Field's begins:

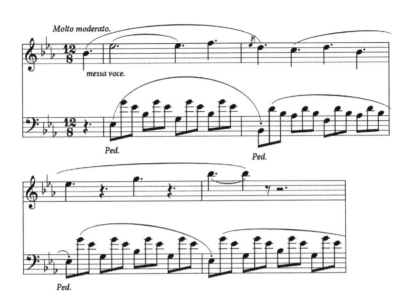

And Chopin's begins:

If you listen to and look at those extracts carefully you will see how similar they are in style. But, of course, though we may *like* Field's piece, Chopin's is the one we *love*. Why? Because to Field's grace and beauty Chopin has added a deeper poetical feeling. It is as if I were to say to you (as the opening of a word-nocturne):

> 'The evening bell is ringing,
> The cattle come home from the fields,'

and somebody were then to read to you Gray's 'Elegy', which begins with just this thought, but ever so much more beautifully expressed:

> The curfew tolls the knell of parting day,
> The lowing herd winds slowly o'er the lea.

But you see what Chopin learnt from Field, and if you will now look at and listen closely to the two Nocturnes you will see many others of Field's ideas that were adopted by Chopin, such as, for instance, this sort of ornamental, running, chromatic-scaly figure:

Field:

Chopin:

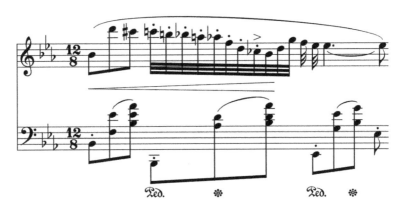

Then notice where Chopin got another of his charming little 'mannerisms', a turn followed by a high leap:

Field:

Chopin:

And so we could go on, comparing these and various other Field and Chopin Nocturnes.

But, since Field is little played to-day, why have I troubled to write a chapter about him? *Firstly,* because his Nocturnes, though not so deeply poetical as Chopin's, are refined and beautiful and worth more playing than they get. *Secondly,* because people so often forget what British composers have done for music, especially piano music, and they should be reminded of it. Look back again at Chapter II of *The First Book of the Great Musicians* and remind yourself of what the British composers did in laying the very *foundations* of keyboard music. Bach's Suites, we may say, are a building reared on the foundation laid by Bull and Byrd, and other British musicians, a century and more earlier. And, similarly, Chopin's Nocturnes are a building reared on the foundations laid by his elder contemporary, John Field.

QUESTIONS

*(To See Whether You Remember
the Chapter and Understand It)*

1. What is a Nocturne? Describe it as clearly as you can.

2. Where and when was Field born?

3. Where and when did he die?

4. What do you remember of Field's boyhood?

5. Mention one or two of Field's teachers.

6. How did Field come to be in Russia?

7. Tell anything you remember of his life there.

8. What did Field write besides his Nocturnes?

9. Mention a few things that Chopin learned from Field.

10. Why should we remember Field?

THINGS TO DO

These have already been mentioned in the chapter itself.

FELIX MENDELSSOHN

CHAPTER III

MENDELSSOHN

1809-1847

The Youth Who Could Do Everything

We will begin with a picnic in Wales, up amongst the hills. The engineer who is in charge of the mines of the district has had a tent carried up, and brought his family to celebrate his birthday among the miners. And with his family he has brought a guest who is staying with them, a young man from Germany, who has the reputation of being a good musician and who has been appearing at concerts in London. But this young man, it seems, is not only a musician. He throws himself into the fun and it really seems as though he can do everything. He can play all the games, or if there is one he cannot play, it has only to be explained to him and he understands it at once. He can sketch, and that quite beautifully. He can dance. In the evenings when they get home he can play chess and billiards and beat them all, he can ride and swim and is a great gymnast, and when he leaves this Welsh family and goes home they find that he can write the most interesting letters, describing all that he sees and does more like a practised author than a mere friendly letter-writer.

But it is the music he makes that pleases them most. He sees a creeping plant in the garden, with little blossoms almost the shape of trumpets. 'Fairy trumpets,' he says, and sits down and plays a piece on the piano— music for the fairies to play. Then he writes it out for one of the children, and draws all up the margin of the paper a sprig of the blossoms.

One morning as he is dressing he hears a boy of the family playing on the drawing-room piano a little tune he has made up in the Welsh style, and in the evening when the visitor sits down to play, out comes this very tune, turned into a long piece of beautiful music.

When they are out in the grounds one evening the young man says, 'What a pity we haven't an instrument out here!' One of the boys rushes to the gardener's cottage and borrows a fiddle. It is a wretched old thing, and all the strings are snapped but one. The young man bursts into fits of laughter when he sees such an instrument, but he takes it, and somehow he draws beautiful music out of that one string, to which his companions listen eagerly until darkness comes and it is time to go in.

That is Mendelssohn 'all over'—the youth to whom everything came easily and who was nearly always in high spirits.

The Boyhood

Mendelssohn had had a wonderful musical boy-hood. He learnt early to play the Piano, and from nine onwards appeared in concerts; he learnt the Violin too, and did a great deal of composition; and he sang alto in the great choral society of Berlin, his native place, 'standing amongst the grown-up people in his child's dress, a tight-fitting jacket cut very low at the neck, over which the trousers were buttoned, into the slanting pockets of these the little fellow liked to thrust his hands, rocking his curly head from side to side, and shifting restlessly from one foot to the other.'

When he was twelve he began to compose more systematically, copying all his pieces into a big album, and, when that was finished, starting another, until, at the end of his life, there were forty-four of these volumes on his shelves—one for each year and a few over.

Sunday Music

Mendelssohn's parents were rich and had a large and beautiful house, with a big dining-room, where every other Sunday they gave concerts for their friends. The children took a great part in the music. Felix, of whom I have been telling you these things, often composed some of the music, and conducted the Orchestra, standing on a stool; Fanny, his clever sister, played the Piano, Rebecka sang, and Paul played the 'Cello. This is the very best way of making music, and more families could do it if they tried, though not all could do it on so big a scale, or do it so well as to be worth their friends' frequent hearing. And of course not all families could provide their own domestic composer.

The Mendelssohn family's music-making was so famous that any notable musicians who passed through Berlin were glad to be present to hear it.

Some Holiday Music

The Mendelssohns lived in music, and when they went on holiday they did not leave it behind. When Felix was fourteen he and his two brothers were taken on a tour in Silesia by their father. At one town a Charity Concert was being prepared, and the committee asked if they might announce that Felix would play a Mozart Concerto with their Orchestra. But at the rehearsal the Orchestra played so much out of tune and out of time that Felix made the schoolmaster go on to the platform and say that, instead of playing the Concerto, Master Mendelssohn would extemporize, and this was done, Felix playing a brilliant improvisation on some tunes out of works by Mozart and Weber.

When they went to the seaside next year they found that there was a wind band there, so Felix wrote for it an Overture, which the band played and which he afterwards published.

The 'Midsummer Night's Dream' Overture

When he was seventeen-and-a-half Mendelssohn wrote a most beautiful overture, intended to precede Shakespeare's *A Midsummer Night's Dream*. To this day, this is the music we generally hear in a London theatre when they perform the play, and to the end of his life the composer never composed anything finer. Its opening is very light and fairy-like, so that somebody has said that Mendelssohn was 'the first composer to bring the fairies into the orchestra.' But there are others besides fairies in Shakespeare's play and so there are in Mendelssohn's overture to it; at one place you can distinctly hear Bottom's 'Hee-haw'.

Mendelssohn later wrote other music for *A Midsummer Night's Dream*—for instance, the famous Wedding March, which is nowadays as much used at church weddings as at stage weddings. And there is also a very beautiful soft Night Piece, or 'Notturno'.

Other Orchestral Pieces

Mendelssohn is famous for his Overtures, some of which were not intended for plays, but just as orchestral pieces to begin a concert. Indeed he may be said to have invented the Concert Overture, writing it much on the lines of the first movement of a Beethoven symphony. One of the best of these concert overtures is the *Hebrides Overture,* sometimes called *Fingal's Cave.* When Mendelssohn was travelling in Scotland, of which country he was very fond, he visited that cave, and there came to his mind a beautiful bit of music, which he wrote down and afterwards used as the opening of this Overture. Some other orchestral works of Mendelssohn are in the form of full symphonies. He gave these names: there are a *Scotch Symphony* and an *Italian Symphony* (in which some of his feelings during his tours in Scotland and Italy are reproduced), and a *Reformation Symphony* with the finale made out of the fine old tune which you will find in all Hymn Tune books to Luther's hymn, 'A Safe Stronghold our God is still'.

Pieces for orchestra and a solo instrument are the very popular Violin Concerto and the two Piano Concertos.

There is also a good deal of Chamber Music.

Mendelssohn's Oratorios

Besides the pieces just mentioned, Mendelssohn wrote a good deal of choral music, and especially sacred music, such as settings of the Psalms, and some Oratorios—*St. Paul, Elijah,* and the *Hymn of Praise.*

The first performance of *Elijah* was at Birmingham, so English people heard it before Mendelssohn's own countrymen. Mendelssohn himself conducted and was delighted with the solo singers and the chorus and the orchestra, and with the audience, too. He wrote home to his brother saying, 'No work of mine ever went so admirably at the first performance, or was received with such enthusiasm as this. I never in my life heard a better performance, no, nor so good, and almost doubt if I shall ever hear one like it again.'

The Piano Music

Mendelssohn was himself a fine pianist, so naturally he wrote a good deal of piano music. Amongst this there is a *Rondo Capriccioso* that you may have heard (you know what a Rondo is, and a Capriccioso piece is naturally one that cuts jolly 'capers'). And you must know some of the *Songs without Words*. The idea of these, of course, is a beautiful tune, of a song kind, with an accompaniment to it going on all the time. And there are other pieces, but these are perhaps the best known. At first nobody in England would buy the *Songs without Words*, and when Mendelssohn, being in London, went to Novello's shop to see how much money they had for him from the proceeds of the first book of six of the pieces he found that they had only sold about a hundred copies in four years and had only a pound or two for him. Afterwards people became even too fond of these pieces, so that every home in England where there was a piano had the full set of them, and other good music was in some cases neglected.

Mendelssohn as Pianist

There must be many young pianists amongst the readers of this book, and they may care to have a description of Mendelssohn's playing, which was very famous.

He was a good sight reader and could play at once anything you put before him. And he was a good memory player, and hardly ever used printed music except when he was sight reading. Train yourself in sight reading and memory playing by all means! And, once his boyhood was past, he *never practised*. But in this you and I cannot, I fear, afford to follow his example—can we? Madame Schumann said that Mendelssohn's playing was one of the most delightful things she had ever heard in her life. She said 'in hearing him one forgot the *player* and only revelled in the full enjoyment of the *music.*'

Joachim said that Mendelssohn's playing in a *staccato* passage was 'the most extraordinary thing possible, for life and crispness.' He had great 'fire' in his playing, yet great delicacy, and he must have listened and trained himself to get very good tone, because in the softest passages everything could be clearly heard, even in the largest hall, whilst in the loudest passages the effect was never harsh. It is in the tone they produce that many well-known players of to-day fail. Mendelssohn's phrasing was beautifully clear, and he used the sustaining pedal with great thoughtfulness. '*Strict time was one of his hobbies.*'

Mendelssohn as Organist

As an organist, too, Mendelssohn was celebrated. Whenever he came to England he had to play on all the greatest organs. He had written six fine Organ Sonatas, which you can often hear nowadays at recitals, and he was very fond of playing Bach's organ fugues, and did a great deal to make these popular amongst English organists. But one thing he could not do that you or I could probably do quite well. After a church service he could not 'play the people out', and once at St. Paul's Cathedral, when the organist got him to play a concluding voluntary, as the congregation did not go, the vergers, who wanted to get home to dinner, went to the organ-blower and made him leave his work, so that the playing came to a sudden end in the middle of a bar, and the people quickly dispersed.

Mendelssohn and Bach

You have read about Bach in *The First Book of the Great Musicians*. After his death, the style of music changed for a time; Fugues and Suites went out and Sonatas and Symphonies came in. And old Bach was almost forgotten, and whilst his sons lived their music was more thought of than his. Then came Haydn and Mozart and Beethoven, and so people went on forgetting old Bach. It was Mendelssohn who did more than any one else to bring Bach to life again. As a youth of eighteen he prepared a choir in the great *St. Matthew Passion*, and gave the first performance of this that had taken place since Bach died, over seventy years before. We owe him a great debt for making us realize the beauty of Bach, as we do also an English organist who did much the same here—Samuel Wesley.

Mendelssohn and an English Composer

Another thing we owe to Mendelssohn is the discovery of Sterndale Bennett. When Mendelssohn first started coming to this country British people had an idea that no Briton could compose fine music. But Mendelssohn went to a concert at the Royal Academy of Music, heard a student, Bennett, play some of his own music, and was so much struck with his compositions that he invited him to Germany and made much of him there, as did other great German musicians, such as Schumann. Then the English musicians, seeing one of their young countrymen taken up in musical Germany, thought there must be something in him, and so gave him a chance in his own country. And so gradually people awoke to the fact that one can be an Englishman and at the same time a composer. Sterndale Bennett wrote some fine music (a little in Mendelssohn's style) and then, unfortunately, left off composing in middle life, so that he never came to his full development. But, all the same, with him the tide of British music turned. *Thank you, Mendelssohn!*

QUESTIONS

*(To See Whether You Remember
the Chapter and Understand It)*

1. Tell anything you remember showing what sort of a youth Mendelssohn was.

2. Were his family musical? If so, tell anything you remember about their musical doings.

3. What do you remember about some music Mendelssohn wrote for a certain Shakespeare play?

4. Mention the names of any other Orchestral pieces by Mendelssohn, and say what you remember about them.

5. What Oratorios did Mendelssohn write?

6. And what Piano music?

7. What do you know about his Piano playing?

8. And his Organ playing?

9. What did he do for Bach?

10. And what for British music?

THINGS TO DO

1. Get the *Midsummer Night's Dream* Overture as a Gramophone record, or a piano piece, and listen to it carefully to see what there is in it, and how it is made

up. If you get the Gramophone record, try to find out, by listening carefully, which instruments are playing the different bits. Get the *Notturno* also.

2. Play, or get somebody to play to you, some of the *Songs without Words,* and then study them to find out how they are made. Do the same with any others of the piano pieces.

3. Get Gramophone records of some of Mendelssohn's Chamber Music, and study it until you know it thoroughly.

4. Get somebody to sing you parts of *Elijah*, or else get these for the Gramophone. Look at a copy of the Piano Score, and find out where in the story of *Elijah* comes each song that you hear.

5. Get a friendly church organist to play you one of Mendelssohn's Organ Sonatas—several times, so that you can study it, and remember it. It will help you if the organist will play the chief bits first, and explain to you how Mendelssohn has worked them up into his 'movements'.

6. There is a favourite Christmas Hymn Tune of yours which is adapted from a work of Mendelssohn's. Look through a Hymn Tune book and find out what it is.

7. Get a Violinist and Pianist to play you part of the Violin Concerto, or get the Gramophone record of one of the movements of this.

CHAPTER IV

ABOUT THE OLD MIRACLE PLAYS AND MASQUES, AND WHAT SPRANG FROM THEM

Where Opera Comes From

This chapter is written to show the origin of Opera. In the first volume there was a short description of Opera. Where does Opera come from? It comes from a human instinct, or rather two or three human instincts—

(1) the instinct to Sing,

(2) the instinct to Act,

(3) the instinct to Dance.

As long as men have been in the world they have felt these three instincts leading them to make Songs and Plays about what interests them, and also to express their jollity, or sometimes their sorrow, by moving rhythmically to music. When you have the singing and acting combined you have OPERA, and many Operas have also dancing in them, which dancing we call BALLET (pronounce *Bal*-ay).

Miracle Plays — A Visit to Chester in 1500

Imagine yourself in some English city at the time of the year when the great plays are performed—say Chester, in Whitsun week, about 1500. These plays are intended to teach the people about religion. At Chester there are, at the date mentioned, twenty-four of the plays, all performed on one day, and the custom of performing them goes back for at least three centuries earlier.

Each play is performed by the men of some particular trade; for instance, the Drapers play the *Creation,* the Water-drawers of the Dee (appropriately) *The Ark and the Flood,* the Barbers and Candle-makers *The Story of Lot and Abraham,* and so on, until we enter the New Testament with *The Birth of Christ,* played by the Slaters, and end it with the Weavers' play of *The Last Judgement.* And thus, in one day, we have gone through the main events of the whole Bible.

Each of these trades has its own Pageant Stage on wheels, and its own simple scenery and very gay dresses. The Drapers will give their play in a certain street, and then move to another street and give it again. Meanwhile the Tanners will come to the place where the Drapers were, and so on—so that all over the city of Chester the people who live in any particular district have each one of the plays brought, as it were, to their very door.

This is to prevent overcrowding in any one spot. And lest there should be disturbances the Mayor has issued a proclamation that whilst the plays are going on nobody is to wear weapons in the city of Chester, on pain of imprisonment by the Mayor, fine by the King, and cursing by the Pope, which is a pretty fearsome combination of punishments. So now all is ready and we will watch just one of these plays. Let us choose the Water-drawers' play of *The Ark and the Flood*.

The Noah's Ark Play

Up comes, with a merry crowd, the Water-drawers' pageant-stage, or pageant-cart, and the play begins. The first character to speak is God. He tells Noah that there is to be a flood, warns him to prepare the Ark and tells him just how to make it, and what animals to put into it.

Then out speaks Shem and says he's got a good sharp axe and will help his father to make the Ark. Ham says he's got the sharpest hatchet in the town, and will do his part too, Japhet says he can make wooden pins, and with his hammer knock them in, and Noah's wife says she will go and gather timber. Shem's wife fetches a block on which they can work the wood with their tools, and Ham's wife has the good idea of going off to get clay to fill up the cracks in the Ark when it is ready for caulking. Japhet's wife gathers the chips from the work and makes it her business to cook dinner for the workers. So very quickly they are all busy.

Then Noah makes a long speech and you will see how quickly a Stage Ark can be made, for by the time he has finished his speech the Ark is finished too.

> Now in the name of God I will begin,
> To make the ship that we shall in,
> That we be ready for to swim,
> At the coming of the flood.
> These boards I join together,
> To keep us safe from the weather,
> That we may roam both hither and thither
> And safe be from this flood.
> Of this tree I will have the mast,
> Tied with cables that will last,
> With a sail yard for each blast
> And each thing in its kind.
>   With topmast high and bowsprit,
> With cords and ropes I hold all fit
> To sail forth at the next weete [tide].
> This ship is at an end.
> Wife, in this castle we shall be kept:
> My children and thou I would in leapt!

But now comes a difficulty, and, as you will soon see, the Monk, or whoever it was who wrote that play, has brought it in just to cheer the audience with a little fun. When they begin to go into the Ark Noah's wife will not budge. In vain poor old Noah says, 'Good wife, do as I bid.' All the animals are supposed to be driven in (Noah's sons have pictures on parchment of cats and dogs, and foxes and hares, and herons and rooks, and lions and leopards, and as each is supposed to be entering they say its name). At last all is ready, and the water is supposed to be rising, but still the silly old woman stays on shore and refuses to join the family unless she can bring with her her 'gossips', or friends. They all try to persuade her, and Japhet cries:

> Mother, we pray you all together,
> For we are here, your children
> Come into the ship for fear of the weather.

In the end they have to put the old lady in by main force, and you may be sure they do it in such a way as to give the spectators a good laugh.

Then the windows of the Ark are shut up and you hear Noah sing a Psalm in Latin, *Salva me, Domine!* At the end of the Psalm you are to suppose forty days have passed, and you see Noah send out a raven, which never returns, and then a dove. When the dove has gone they have another one ready with an olive branch in its mouth, which they let down by string (a stuffed dove, or a wooden one, perhaps, but supposed to be the first one come back), and Noah takes it in, and so the play goes on until at last it ends with a long speech by God, and the words:

> My blessing now I give thee here,
> To thee Noah, my servant dear;
> For vengeance shall no more appear;
> And now farewell, my darling dear!

So that is how our ancestors amused themselves and taught the scripture stories at Whitsuntide; and at Christmas and Easter and on Corpus Christi day there were other plays suited to the season. You can get some of the Chester, Wakefield, Coventry, and York plays, and the Cornish Mystery-Play of the Three Maries, and the old play, *Everyman*, and similar things quite cheaply in the 'Everyman Library', if you want. You will find that some of them have more music in them than the one I have described. For instance, the Coventry Christmas Play has the song of the Angels, and songs by the Shepherds, and a Lullaby by the mothers of the Innocents. Plays of this kind were not only common in England but all over Europe, and we may fairly see in them the origin of:

    (a) our Drama—that is, plays without music,

    (b) our Opera—that is, plays set to music,

    (c) our Oratorio—that is, sacred plays with music but not acting (and therefore, really, plays no longer).

The Masques

Another form of entertainment the influence of which we see in Opera is the Masque. The Miracle Plays were for the common people, the Masques for the rich nobles. The Masque was a sort of private theatricals, popular in the sixteenth and early seventeenth centuries. It first came about by people introducing into festive processions men wearing masks, who represented allegorical personages, such as Virtue, or Vice, and acted in dumb show. Then it became more elaborate, and turned into a sort of play of an allegorical kind.

Very often a wedding was celebrated with a Masque after the feast, and so was a royal visit to any great house. For instance, when Queen Elizabeth went in state once to visit the lawyers of Gray's Inn, in London, they entertained her with a Masque.

A Seventeenth-Century London Masque

Next time you go down Whitehall have a good look at the Banqueting House, which is now a naval museum (you can go in for sixpence). This is the building from which Charles I stepped out on to the scaffold (which was erected in front of it), and before that time it had been the scene of many events. For instance, in 1613 there was a famous Masque performed there to celebrate the marriage of the Earl of Somerset and Lady Frances Howard. In the upper room, which you can still see, they put up pillars and platforms, and a triumphal arch in front of these. They had a painted canvas sky above the platform, and on each side of it a high promontory with three big golden pillars. Between the promontories was what appeared to be the sea, with ships, some just painted on the background and others made to move. In front of the sea was a beautiful garden, where the masquers were.

The King and Queen and Prince were present, and after the trumpets had blown and they had entered and taken their seats in the audience, the Masque began with four Squires approaching them and explaining what was about to befall. At the end of these four speeches appeared Error, 'in a skin coat scaled like a serpent,' and Rumour, 'in a skin coat full of winged tongues,' and Curiosity, 'in a skin coat full of eyes,' and Credulity, 'in a like habit painted with ears.'

When these had acted awhile there came in the Four Winds, the East Wind 'in a skin coat of the colour of the sun-rising,' the Northern Wind 'in a grisled skin coat of hair,' and so on. All these Winds had wings on their shoulders and feet.

Then came in the Four Elements: Earth, in a coat grass-green, a mantle painted with plants and flowers, 'and on his head an oak growing'; Water, in a coat 'waved, with a mantle full of fishes, on his head a dolphin'; Air, in a sky-coloured coat, with birds on his mantle, and an eagle on his head; and Fire, with a flame-coloured mantle, and on his head a salamander. Then came the Four Continents, suitably dressed, and the Three Destinies, and at last Harmony, with nine musicians with garlands, playing and singing.

Then followed a great deal of dancing, and solo singing and chorus singing, and at the end the Four Squires came on again and wished the newly married couple happiness, and the people on the stage got into boats and sailed away, whilst a song was sung.

That gives you a sort of rough idea of a Masque. Shakespeare sometimes introduced Masques and Masquers into his plays (for instance, in *The Tempest* there is a Masque to celebrate the engagement of Miranda and Ferdinand). Milton wrote the most famous Masque of all, *Comus*.

QUESTIONS

*(To See Whether You Remember
the Chapter and Understand It)*

1. Describe, as well as you can, what Miracle Plays were.

2. Do the same for Masques.

3. What is a Ballet?

4. What three human instincts come out in Opera?

THINGS TO DO

A good Christmas entertainment would be a Play made out of the Christmas Miracle Plays. In the Wakefield Second Nativity Play (in the volume mentioned on page 44) there is a very funny part about one of the shepherds who steals a sheep belonging to another shepherd, carries it home, puts it in a cradle, and pretends it is a new baby. Don't leave this bit out if you act the play. The Coventry play has rather more opportunity for music, and I do not see why a class of children should not, amongst them, make up tunes for the songs. Or a good play could be made by taking parts of each of these plays. Instrumental music for the Shepherds' Watch, or for the overture, could be taken from *Messiah,* and parts of Bach's *Christmas Oratorio* might come in. But, of course, an ambitious class with an intelligent teacher could do things in a more 'authentic' way than this—giving one of the plays as it stands, and composing the music, with or without the help of the best musician in the neighbourhood.

CHAPTER V

ABOUT ORATORIOS

What is an Oratorio?

An Oratorio is a long sacred piece, with vocal solos and choruses and instrumental music, and generally it tells a story, which is often taken from the Bible. Handel's *Messiah* is an Oratorio, and so is Bach's *Passion according to St. Matthew,* and so are Haydn's *Creation* and Mendelssohn's *Elijah,* and Elgar's *Apostles* and *The Kingdom.* In all those works the story told comes from the Bible. In Elgar's oratorio, *Gerontius,* a story is also told, and a very beautiful one, but here the story comes not from the Bible but from a modern poem describing the death and after-death of a saint of the Church.

The First Oratorios

It is always difficult to say what was 'the first' of anything, but the first pieces to which the name 'Oratorio' was given were some which were performed in Rome in the sixteenth century, by a very good priest, who has been canonized by the Roman Catholic Church and is called St. Philip Neri (pronounce *Nay*-ree). You must know about him, for he was a great man.

ST. PHILIP NERI

Neri was born in Florence in 1515, and his father was a lawyer. He did so much good even as a boy that everybody called him 'The Good Pippo' ('short' for Philip). A very rich man, his uncle, wanted to make him his heir, but Philip refused, and when he was eighteen decided to go to Rome, and to put aside all thoughts of worldly success. When he got there he found a gentleman from his own native city, who gave him a small room and a daily allowance of meal of which to make his food. He spent his time in visiting the poor and sick, and in prayer. This went on for a long time, but when he was thirty-six he was persuaded to become a priest. He then started a sort of prayer-chapel or oratory, which he built on the roof of his church. A great many young men, many of them rich, used to come to his daily meetings.

Philip wanted to make religion attractive to the boys and young men, so he started the acting of religious plays, with music. These were called Oratorios, because they took place in the Oratory. Later Philip built a larger church in another part of Rome, and his Oratorios here became very popular and famous. Before Philip's time, and in Italy as in England, there had been religious 'Miracle Plays' and 'Mysteries', and some of them had a little music. But Philip's were very notable.

Philip died in 1595, and five years later a composer in Rome, CAVALEIRI (Cav-al-ee-*ay*-ree), composed a piece of something the same kind, but set to music throughout, and with scenery, acting, solo and chorus singing, instrumental music, and even dancing (Philip had sometimes had dancing—dancing not being in those days a mere amusement, as it generally is to-day). Cavalieri's oratorio was called *The Representation of the Soul and the Body,* and the characters in it were Time, Life, The World, Pleasure, Intellect, The Soul, and The Body. This was performed in 1600, and is generally considered the foundation-stone of the modern Oratorio, but the acting part was dropped by composers who followed Cavalieri, and to-day we do not have acting in an Oratorio as a rule, nor even scenery.

Passion Music

In Germany and elsewhere another sort of piece had come into existence, which was also a kind of Oratorio. In Holy Week the clergy would hold services for the singing of the story of the Passion of Christ, taken from one of the Gospels. They would have one singer, called the Evangelist, who would sing all the Narrative parts, and another for Christ, who would sing all the words of Christ when they came into the narrative, and another called the Crowd, who would sing such words as 'Crucify him!', or other words spoken by the body of people present in the story. By and by skilled composers took up this form of music and made it more elaborate. One of the greatest of these was the German composer Schütz, who was born exactly a hundred years before Bach.

When Bach himself arrived he became the very greatest composer of Passion Music there has ever been. He wrote five settings of the Passion, and of these three remain to-day—those according to St. Luke, St. John, and St. Matthew. The last is much the finest, and you can hear it in most large towns every year, in Holy Week. It is one of the greatest pieces of music ever composed. Bach has a Narrator (whom, he, also, calls 'The Evangelist'), another singer for Jesus, another for Peter, another for the High Priest, and so on. The Choir takes the part of the Crowd, and both certain soloists and the choir have some pieces of musical meditation (so to speak) on each little bit of the story as it is told.

Amongst the meditations are verses of hymns, very finely set by Bach to the old German hymn-tunes, or Chorales, with beautifully flowing alto and tenor and bass parts and lovely harmonies.

Another work of Bach's is *The Christmas Oratorio,* and he wrote about 200 Church Cantatas, which are something between a big Anthem and a small Oratorio.

Handel's Oratorios

Handel, who, as you remember, lived at exactly the same period as Bach (both born in 1685), wrote a great many fine oratorios. They were written in England, for the English people, and were very popular here, but of late years they have been much less performed—all except our favourite Christmas piece, *Messiah,* which, happily, still goes on.

Here are the names of some of Handel's Oratorios:

Saul (from which comes the solemn *Dead March,* played by the band at military funerals, and by organists at funeral services in church).

Theodora (from which comes the lovely song, 'Angels, ever bright and fair').

Samson.

Judas Maccabaeus (an Oratorio all about fighting).

Israel in Egypt (which has a 'Hailstone Chorus', and music for the Plague of Frogs, and other descriptive things, and also very fine double choruses, i.e. choruses for two choirs singing together).

Haydn's 'Creation'

A little later than Handel we get Haydn. When he came to England and heard Handel's Oratorios here, and especially *Messiah,* he said he felt that he, too, would like to write an Oratorio, and *The Creation* is the result. It has fine choruses in it, such as 'The Heavens are Telling', and beautiful solo tunes, such as 'With Verdure clad'. When it was finished some enthusiastic Austrian noblemen arranged a performance, paid all expenses, and gave Haydn the money taken at the doors, which was over £300. When Haydn first heard it performed (at Vienna in 1799) he was so excited that he said, 'One moment I was as cold as ice, and the next I seemed on fire.'

The Creation has been very popular in England, and is still often to be heard, though not so often as formerly.

Mendelssohn's Oratorios

In a previous chapter something has been said about Mendelssohn's Oratorios. The greatest is *Elijah,* which tells its story very vividly. Many of the solos from *Elijah,* such as 'O rest in the Lord', are known to almost everybody, everywhere.

Elgar's Oratorios

These have already been spoken of. *The Apostles* tells the story of Christ's choosing of his twelve Apostles, and the doings of Christ and of them, the betrayal of Christ by Judas, and the Crucifixion, Resurrection, and Ascension. *The Kingdom* takes the story forward with the doings of the Disciples after Christ had left them.

Gerontius, or, in full, *The Dream of Gerontius*, is a setting of a very beautiful poem by Cardinal Newman.

Besides these there are a great many other Oratorios by composers British, and American, and foreign, but those mentioned are the chief Oratorios that you are likely to have a chance of hearing.

QUESTIONS

*(To See Whether You Remember
the Chapter and Understand It)*

1. How would you describe an Oratorio?

2. Tell, in your own words, what you know of St. Philip Neri.

3. How was Cavalieri's Oratorio *Soul and Body* different from Oratorios to-day?

4. Describe Passion Music, and mention the chief writers of it.

5. Which is the finest 'Passion' ever written?

6. Give the names of four or five of the most important of Handel's Oratorios.

7. And the name of one of Haydn's.

8. And the name of the most popular Oratorio by Mendelssohn.

9. And the names of three by Elgar. Tell anything you know about these.

THINGS TO DO

1. Get Mendelssohn's *Elijah*, or Handel's *Messiah*, or Haydn's *Creation* and look through the words at the beginning (they are generally printed out in full, before the music begins).

2. Then play, or get some one to play, some parts of the Oratorio, such as the Overture and some of the choruses and solos. Or get Gramophone records of these. Try to get a pretty good idea of what the Oratorio is about, and how the composer has treated his subject.

3. Get somebody to sing (or play) you some of the best bits of Bach's *Christmas Oratorio* (such as the Cradle Song).

4. And also some of the Chorales or Hymn Tunes in the *St. Matthew Passion* (notice the flowing voice parts in these).

5. If you can get somebody to play you parts of an Elgar Oratorio, so much the better. You can enjoy a few things as Gramophone records if you are rich and intelligent—and I hope you are both!

CHAPTER VI

THE EARLIEST OPERAS

ONE of the greatest dates in history is 1453, the date when the Eastern Empire fell and the Turks took Constantinople. You may wonder what that has to do with music, but you will soon see.

The Renaissance

Constantinople had been a great centre of scholarship. Many learned and studious Greeks were living there, and there were great collections of Greek literature and art. When the Turks entered the city the Greeks fled, and took with them such of their ancient manuscripts as they could carry. Wherever they could find a wealthy patron to support them they settled, and so the study of the ancient Greek language and literature was spread over Europe, and, as a result, the very thought of Europe was changed. This change of thought is called by a word meaning 'Re-birth'—RENAISSANCE (or RENASCENCE). The new ideas which sprang out of the revival of the old ones altered men's views on Politics and Religion and science, changed the course of Literature, and brought in a new Architecture based on that of ancient Greece.

It will give you a rough but sufficient idea of the change in Architecture if you think first of Westminster Abbey, and then of St. Paul's Cathedral. The Abbey, with its pointed arches, and interlacing lines, and slender columns, belongs to the older style of mediaeval architecture; the Cathedral, with its massive blocks of masonry, its great round arches, its pillared portico, and its dome, illustrates the Renaissance style, which is based on that of the ancient Greek temples.

In the Abbey you feel a sense of awe and mystery that you do not feel in the Cathedral, where everything is much more open and simple in style. The Abbey, we may say, is graceful and mysterious, the Cathedral massive and striking. It is worth while to look at some pictures of these great churches, if you have them, and think out what has just been said, because it will, in a moment, illustrate a similar change that the Renaissance a little later brought about in music.

What Happened at Florence

As Italy was so much nearer to the East than Germany or France or Britain, of course a great many Greek scholars settled there, and Florence, in particular, became a great centre for the study of the Greek language and literature, and art, for in Florence there long lived a great and rich family called the Medici family (pronounce Med-*ee*-chee) who made their palace a meeting-place for learned and cultured men of every kind, and there were other palaces, of other families who followed the Medici fashion, and monasteries, too, where the studies went on very actively.

The Renaissance in Music

One little group of learned men used to gather at the palace of a Count Bardi at the end of the sixteenth century (a century and a half after the Renaissance had begun). They discussed the Greek plays and Greek music, and wondered if these could be revived, and at last one of them, Vincenzo Galilei (father of Galileo Galilei, the great astronomer), wrote a piece modelled on what, from his reading of the Greek classics, he imagined to be the Greek style. The idea was, instead of the elaborate madrigal style of which you read in the first volume of this book, and which was at its height just then, to have a single voice, declaiming rather than singing, and to support it with a few chords on Lutes or similar instruments.

Other composers took up this idea, and by and by real Operas were composed, chiefly treated in this way (dialogue supported by chords), but with bits of simple chorus (also largely in plain chords), and with an orchestra of any instruments that were to be had, used both to accompany the voices and also to play little bits of music in between the vocal parts. A line of one of these earliest operas will show you the style of thing.

(Free translation: I, that from above breathe plaints and sighs.)

There you see the voice part imitating the speaking voice rather than singing a tune, and under it a plain accompaniment of chords.

Generally the Operas of this time were on subjects taken from Greek mythology. For instance, the story of Orpheus and how he went down to the place of death to bring back his Eurydice, was used. So altogether the early operas were very much influenced by the study of Greek thought, and the invention of Opera may fairly be considered one of the results of the Renaissance.

The Old Style and the New

If you will look at that little bit of music, made out of plain chords, one after another, and compare it with a bit of a song with lute accompaniment belonging to the same period, you will see what the difference amounts to.

Be still, for if you ev-er do the like

Here you will see how the lute player, instead of playing mere chords (i.e. just 'Harmony'), weaves a combination of melodies (i.e. 'Counterpoint').

Now let us look at the same sort of thing in a three-part chorus. Here is a bit of one of the new Florentine works—

And here is a bit of one of the older style pieces—

Again you see just the same difference. The newer style of piece is in chunks of harmony, and the older style of piece is a weaving together of counterpoint.

Both these styles of writing were going on at the same time. The older-minded composers sometimes had 'chunks', and the newer ones tended more and more to fall back into the 'weaving' process. But you see the difference, and you will realize that these new Opera and Oratorio composers brought about a new way of looking at music—as we may say, a *perpendicular* way instead of the old *horizontal* way. After a time composers learnt more and more to look at music in both ways together.

If you recall any music you heard in illustration of the Elizabethan Composers (Volume I, chapter II) you will remember that it was nearly all *horizontal*. And if you then recall any of the Purcell music you heard (Volume I, chapter III) you will remember that some of it was *perpendicular* or 'chunky' (for instance any Recitatives and some parts of the Choruses) whilst other parts were *horizontal,* or woven. But even when composers wrote horizontally they now had a clear idea of the chords they were using; in other words, they were writing both horizontally and perpendicularly at the same time.

Frozen Music

Now let us look at some Architecture. Somebody has called Architecture 'Frozen Music', and it is true that there are lots of things in Architecture that remind us of Music. If you glance at the picture opposite you will see a bit of old-style (early Gothic) 'frozen music'—Counterpoint, etc., woven lines. Now if you will look below you will see also a bit of new-style (or 'Renaissance') 'frozen music'—Harmony, one thing just above or against another, architectural 'chords' as it were.

Remember as much of this chapter as you can. It tries to give you, in a rough-and-ready sort of way, an idea of the beginnings of Opera, and then to show you in what sort of style the early Opera writers composed.

COUNTERPOINT IN ARCHITECTURE

HARMONY IN ARCHITECTURE

QUESTIONS

*(To See Whether You Remember
the Chapter and Understand It)*

1. When were the first Operas written?

2. And where?

3. What was the chief idea of their writers, i.e. what were they trying to do?

4. What sort of music did they write, and how was it different from what went before?

5. Why is Westminster Abbey like an Anthem of Queen Elizabeth's day, and St. Paul's like some of the Anthems of Charles the Second's time? It is rather difficult to put this into words, but you might try.

THINGS TO DO

There are none—unless perhaps you were to get hold of a Gramophone record of one of Purcell's or Handel's or Mendelssohn's Recitatives, and see how the speaking style of song, supported by chords, was still going on long after those people in Florence invented it. Also if you cared you could put on the Gramophone a record of some Handel chorus and notice whether the composer has written it in *(a)* the Harmonic style, or *(b)* the Contrapuntal style, or *(c)* sometimes a bit in one and sometimes a bit in the other (the 'Hallelujah Chorus' is a good example of the mixed styles).

CHAPTER VII

MORE ABOUT OPERA

If You Were Writing an Opera

If you were writing an Opera which should you consider more important—the play or the music? Just think a moment. Suppose we imagine a school opera. Let us make up a plot. How would this do—taken from *Tom Brown's Schooldays?*

ACT I. SCENES 1 AND 2.

The Head, distressed that Tom Brown is always in mischief, hits on a good idea—to put a young and nervous new boy into his study and in his charge, so that he will feel a sense of responsibility. On the first day of term he invites Tom to tea and introduces him to Arthur, the new boy.

ACT II.

Tom looks after Arthur as well as he can, but feels that Arthur needs something to wake him up. Suddenly Arthur begins to take an interest in a boy who is a great naturalist, and in his collection of birds' eggs (the boy's nickname is 'Madman'); Tom thinks that this is just the thing. He invites Madman to supper and they all plan a great birds-nesting expedition together.

ACT III.

Coming home after their expedition they throw stones at a guinea-hen, and are seen by the farmer and chased by the farmer's men. They see a Prefect and go and surrender to him. The Prefect has a great argument with the farmer, who wants half-a-sovereign in compensation, although the guinea-hen was not hurt. In the end, after a thrilling dispute [a lot of agitated recitative here], they agree to pay three shillings, and the Prefect, as they all go back to school, gives them some good advice about keeping out of trouble in future.

Now all that is very brief and bald, is it not? But, of course, there is a lot of detail to be worked in when the libretto (or word-book of the opera) is written, and those who have read *Tom Brown's Schooldays* will see that quite an exciting little opera could be made out of the incidents.

Two Ways of Doing It

Now there are two ways of setting the words:

(a) We can set them so as to make a lot of opportunities for pleasant music.

(b) We can set them so as to make the tale *really* live.

And either of these ways might be quite successful.

The Musical Way

Suppose we try the first way. We shall have, to begin with, a long chorus of boys back from the holidays, saying 'How jolly to be back at School', or words to that effect. Then we shall have a bit of recitative for the Matron as she says that Tom is invited to tea in the Head's drawing-room. And we shall have solos from various boys, telling at great length what they did in the holidays, or what they mean to do at school this term, and there will be various little bits of fun in between the solos, to keep things going. The first scene will then close with a solo from Tom, who is wondering why on earth the Head has invited him to tea, with little bits of chorus by the other boys, saying '*We* wonder too.' This chorus will work up loudly and excitedly as Tom goes off the stage to see the Head and the curtain falls.

And all those solos and choruses will be beautiful tunes, so that as you hear them you will be saying, What lovely music! (for of course *our* music would be lovely, wouldn't it?). But, as you can see, the Scene will not be very much like real life because schoolboys do not make soliloquies and long speeches while their companions stand quietly by. Probably that scene would have about three good set choruses, and about five good solos, and little bits of recitative here and there when we wanted rapid dialogue such as could not well be set to a real 'tune'.

The Dramatic Way

Now imagine the other way of setting. This time we are not going to think so much of the music, though, of course, we shall try to make that as good as possible; we are going to think of making the schoolboys lifelike, so that any old Rugby boy present when our Opera is given will say, 'That's just what *did* happen on the first day of term!' Of course, we shall have singing instead of speaking, but it will not be so much in long tunes as in short natural bits of recitative, only rising to a tune or chorus here or there in some very suitable place.

The Two Ways Compared

If you took the first setting you would find it had in it a lot of pieces that you could sing at a school concert, quite apart from the opera and just as ordinary songs or choruses; if you took the second there would be very little you could take apart in that way, because it would all be just suitable for its special purpose and for no other.

Both these ways of writing an opera may be quite good, but the first will make a more *musical* opera, and the second a more *dramatic* one.

Now the early operas, as you have seen, were dramatic operas, but very soon composers began to make them less dramatic and more musical. They began to put long tunes into the operas, and very beautiful and often difficult ones. When the performance arrived at one of these, the singer who had to give it would go to the front of the stage and sing it more like a concert song than a bit of a play, and meantime the other characters of the play had to stand quietly by and listen. So you see the plot could not move very quickly, for it was always being held up by some long song. Yet, as *music,* many of the operas of this period were very beautiful.

Both in Italy and in France such operas as these were very fashionable, and opera singers who had lovely voices, and who could do justice to the difficult music, earned enormous fees. Opera Houses were opened everywhere. The first one was opened at Venice in 1637, and in that city opera was so popular that even the nuns had performances of it in their convents. Half a century after Opera began it had almost ceased to be dramatic, and was just a pleasant musical entertainment, and half a century later still, so much was thought of good opera singers that they lived almost like kings and queens and made huge fortunes.

Opera in France

A great opera composer in France was Lully, who was under the patronage of Louis XIV. He had been born in Florence, where a monk taught him to sing. A French princess took him home with her as a scullion, and he used to sing and play his fiddle in the kitchen. One of the princess's guests heard him one day and spoke to his mistress about him; she then promoted him, making him a fiddler in her private band. Then he made up a song poking fun at the princess and she found it out and dismissed him, but this turned out well for him, for King Louis (then a youth of fifteen) took him into his famous band of 'Les Vingt-quatre Violons du Roi', and later started a new and additional band, called 'Les Petits Violons', with Lully as the master of it.

Lully became both a clever courtier and a clever composer, and collaborated with the great Molière in writing Ballets for performance at Court, and also wrote operas that were very graceful and pleasant. He was a horrid character, but made a lot of money by pleasing people.

This is just a glimpse at the life of a successful opera composer of the seventeenth century. It will at any rate show you how popular opera had become amongst royal and aristocratic people. Lully had an English pupil called Pelham Humphrey, and Pelham Humphrey was one of the masters of Purcell. And in that way something of Lully's graceful way of writing tunes, and his style of dramatic recitative, crept into English music.

Opera in England

Purcell himself, as you know, wrote a good deal of music for stage plays, and one or two real Operas, and he also set some Ballets, or dance pieces. The earliest opera in the world that is still performed is a very fine one by Purcell—*Dido and Aeneas:* he wrote it for the pupils of a ladies' school near London. After Purcell was dead Handel came to London and for years wrote operas. He wrote them in Italian, which was the

GLUCK

fashionable language for opera, most of the best singers then being Italian. His operas were much more musical than dramatic, and you never hear one of them to-day, though some of the Handel songs you hear at concerts come from his operas.

Gluck (1714-87)

Roughly half a century later than Lully came Gluck, a great reformer of opera. He was a German. He came to England, but his operas could not then compete with those of Handel. After many years his works took on a new style, and then they made him famous. He realized that opera had become too entirely musical, and he started to make it dramatic once more. At first people did not like this, but by and by they saw Gluck's point.

Just to illustrate this, in his famous opera *Orpheus*, which you can still sometimes see (it is the next earliest opera still performed after Purcell's *Dido)*, he made the chorus move about the stage and take part in the play, instead of standing on each side of the stage and just singing. Also he used his orchestra very cleverly. And his Ballets in *Orpheus* were really a part of the play, and, indeed, one of the most important parts, instead of being a bit of entertainment stuck in without much reference to the plot.

Mozart's Operas

Mozart's operas are very beautiful, though some of them have silly stories, for he was one of those men who could set anything to music—and to lovely music, too. You ought to know the names of one or two of the best.

Figaro (*Feeg*-gar-o).

Don Giovanni (Don Jo-*vahn*-nee).

The Magic Flute.

The Seraglio (Say-*rah*-lee-o).

All these can often be heard. You would probably like *The Magic Flute* best.

Some Other Opera Composers

Beethoven only wrote one opera, *Fidelio* (Fee-*day*-lee-o).

Weber(*Vay*-ber), a German, wrote *Der Freischütz*, (something between *Fry*-sheets and *Fry*-shoots; it cannot quite be spelt in English) and *Oberon*.

Rossini (Ross-*een*-ee), an Italian, wrote *The Barber of Seville* and *William Tell*.

Bizet (Bee-*zay*), a Frenchman, wrote *Carmen*.

Gounod (Goo-*no*), a Frenchman, wrote *Faust*.

Some more operas and opera composers will be mentioned later in this book, especially those of Wagner (*Vahg*-ner), a German.

Grand Opera and Light Opera

Some operas have spoken dialogue mixed up with the music. Others are set to music all through, and these last we speak of as 'GRAND OPERA'. An opera with a libretto of a not very serious nature, set to music which is also not serious, we call a 'LIGHT OPERA'. A short light opera is called an 'OPERETTA'. There is an opera popular both in Britain and America just at the time this book is written, called *The Beggar's Opera*. It is nothing but a string of jolly tunes of the time when it was written (two centuries since, 1728), and so is called a BALLAD OPERA.

QUESTIONS

*(To See Whether You Remember
he Chapter and Understand It)*

1. If we were writing an Opera, what two different styles would we have to choose from? Which would *you* choose?

2. When composers began writing Opera, about 1600, which way did *they* choose?

3. And what did the composers who followed them do?

4. What do you know of Lully?

5. What do you know of Purcell?

6. What do you know of Gluck?

7. What do you know of Handel's Operas?

8. Mention any Operas by Mozart.

9. Mention any Operas by Beethoven.

10. Mention any Operas by Weber.

11. Mention any Operas by Bizet.

12. Mention any Operas by Gounod.

13. Give the nationality of Lully, Purcell, Handel, Gluck, Mozart, Beethoven, Weber, Bizet, Gounod, and Wagner.

14. What do you mean by Grand Opera?

CHAPTER VIII

WAGNER

1813-1883

A Schoolboy Playwright

A Leipzig schoolboy of fourteen sat puzzling over something that for days had kept him busy—a grand tragedy he had written. It was based on Shakespeare—characters from *Hamlet* and *King Lear* being introduced, with others too, so that, altogether, there were forty-two characters in the play. And now, at the end of the fourth act, with a fifth needed to finish off the plot, there was nobody left to do it. By one disaster or another all the forty-two had been killed. Happy idea! Let some of them return as ghosts! And so the tragedy was at last finished.

A Mania for Music and Drama

This boy was Richard Wagner and he was always thinking about drama—except when he was thinking about music.

RICHARD WAGNER

Sometimes, sitting at the window, he would see the great opera writer, Weber, pass, and then he would think what a fine thing it must be to be a great composer of operas! And he would sit down at the piano and dash away at the overture to Weber's *Freischütz,* with any sort of fingering so long as he hit the right notes. Then he would take out his own great tragedy and wonder if he knew enough about music to be able to set it as an opera. He got hold of one or two text-books of musical composition at a library, but they did not seem to help him much, and in the end the tragedy never was set to music.

One reason that play-writing and music were so much in the boy's mind was this—his step-father was an actor, and so were one or two other members of the family, so you may be sure that plays and acting were talked about every day in that household.

At school the boy made good progress in Latin and Greek, and he loved Shakespeare and studied him thoroughly. Once there was a competition, the writing of a poem about a school event, and his poem was the best and was printed.

Concert Going

At Leipzig there was plenty of music to be heard. Bach had lived at Leipzig, you remember, and the music at the Thomas Church, where he was musical director, has always been famous. Wagner would hear this sometimes—especially as he attended the Thomas

School, of which Bach had once been 'Cantor'. Then there were some very famous concerts at the hall called the Gewandhaus, and young Wagner used to go to these and especially delighted in Beethoven. In *The First Book of the Great Musicians* I told how Elgar, at a later date, was 'awakened' by the sight of a Beethoven symphony. Hearing Beethoven at these concerts had a great effect on Wagner in something the same way, and soon he knew well almost everything of Beethoven's.

Learning to Compose

Perhaps stirred by the *Freischütz* overture, or perhaps by one of the overtures of Beethoven, young Richard thought he would write an overture himself. He did so, and managed to get it performed at a concert one Christmas Day, but people only laughed at it, because it was so queerly written and had a bang on the drum every four bars from beginning to end.

At last he found a first-rate teacher (one of Bach's successors as 'Cantor' of the Thomas School). He worked hard at his studies, and wrote pieces under his master's direction until he gained a good deal of proficiency. He still went on poring over Beethoven's scores and hearing Beethoven as much as he could, and all his life through Beethoven was one great influence behind his music.

You remember (from the first volume) what Beethoven did. He made music *express more feeling*— made it more dramatic. And this is what appealed so much to Wagner.

All this time he was studying at the University, but he gave a great deal more attention to music than to his studies there.

The Young Conductor

By and by Wagner got a small post as conductor, and then a rather better one. Then he thought he would like to go to Paris, which has always been a city famous for its love of opera. He went first to London, by sailing boat from a North German port. The voyage was a terrible one and lasted three weeks. He thought of the old legend of the Flying Dutchman, who was driven for his sins from sea to sea, always sailing, sailing, sailing, and he resolved to make this legend into an opera.

Starving in Paris

When he got at length to Paris he had many bitter disappointments. He had finished one opera called *Rienzi*, and wanted them to perform it at the great opera house in Paris. But he could not persuade them to do so, and for a bare living he had to work hard at any sort of musical drudgery he could get. Then he retired to a village near Paris, and worked hard at *The Flying Dutchman*. He put into it some of the salt of the air and the sting of the wind, as he had himself found them in the North Sea, and made a very fine thing of it. But he could get nothing of his performed in France, and at last he went back to Germany—this time to Dresden, where, at length, he had the joy of seeing *Rienzi* performed, and the people in delight about it. His *Flying Dutchman* was performed, too, and he was made chief conductor of the opera house there. So now he seemed to have found his feet.

Some More Operas

The next opera he wrote was *Tannhäuser* (*Tann-hoy-zer*). This is a finer opera than *The Flying Dutchman*, and very much finer than *Rienzi*, but the public did not at first like it, for Wagner was beginning to find his own way of doing things, and it was a different way from that of composers before him.

Then he wrote another opera called *Lohengrin*. Both *Tannhäuser* and *Lohengrin* are very popular to-day everywhere, but in those days they were in advance of their times.

Note this—unlike other composers Wagner wrote both the words and the music of his operas. All the time he was getting more and more away from the idea of those days that an opera was a *musical work* (you have seen something about this in the last chapter). His view was that an opera should be a *drama* (a real strong, fine play) *set to music*—music and words being equally important, instead of the music being the chief thing and the words of slight importance. You see then that Wagner had got back to the old idea of Gluck, who in his time went back to the old idea of the Florentines, who first began opera. But, of course, in Gluck's day music could do a good deal more than it could in the Florentines' day, and in Wagner's day it could do still more. So now, the art of music being so greatly developed, and able to express emotions so clearly and strongly, Wagner had a real chance of bringing into existence not mere 'opera', but actual 'Music Drama', and that is the name he before long adopted for his compositions.

Revolution

Troubles broke out in Dresden. The poor people, who were suffering very much, rioted, and the King and Court had to flee. Then the soldiers got the upper hand, and this time it was Wagner who had to flee, for he was accused of making speeches that had incited the revolutionists. He went to Weimar (Vymar), where his friend Liszt was the opera conductor. But this was not safe, and at last he got quietly away, right out of Germany, going first to Paris and then to Switzerland, where for some years he continued to live.

Meantime, at Weimar, the great musician Liszt began to perform his works, and to perform them very beautifully, so that people realized how wonderful they were, and began to see that their composer was a really great man.

Wagner and England

One year Wagner came to England to conduct the season's concerts for the Philharmonic Society in London. He proved successful as a conductor. One thing that astonished people was that often he would conduct a piece without a score, which is pretty common now but was not so then. Beethoven's *Heroic Symphony* he conducted in this way, but, as you have already heard, he had long known Beethoven by heart.

At last the banishment was withdrawn, and Wagner could return to his native Germany.

In later years he came to London again, to conduct concerts of his own music at the Albert Hall. But somehow this time his conducting was unsuccessful, and it was found better to have another conductor, whilst he sat beside him on the platform in an arm-chair facing the audience.

The Mad King

At that time, as you know, Germany consisted of a number of different states, with their own rulers. The kingdom of Bavaria was then ruled by King Ludwig II, who was very much interested in music, but a little mad. Wagner had written and published the libretto of a wonderful series of four music dramas, to be performed on four consecutive days. It was called *The Ring of the Nibelungs* (or for short, just *The Ring*). To produce such elaborate music drama as this would be very costly and difficult, and the ordinary opera houses were very unlikely to undertake to do so. So in his published preface Wagner asked 'Is the monarch to be found who will make performance possible?'

Ludwig was then Crown Prince, and when he read

this he said to himself that as soon as he came to the throne he would show Wagner that one monarch did prize his genius. And hardly a month after his accession he sent his secretary to seek Wagner. The secretary had some trouble about this, for Wagner had got into debt, and to escape arrest was in hiding. At last he was traced and the secretary gave him a photograph of the King and a ruby ring, and said, 'As that stone in the ring glows, so does my ruler's heart burn with longing to see you!'

This reads like a fairy story, doesn't it? But it is true. And when Wagner reached Munich and saw the King, his debts were paid, and a beautiful villa on the shores of a lake was given to him so that he might live and work happily. Wagner was now over fifty.

Bayreuth

Yet *The Ring* was not first performed at Munich, after all. Others of Wagner's works were given there, including *Tristan* and the very jolly comic opera *The Mastersingers of Nuremberg*, but before *The Ring* could be finished and performed trouble had occurred. Wagner was not always wise, and did many things that gave his enemies a handle against him, and at last, though the King still loved him, he had to leave Munich. He determined to settle in the little Bavarian town of Bayreuth (By-royt), build a special theatre and hold festivals there to which people from all over Germany could come. There, in 1876 (when Wagner was sixty-three), *The Ring* was at last given, and people came not only from all parts of Germany, but from Britain, and, indeed, every country in Europe, and from America.

The four dramas that make up The Ring are:—*Rhine Gold, The Valkyries, Siegfried,* and *The Dusk of the Gods.*

Later Wagner wrote *Parsifal,* a sacred music-drama, which was to be performed at Bayreuth and nowhere else, and so it was, until the copyright expired, and then opera managers all over the world were free to perform it.

The Death of Wagner

Six months after the first performance of *Parsifal* Wagner died—at Venice.

What Wagner's Music Dramas Are Like

Here is a recapitulation of a few points about Wagner's Music Dramas—

1. Except for one or two early works, they are founded on national legend.

2. They are very dramatic.

3. Their vocal music is largely a sort of Recitative, which rises into real songs when the occasion is suitable.

4. They are not cut up into a number of quite separate songs and choruses, etc. Each act goes on without break.

5. The orchestral part is largely made up of 'Leading

Motives', as they are called—little bits of music, each attached to some particular thought that keeps recurring in the play, or to some particular character in the plot.

6. A very large orchestra is needed, and the orchestration is very beautiful indeed, and more elaborate than anything written before Wagner's time.

7. Wagner wrote both words and music of his dramas.

8. He considered words, music, stage setting, and acting equally important, and wanted all to have equal attention.

The Three Attempts at Music Drama

Remember the three sets of really *dramatic* attempts at opera:

(a) Those of the Florentines (early seventeenth century);

(b) Those of Gluck (eighteenth century);

(c) Those of Wagner (nineteenth century).

All these composers were aiming not so much at making the music beautiful (though they did that) as at making the play tell its tale vividly by means of music.

Get the dates of Gluck and Wagner in your head (roughly at any rate). Notice that they are practically just a century apart—

Gluck born 1714: Gluck died 1787.

Wagner born 1813: Wagner died 1883.

Perhaps the best plan will be to learn Wagner's dates, and then remember that Gluck's were a century earlier.

QUESTIONS

(To See Whether You Remember the Chapter and Understand It)

1. When and where was Wagner born?

2. Tell what you remember of Wagner's boyhood.

3. And of his later travels to England and France.

4. What was his first bit of real success, and what happened to destroy it?

5. Who was the conductor who first had faith in Wagner and made people realize what a great composer he was? Where did he live?

6. What do you remember about the King who helped Wagner? What happened in the end?

7. What was the name of the place where Wagner set up his great theatre?

8. Give the names of as many of Wagner's Music Dramas as you can recall.

9. What are the special characteristics of Wagner's works?

10. What are the dates of Wagner and (roughly) Gluck?

THINGS TO DO

1. If you can get hold of a book with the stories of the plots of any of Wagner's Music Dramas, read it. If you are learning Musical Appreciation in a class, perhaps your teacher would read one of these stories aloud to you.

2. Get a volume of Wagner's Overtures for Piano (solo or duet) and practise them (if you are a good enough player; they are fairly difficult, as a rule). Or get them as Pianola rolls, if you have a Pianola.

3. There are a very great many Gramophone records of pieces from Wagner's works. Hear all of these that you can, and listen to them often, until you know them well. Find out where each piece comes in the plot of the drama.

CHAPTER IX

VERDI

1813-1901

The Boy and His Spinet

In a little Italian village, called Roncole, in the year 1813, lived two good people who kept a little inn, and sold groceries and tobacco. Their name was Verdi (*Vair*-dee), and they had a little son called Giuseppe ('Jew-seppy' is as near to the pronunciation as we can get in English spelling), who seemed to have a great talent for music. So they contrived to buy an old Spinet (a sort of harpsichord), and of this their little boy was very proud.

I think they gave Giuseppe the Spinet while he was rather too young, for this tale is told about him. He was trying one day to play notes together so as to make good 'chords'. He found one chord he liked very much, but when he tried to find it again he could not do so. He got into a childish rage at this, and taking up a hammer began to smash the Spinet. Fortunately his father came into the room and stopped him before much damage was done. Verdi afterwards made up for his foolish

GIUSEPPE VERDI

treatment of the instrument, for he kept it carefully all his life, and when, about eighty years after, he came to die, this old Spinet was still in his possession.

Verdi must have been a hard worker and his practice must have been very thorough, for the repairer who mended the instrument wrote inside it a description of the repairs he had done, and ended:

'This I do gratis in consideration of the good disposition the boy Giuseppe Verdi shows in learning to play on this instrument, which quite repays me for any trouble. [Signed] STEPHEN CAVALETTI, A.D. 1821.'

So we see that though in a fit of temper Verdi was capable of damaging his spinet, yet he really loved it, and worked hard to master it.

The Wandering Fiddler

There was a wandering fiddler who used to come to the village in those days. No doubt he was in great request when there were weddings or dances, and perhaps on festival days he played on the village green, which lay just before the inn where the little boy lived. We can be quite sure that Verdi liked to listen to the fiddler. You can imagine him standing open-mouthed, and watching his friend as his active bow brought jolly dance-tunes out of the instrument. And the fiddler, on his part, was very much interested in the boy, and I suppose would listen to his playing on the Spinet. Perhaps the man and the boy sometimes played their instruments together.

Now this fiddler, whose name was Bagasset, used to urge Verdi's father to allow him to become a musician by profession, and in other ways encouraged the boy in his studies. And when, long years after, the little boy had become a famous man, he remembered this with gratitude, and finding Bagasset again (now a very old and poor man), he did all he could to help him.

Verdi and the Priest

When Verdi was only seven years old, he used to help in church as an acolyte (that is, a helper for the priest in the smaller duties of the service). But the music he heard used to take his attention too much, and sometimes he forgot his duties. One day, after the part of the service called the Elevation of the Host, the organ music seemed so lovely that he was wrapped up in listening to it, and the priest had to ask him three times for water, and still he did not hear. So the priest knocked him down the altar steps, and he hurt his head so badly on the floor that he had to be carried unconscious into the vestry.

Verdi as Organist

The village organist was soon called in to be Verdi's teacher, but the boy learned so fast that after a year he knew as much as his master, and then the lessons had to stop. Two years after this, the organist left and Verdi took his place, retaining it until he was eighteen years old. He got a small salary, which was very useful to him, and when there were weddings or funerals he made a little more money. One dark night, when he was coming home from his work at the church, he fell into a deep stream and nearly lost his life. Fortunately a country-woman who was passing just then heard his shouts and was able to help him.

Verdi's Great Helper

In the neighbouring town of Busseto lived a well-to-do man named Barezzi, who was a great music-lover, and played several instruments. There was in Busseto a Musical Society, and this used to meet at Barezzi's house. Now, Barezzi took a great fancy to Verdi, and did all he could to help him. He used to invite the boy to his house, allow him to practise on his piano, and introduce him to all the musical people of the place who would be likely to be useful to him. All this was of great value to Verdi.

At this house, too, he met the organist of the Cathedral of Busseto, and this musician now became his teacher.

Verdi Goes to Milan

The people of Busseto had a fund with which to help clever boys to carry on their studies, and Barezzi persuaded them to give Verdi money to go to Milan to study music there. Milan had always been a very great place for music study, and it still is so. It has a great

Conservatory, or School of Music, and also an Opera House which is famous all over the world.

When Verdi got to Milan he applied to be admitted as a student of the Conservatory. He showed some music he had composed, and also played the piano to some of the professors. After waiting a week he went to ask what was the result of the examination, and was told he could not be admitted. This is one of the surprising things in the history of music—that this great Italian music school should have refused, 'on account of lack of talent,' to admit as a pupil the boy who was afterwards to become the greatest Italian musician of his day.

Verdi as Conductor

Verdi was then advised to study privately with a well-known composer called Lavigna, and under him he made great progress.

Musicians need to take every chance of hearing music played and sung, and so it came about that Verdi attended the rehearsals of the Milan Philharmonic Society, which was then studying Haydn's oratorio, *The Creation*. Three conductors took it in turn to direct the practices, but one day none of them turned up, and the secretary, not knowing what to do, asked Verdi if he thought he could manage to accompany. 'You needn't trouble to put in anything but the bass, you know, if you find it difficult,' he said. The singers, who thought they were very important people, were inclined to sneer at such a young and inexperienced director, but, adds Verdi, 'however that may be, we began the rehearsal, and little by little, becoming warmed and excited, I did not confine myself to accompanying, but began to conduct with the right hand, playing with the left alone.'

Afterwards every one congratulated him most warmly on his success, and it ended in his being appointed to conduct the performance of *The Creation*.

Back at Busseto

When the period of study was over, Verdi went back to Busseto. He had been made to promise, before he went to Milan, that he would come back to be organist of the Cathedral at Busseto when the then-organist, his old master, died. But the priests said that as he had been studying opera-music at Milan, instead of church music, they would not have him. Because of this, riots broke out. The Musical Society, which met at Barezzi's house, was very indignant and broke into the cathedral and took away all its own music which it had kept there. Verdi was for three years Conductor of this Society, but at the end of this period he removed to Milan, with the wife he had married—Barezzi's daughter.

Verdi's Great Sorrow

At Milan he was asked to write a comic opera, but just when he was beginning to be busy with this, he fell seriously ill. This caused him to be short of money, so he had trouble in paying his rent. Then one of his children fell ill and died, and a few days after the other died too. Soon after this his wife died. So in three months he had lost his whole family—and all this time he had to be hard at work writing a comic opera!

No wonder that the opera was not a success. The theatre manager, however, had faith in him and was always urging him to write another. At last he persuaded him to do so, and then Verdi began a long series of operas which, as it turned out, made his name famous all the world over.

Verdi's Operas

The Italians are particularly fond of operas. Indeed, as you already know, we may say that opera was *invented* by them. So Verdi, when he showed what skill he had in composing opera music, became one of the most popular men in Italy, and every one there is tremendously proud of him. There is little need to tell more of Verdi's life. It was a long one, and a successful one, and when he died, at the age of eighty-eight, the whole of Italy mourned for him.

Some of Verdi's Operas

Rigoletto.

Il Trovatore (= 'The Troubadour').

La Traviata.

Un Ballo in Maschera (Oon Ballo in *Mask-ay-rah* = 'A Masked Ball').

Macbeth (founded on Shakespeare's play).

Aida (Ah-*ee*-dah; an opera about Egypt, written for the Khedive, and first performed at Cairo).

Otello (founded on Shakespeare's play, 'Othello').

Falstaff (a very jolly opera, founded on Shakespeare).

Amongst other works than operas the most important is a fine *Requiem* (a mass to be sung for the dead) written in memory of the great Italian poet, Manzoni.

QUESTIONS

*(To See Whether You Remember
the Chapter and Understand It)*

1. What do you know of Verdi's childhood, and especially of his musical doings as a child?

2. Mention all the people who are spoken of in the chapter as having helped him (it does not matter about their names, if you remember who they were and what they did).

3. Mention one or two of his great successes, and one or two of his disappointments and sorrows.

4. Give the names of seven or eight of his Operas and one sacred work.

THINGS TO DO

Get all the Gramophone records you can of Verdi's music and listen carefully, until you know the pieces.

CHAPTER X

THE GAME OF 'CAMOUFLAGED TUNES'

IN Volume I of *The Book of the Great Musicians* were given a number of 'Camouflaged Tunes', with directions for playing the game. Here are some more. You remember what to do. You get somebody to play these tunes to you on the piano and try to hear the lower one, and to say what it is. Full directions for playing the game of 'Camouflaged Tunes' are given in Volume I.

A Christmas Tune—

A Tune we all know—

A Hymn we sing once a year—

There is something a little curious about the last two bars here; perhaps you will listen carefully and find it out.

Two Carol Parties in the same street—

A solemn Hymn Tune—

Another Hymn—

A favourite Scots song—

A favourite Hymn—

A fine old Psalm Tune—

A soldier's song, with Trumpets above it—

CHAPTER XI

ORGANS

A Human Organ

I do not know whether this game is worth playing. You might try it, and write and tell me.

You pick about a dozen intelligent boys—really serious, well-behaved ones, though, for they must not spoil the game by laughing. (Girls will do if they can whistle.)

You then stand them in a row and make each hold out his right hand (as if for caning, but of course you promise them they shall not have that). You then give each of them a note. No. 1 is to whistle C, calling it *Doh* (and only *Doh*), No. 2 *Ray,* No. 3 *Me,* and so on up the scale, including, I should think, *Fe* and *Ta.*

(This needs 12 boys or girls.)

You might make *Fe* and *Ta* (as 'black notes', so to speak), stand a little back from the others, so that you will not forget which they are.

THE 'CONSOLE' OF A BIG MODERN ORGAN

The 'Human Organ' is now ready to play, and you walk along pressing down the keys (the hands). As you press each key the boy to whom it belongs whistles his note, and keeps it on until you let his hand come up again.

First of all, for practice, you go up the scale and down again. Then you play a sort of voluntary, like a modulator exercise, bringing in an occasional *Fe* or *Ta*, something like this:

When your Organ can do that sort of thing smartly, you begin to practise tunes—easy ones at first, such as the *Old Hundredth* and *God Save the King*.

Then, if you like, and know how, you can put in a bit of harmony like this:

But you may find that harmony is too difficult for you, and for your Organ, and if so don't trouble about it.

Should you find your organ pipes (for that is what they are) prone to smile, try letting each sing his note (either to its *Doh-Me-Soh* name, or to *laa* or *oo*) instead of whistling it, as it is easy to sing even with a smile on one's face, whereas a quite small smile, by altering the shape of our mouth, prevents us from whistling.

This is perhaps not a game to spend much time upon, but it is worth trying, and your singing teacher may care to try it some time, setting various members of the class to play particular tunes on the Organ, as it is a good 'ear test' to find the right notes.

Tin Whistles and a Pair of Bellows

Now if we wanted to make a simple *real* Organ, how should we go about it? Something like this:

Take a box that does not leak, and a dozen tin whistles. Make a hole in the top of the box for each whistle to stand in. Stick gummed paper over the holes of the whistles so that each will play just the one note you want and no other. Bore another hole in the *side* of the box, this time for the nozzle of the kitchen bellows to go through. Then blow.

Yes! but when the box is filled with air all the whistles sound at *once,* making a horrible noise. That won't do! So next we fix a little cap inside the box under the mouthpiece of each whistle, close it with a spring, and have a string from it running through the bottom of the box by means of a hole we bore for the purpose. This cap is called a 'Pallet'. Now whilst your brother blows the bellows you pull the strings of the notes you wish to sound, and you have a 'Tin Whistle Organ'.

Here is a diagram of it:

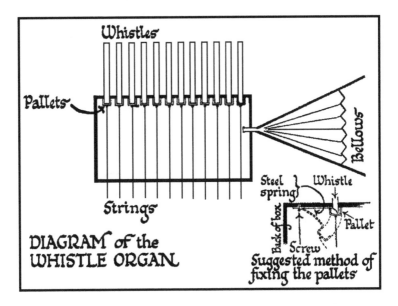

I do not say you could actually make a very good Organ of that sort, though a mechanically-inclined boy might, especially if he had an elder brother, or a father, who was an engineer. But I am explaining the subject this way because I think it makes it easier.

Tin Whistles and Toy Trumpets

Next we have a very good idea. We are tired of having all one sort of tone—Tin Whistle tone, so we decide to have also Toy Trumpet tone. We bore another set of holes behind the Tin Whistle holes and (being millionaires) buy a dozen good Toy Trumpets (the expensive sort on which you can play different notes, and we so fix down the trumpet keys that they shall do this), and add them to our Organ. We now have a big cap for each note, so that it will cover the mouth both of its Whistle and its Trumpet. When we pull down the C string, or the D string, we now have both Whistle and Trumpet sounding together.

Yes, but sometimes we may want to play for a time on Trumpet alone or on Whistle alone. So we have another little difficulty to get over. We invent sliders like this:

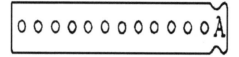

That, you notice, is just a plain strip of wood, with a hole for each note. We have two sliders, one for the Whistle, and the other for the Trumpet. The sliders move under the note-caps (or pallets). The part (A) projects through the side of the box. When we want the Whistle to sound we pull the whole Whistle-slider, so that the holes of the slider come under the mouthpieces of the Whistles, and then, as each pallet is pulled down by its string, the Whistle belonging to it can sound. Or we can push in the whole Whistle-slider and pull out the Trumpet-slider. Or we can pull both out together and then for every note we shall have a combined Whistle-Trumpet sound.

Now if we were to do two things more we should have a small complete organ. (a) Instead of pulling down the strings with our fingers we should make a keyboard and tie each string to the back part of its appropriate white or black Key. And (b) instead of pulling out the sliders with our hands we should put beside the keyboard two 'Stops' labelled 'Trumpet' and 'Whistle', by which we could do this without leaving the keyboard.

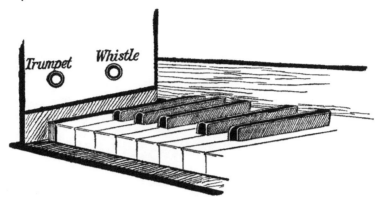

Now for a Real Organ!

If you have read carefully that description you have really got a very good idea of what an organ is like, and you can now go and ask some kind-hearted organist to let you see his instrument. Tell him I sent you, show him this chapter, and say that he is please to take you inside his organ and show you how it is just as I described, except that it has modern improvements, such as:

(a) more elaborate bellows, probably blown hydraulically (i.e. by water-pressure) or electrically;

(b) far more rows of pipes, and so more stops—say thirty or sixty, and no two sounding just alike in tone;

(c) the keys arranged in two or three separate Manuals, or keyboards (so that if the organist wants he can play with one hand on one Manual and the other on another, and can do other clever things); and

INSIDE A BIG ORGAN

another row for the feet ('Pedal Board');

(d) a much neater connexion than our strings between the Keys and the Pallets (perhaps, in a modern pneumatic connexion, or even electrical);

(e) instead of the Tin Whistle stops being all the same length like ours, but having holes in their sides, they are different lengths and have no holes. The big ones play low notes and the small ones high notes. In a very big Cathedral Organ there may be some 'Whistles' (i.e. organ pipes) thirty-two feet long and some but a few inches (every organ, even a small one, has at least one pipe sixteen feet long);

(f) in a very modern organ, instead of the Stop knobs (to pull out), there are little pneumatic pistons (to push in) or some other clever device of that kind.

The Difference between Whistles and Trumpets

You have now got a rough idea of an organ. But before the description is finished you must come back to the Tin Whistle and the Trumpet, and know something about the difference between them. If you break open a Tin Whistle, you find it is just a tube with a mouthpiece. If you break open a Toy Trumpet you find inside it a little strip of brass (called a Reed) which vibrates when you blow the Trumpet, and makes the sound. Mouth Organs and Concertinas have similar reeds (real Trumpets do not, nor do Horns, nor Flutes; but Oboes, Clarinets, and Bassoons do, as you learnt in the Orchestra chapter of the first volume of this book).

Now your organist friend will, tell you that his Organ, like the one I have just imagined our making, is made up of 'Flue Stops' as he calls them (with plain pipes like Whistles) and 'Reed Stops' (with pipes that have reeds inside, like those of a Toy Trumpet). Get him to play you a few notes first on a Flue stop and then on a Reed stop and you will know the difference in a minute, and remember it ever after.

That is all I am going to tell you now about the way an organ is made, but do go and talk to an organist and get him to let you sit by him as he plays. You will find that to play a big Organ is just as fine a thing as to drive an engine or a car.

Some Pictures of Organs

Now, to end with, here are a few pictures of organs, showing how the instrument developed out of something even simpler than our box of whistles.

SCULPTURE OF AN ORGAN OF THE TENTH CENTURY,
AT ARLES IN FRANCE

Note that here we have 'human bellows'—men who blow into tubes, having turns, I suppose, to take breath.

A STILL EARLIER ORGAN

Earlier, yet really more advanced, because it is blown by bellows. The men stand on the bellows to press it down with their weight, then get off till the bellows goes up again, stand on it again, and so on. Some organs on the Continent are still blown in much that way, and the writer of this book used to be organist of a church in Switzerland where this was done.

A TENTH-CENTURY ORGAN WITH
FOUR (HARD-WORKING) BLOWERS AND
TWO (BAD-TEMPERED) PLAYERS

Apparently the tenth-century organ had no keys. It looks as though the players stopped and unstopped the holes in the pipes with their fingers.

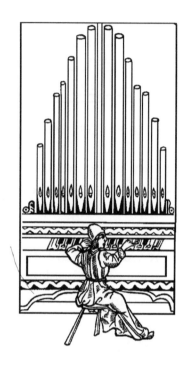

A FIFTEENTH-CENTURY ORGAN, WITH KEYS, BUT THESE SO BROAD THAT THEY WERE PLAYED NOT BY SINGLE FINGERS, BUT BY THE WHOLE HAND.

QUESTIONS

1. What is a Flue Stop?

2. And what is a Reed Stop?

3. What is a Manual?

4. What is a Pedal Board?

5. When the Organist pulls out a Stop what does it do? When he pushes it in, what does it do?

6. When he puts down a key, what does it do? When he lets the key go up, what does it do?

THINGS TO DO

1. Go and talk to an Organist, as I have already advised you.

2. When you come back, write a little essay called 'How an Organ Works' or (if you prefer) '*A Visit to Mr.____'s Organ, and what he showed me*'.

CHAPTER XII

DEBUSSY

1862-1918

ALTHOUGH Debussy died only recently, very little is known about his life—not a twentieth part of what we know about that of Bach, who died in the middle of the eighteenth century. Debussy was a shy man and did not like to talk about himself. What talking about himself he did was done not in words, but through his music—and that, though it tells us a good deal about what manner of man he was, does not tell us what he did in his boyhood, and what people he met, and what difficulties and triumphs he had. So though I have told you, in this volume and the one that went before, quite a lot about the boyhood-life of a great many composers, I cannot do so about Debussy. For this I am sorry, but—there it is!

Debussy at the Conservatoire

This I do know. He showed talent for music quite early, and, as he was a French boy, was sent to study at the Paris Conservatoire of Music when eleven or

CLAUDE DEBUSSY

twelve years old. In the years that followed he won a number of medals for Sight-Singing, a prize for Piano Playing, another for Accompanying, and another for Counterpoint and Fugue. So it looks as though he worked hard.

Now every year at the Conservatoire there is a competition for what is called the 'Prix de Rome'. The competitors are all supposed to have learnt whatever can be taught them about composition, and to need merely the opportunity for quiet practice in composition and self-development. The winner is sent to Rome to a large house called the Villa Medici, where other young musicians and painters are already living. He joins them and works quietly there for two or three years, and is expected to send home every year some composition to show what progress he is making. As you may guess, life in that wonderful city is very stimulating to the imagination of a young genius, and so is the association with other young artists.

When Debussy was twenty-two he won this prize, the composition with which he won it being a Cantata called *The Prodigal Son*. This has been given as an Opera in London in recent years. It is now quite old-fashioned and does not strike one as very wonderful, but it is well written, and it is quite clear that the judges were right in thinking it showed promise, for Debussy's after-career showed that no mistake had been made.

Early Compositions

But the authorities at the Conservatoire did not so much approve of the compositions Debussy sent home from Rome, according to the regulations. The first year he sent a Suite for Orchestra called *Spring,* and the judges said its form was too 'vague'. Next year he sent a cantata for Women's Voices and Orchestra, a setting of our English poet Rossetti's beautiful poem, *The Blessed Damozel,* and the judges said that this was still more 'vague'. Remember this criticism about 'vagueness', for we shall come back to it in a moment.

Debussy in Russia

When his time in Rome was up, Debussy came back to Paris, and then, before long, went off to Russia, earning his living by giving lessons to some young Russians. He took the opportunity of studying Russian music, both folk-music and art-music, and especially that of a composer named Moussorgsky, who was a very free and independent sort of composer—one who went his own way and made up music in the way he liked, and not according to the rules and settled plans of other composers before him. Remember this too, will you? for you will soon find that it has its bearing upon Debussy's own manner of composition.

When Debussy returned to Paris he lived quietly for a time, and then people began to pay attention to him and to perform his music. A choral society gave his *Blessed Damozel,* which had had to wait eight or nine years unheard; a famous string quartet party (the Ysaye Quartet—pronounce Ee-sye, and you will be near it) gave his Quartet; and his Orchestral Prelude, called *The Afternoon of a Faun,* was performed and soon became very popular. This last is the piece of his which we hear most often at orchestral concerts. It gives a wonderful feeling of a sultry summer afternoon, in which we are to suppose a faun (one of the woodland deities—with the face of a man and the legs, feet, and ears of a goat) half asleep and lazily day-dreaming. The music gives us the feelings that we may suppose would pass through his mind. It is a very delicate piece, and, again, vague—like the haze of a hot summer day.

Debussy's Vagueness

That brings me to the point of explaining what I mean by Debussy's 'vagueness', but it is a difficult thing to do. Let me put it this way. He loved in his music to picture nature, but the aspects of nature he loved most were mists and clouds and dusk, and bright sunbeams, and waves in the light of the moon. Now all these things, if you think for a moment, are vague rather than clear-cut and precise, and Debussy's music was often like them. It had its clear lines, but they were so arranged that they gave one the vague feelings of wonder and beauty that such sights as I have mentioned awaken in our minds.

Something about Scales

Go to the piano and play a Whole-tone Scale—that is, a scale with all tones and no semitones, like this:

Debussy had picked up that scale in Russia, where one or two composers had used it a little, and he then used it a great deal more than they did. It, in itself, has a strange effect of vagueness, all the intervals being just alike, so that if you play it up the piano for an octave or two and listen, you will find you can hardly tell where you have got to, whereas with the ordinary major and minor scales the mixture of semitones keeps you alive to where you are, and you can say in a moment (if you have a well-trained ear) 'we have now got to *Soh*', or 'that note is *Lah*'. So when Debussy made a melody out of this scale there came about that feeling of 'vagueness' that I have mentioned.

Something about 'Harmonics'

And his harmony had a vague feeling too.

Go to the piano again, and this time strike a low G.

How many notes did you hear? 'One'!... Nonsense! you *struck* one note, but *heard* hundreds—and never knew what you were hearing.

Let me tell you something about rainbows. Do you know what colour Homer thought a rainbow was?— Purple! Now Homer lived probably about 3,000 years ago.

But Xenophon, besides the purple, saw in the rainbow red, yellow, and green. Now Xenophon lived, roughly, 2,350 years ago.

But Aristotle saw red, green and blue, and said that sometimes yellow could also be seen. Now Aristotle lived, roughly, 2,300 years ago.

But Ovid saw in the rainbow a 'thousand dazzling colours that the eye cannot distinguish separately.' Now Ovid lived, roughly, 1,950 years ago.

You see how gradually people learnt to see the colours of the rainbow. The latest in date of those I have mentioned is Ovid, who came the nearest to the truth, but even he was bewildered, and could see that many colours were there which he could not, as it were, seize. And some people actually went on, up to six or seven hundred years ago, saying 'a rainbow has three colours.' How slowly people's eyes get trained!

Now apply this to music. If you will listen again to that note G, you will hear not only the note you strike, but also what Ovid would perhaps call 'A thousand dazzling sounds that the ear cannot distinguish separately'. You really hear a *cloud of sound*, something like this:

Try the experiment again, this time with the right pedal down, and listen very closely indeed. You can hear that 'cloud', can't you? But I defy you to pick out all the separate sounds given in the diagram, though they are there. Yet if you trained yourself, you could gradually come to recognize many of the sounds—especially the lower ones.

Next time you hear a church bell, go near to it and listen to the 'harmonics', as we call the sounds of this 'cloud'. You will find that you can pick out some of them quite clearly. Debussy was very fond of listening to bells and, with his quick ear, could take in a good deal more, probably, than you or I. At all events the bells taught him harmony—in a sort of way.

Chords

If you look at that diagram again you will find that the first five sets of notes (counting from the bottom) make up an ordinary common chord, and the first seven sets make up the Chord of the Dominant Seventh, which is our most usual 'discord', as we call it. All composers use common chords and chords of the seventh.

Composers have also long used other chords, taking in some of the slightly higher harmonics. But Debussy loved chords made out of the still higher harmonics, chords that he heard the church-bell play when he listened to it very keenly. And if you listen to Debussy's music (his later music, not the earliest, written before he had developed his personal style of writing) you will find a 'vagueness' in the chords that will remind you a little perhaps of the bells from which this composer learnt so much.

How Harmonics Come About

It may be worth while to tell you how those harmonics come about. When you strike the note I told you to strike, the whole string vibrates and makes the low G. But at the same time the two halves of the string vibrate, and give us the two G's an octave higher. And at the same time the three thirds of the string vibrate and give us the three D's—and so on. It sounds a bit unlikely, doesn't it, that a string should vibrate both as a whole and in parts, at the same time? But ask your physics teacher and you will find it is true enough. Possibly your physics teacher can show you some interesting experiments to make the matter clearer.

Debussy's Rhythms

All his life Debussy was not merely a maker of music, but also a *listener.* He heard the bells, and the bugles, and the winds and waves, and other sounds of nature, and learnt something from each, but he also listened keenly to the gipsy bands of Russia, and to the old plainsong in the French churches. The rhythms of the gipsies were very wild, and those of the plain-song very free (I mean, not just two-in-a-bar or three-in-a-bar, but in varying groups so that you could hardly put bars in the music at all). All this taught Debussy something, and in his music you can find the rhythmic influences of the gipsies and of the old church song.

A feature of Debussy's music is that he did not stuff it full of notes, as some composers do. He wrote just as many notes as were needed to get the effect he wanted, and no more. A living Swiss composer, called Bloch, has said that he knew Debussy well and knows Strauss, and has seen both composing, and that when Debussy had written a piece for orchestra he would go through it carefully, taking out every note he could, whilst Strauss would go through just as carefully, adding bits here and there, for the different instruments, until he could add no more without spoiling the piece.

Some of Debussy's Music

Debussy wrote a good deal of piano music, such as *Children's Corner, Gardens in Rain, Reflections in the Water Bells heard through the Leaves, Goldfish.*

Then he wrote a good many beautiful songs.

And for Orchestra he wrote the *Afternoon of a Faun* (already mentioned), *The Sea* (three pieces, one of them depicting morning on the sea, another the waves, another a dialogue between wind and waves), and *Three Nocturnes* (1. Clouds; 2. Fêtes; 3. Sirens).

Then there is some Chamber Music, including the String Quartet.

And there is a very beautiful opera, called *Pelléas and Mélisande.*

Debussy's Death

Debussy died in 1918, when you were __ years old.

QUESTIONS

*(To See Whether You Remember
the Chapter and Understand It)*

1. When was Debussy born?

2. What was his nationality?

3. What do you remember of his early career?

4. What do you understand by the 'vagueness' of his music?

5. What are 'Harmonics'?

6. What is the 'Whole-tone Scale'?

7. Mention all the names you remember of pieces by Debussy.

THINGS TO DO

1. Play any of Debussy's music that is within your capacity.

2. Get some good pianist to play you other pieces.

3. Get *L'Après-midi d'un Faune* ('The Afternoon of a Faun') as a Gramophone record.

4. If you have a Pianola get some records of Debussy's music (there are lots of these).

CHAPTER XIII

MILITARY MUSIC

WE may be sure that as long as men have fought they have had fighting music of some sort. For bold music stirs us and excites us, and makes us feel brave. And for marching it is, of course, a great help, for it not only keeps men in step but also cheers them so much that the way seems only half as long. So we can rely upon it that all the great generals of the past have had music for their armies.

Queen Elizabeth's Soldier-Music

In England soldiers have had their music as far back as history goes. For instance, in Queen Elizabeth's day the soldiers had lots of music. We can see this very quickly if we look at any of Shakespeare's plays, for we shall find that in them all, whenever soldiers are on the march or whenever fighting is going on, there is the roll of drums and the blast of trumpets.

Whatever country Shakespeare's soldiers come from, and whatever age they belong to, he gives them the sort of instruments he himself was accustomed to hear in his and our country in the days of Elizabeth and of James I. There are Drums and Trumpets, of course, as I have already mentioned. But, in addition, there are Cornets (which in Shakespeare's day were wooden instruments, not like our brass Cornets), and Sackbuts (something like our Trombones), and Hautboys (like our Oboes, but rougher in tone).

No doubt Shakespeare had sometimes seen Queen Elizabeth's soldiers marching about the city, and had noticed that these were the instruments they played.

Bands in Charles the Second's Day

Charles II had much the same sort of soldier-music. Like Queen Elizabeth he was very musical, so I should think that he would see that his soldiers had a few good players attached to their regiments, and good instruments for them to play upon. When the King walked out he had a little troop, consisting of a Captain, two Lieutenants, three Sergeants, three Corporals and eighty Privates, with two Drummers and two Hautboy players to provide them with music, and the Queen and the Duke of York had similar troops as their bodyguards.

We do not know what music the Hautboy players and the Drummers played.

Turkish Music in the British Army

It is a curious thing that in the eighteenth century the British Army began to imitate Turkish army music.

Probably this was because the Turks were very fond of instruments of percussion (that is, banging and rattling instruments, such as Drums and Tambourines and Cymbals and Triangles). Such instruments as these, though not very musical, are splendid for keeping time, and helping the soldiers to march in step. And so British soldiers marched to the sound of a few Fifes and Hautboys, with the addition of lots of these noise-making instruments, and they even had one curious Turkish bell instrument which the soldiers called 'Jingling Johnny'.

In those days it was thought to be a great thing to have black men in the band, and sometimes these black men were allowed to behave very strangely, dancing and jumping to the music, or throwing their arms about in time to it. The other day I saw the band of a public school Officers' Training Corps, and the boy with the big drum threw his arms about in a way that has evidently come down as a tradition from those Turkish Band days. To hit the left side of the drum he sometimes used his right arm, swinging it over the top of the drum; and to hit the right side he used his left arm in a similar way. I don't suppose he knew he was imitating our recent enemies, the Turks, but I believe he was.

The Second Life Guards, the Coldstreams, and the Scots Guards had blacks in their bands until about sixty or seventy years ago.

German Bandmasters in the British Army

You know that the British people for some time had a silly idea that they were not musical, and that if they wanted to get good musicians they must send abroad for them.

So during the last century nearly all the Bandmasters for the British Army were brought from Germany, and often the Bandsmen too. If you ask any really old British Soldier he will tell you that in his day his regiment had a German Bandmaster. Indeed, a regiment that had not one would have felt rather ashamed. Occasionally, instead of a German, they would have an Italian.

Nowadays, of course, we have British Bandmasters and British Bandsmen, and there are no better conductors and players in the world. They are most of them trained at the very fine Army Music School, which is called Kneller Hall, near London, and this has become so famous that the Germans have founded one like it. So now they are learning from us, not we from them!

But the French Army Bands are even better than ours in some ways; they have a greater variety of instruments, as a rule.

QUESTIONS

*(To See Whether You Remember
the Chapter and Understand It)*

1. What sort of military music did Shakespeare hear?

2. What other nations have influenced British Army Music, and how?

3. Where are British Army bandmasters trained to-day?

THINGS TO DO

1. Look through any Shakespeare historical play you happen to know, and see if there is any military music in it, and if so, what instruments are mentioned.

2. Write an imaginary description of a visit to London in 1670, and the sight of a procession through the streets with Charles II attended by his bodyguard. Mention some of the great people you happened to see watching the procession, and bring in a little group of the King's choir boys and their remarks on the music (you have learnt something about them in *The First Book of the Great Musicians*).

If you like, put this in the form of a short letter to a musical friend in the country.

CHAPTER XIV

ARMY BANDS OF TODAY

HOW TO KNOW THE INSTRUMENTS

WHEN you hear a military band playing you would, I am sure, like to be able to tell the different instruments one from another. Many of the instruments have already been described in the chapter on the Orchestra in the first volume. But there is no harm in repeating. In fact, it is time you did recapitulate your knowledge of the instruments.

I. — The Wood Instruments

1 Flute (or Piccolo = a little, high-pitched Flute).

2 Oboe.

1 E flat (i.e. high-pitched) Clarinet.

8 B flat (i.e. low-pitched) Clarinets.

Bass Clarinet (probably).

1 or 2 Saxophones (probably).

2 Bassoons.

131

Flute

You all know a Flute when you see it. It is really a simple tube of wood with a hole to blow into and a number of other holes to make the different notes. As you all know, the Flute has a clear smooth sound.

The Piccolo, or little Flute, has a very high tone, and can if it likes play in a shrill piercing way, so as to be heard above all the other instruments.

Oboe

The Oboe is what we call a *Double Reed Instrument.* That is to say, the sound is made by two pieces of thin wood, or cane, placed together, much as you have sometimes placed two pieces of leaf to make a squeaking noise, or two pieces of tin with a piece of tape round them to imitate the Punch and Judy man.

The Oboe has a rather gentle but piercing sound (if that is not a contradiction). It is not smooth in sound like a Flute.

Clarinet

The Clarinet is another Reed Instrument, but it has a *Single Reed*—a single thin piece of wood placed against a sort of mouthpiece.

The Clarinet has a much smoother, fuller tone than

PICCOLO

FLUTE

CLARINET

OBOE

BASSOON, OR FAGOTTO

SAXOPHONE

BASS CLARINET

THE WOOD INSTRUMENTS

the Oboe. If you can ever catch the Oboe man playing alone for a few bars, and then do the same with the Clarinet, you will know the tone of their instruments ever after, as it is very different.

You will note that there are in the band more of the Clarinets than of any other instruments. The Clarinets in a Military Band take the place of the Violins in an Orchestra.

Besides the ordinary sized Clarinets (B flat Clarinets), there are in a band one or two smaller ones (E flat Clarinets), and perhaps also one big Bass Clarinet.

Bassoon

The Bassoon is really nothing but a grown-up Oboe, with a *Double Reed* like that instrument. It has a tube so long that it would be inconvenient if it were not doubled on itself in the way the picture shows you.

Saxophone

Though the Saxophone is made of metal we class it with the wood instruments, because it has a reed like a Clarinet. There are two sizes of Saxophone used in Military Bands (just as there are two sizes of Clarinet), a higher one (in E flat), and a lower one (in B flat).

II. — *The Brass Instruments*

3 Trumpets.

3 Cornets.

2 French Horns.

3 Trombones.

4 Tubas.

Trumpets and Cornets

Do you know the difference between a Trumpet and a Cornet when you see them? Look at the pictures of both.

The Trumpet has a much bolder, more bracing tone than the Cornet. But here again, you must watch until you catch the players doing a little bit of a solo, and then you will have a chance of grasping the difference.

French Horns

The Horn is a tube so long that if it were straight it would stick out from the player's mouth for about twelve feet. That would never do, would it? So it has to be curled round and round as you see in the picture.

Horns can play boldly and loudly, almost like Trumpets, or they can play beautifully softly and gently, and then they sound lovely. Just you watch them and listen.

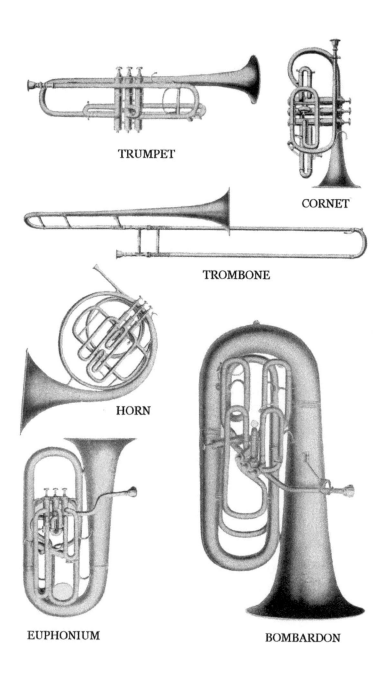

TRUMPET

CORNET

TROMBONE

HORN

EUPHONIUM

BOMBARDON

THE BRASS

Trombones

I suppose you now know a Trombone when you see it. It is a sort of Trumpet with a sliding dodge for making it longer or shorter, and for so making lower or higher notes.

Tubas

The Tubas are rather like very big Cornets in appearance.

There are three sizes. The smallest of them is called the *Euphonium.*

The bigger Tubas are called *Bombardons.*

III. — The Percussion Instruments

The picture shows you three different kinds of drums:

(*a*) **Kettledrums** or **timpani** (these can be tuned to any particular kind of note, by means of the screws shown).

(*b*) **Big Drum,** which just makes the same low sound all the time.

(*c*) **Small Side Drums** (by a Side Drum we mean one with the parchment at the side—not at the top like the Kettledrum).

BIG DRUM

KETTLE DRUM
(OR TIMPANI)

SMALL SIDE-DRUM

THE PERCUSSION

In addition there are **Cymbals** (brass clangers; you know them, I am sure), and the little tinkling **Triangle** (this also you know). Some Army Bands have more instruments than those I have mentioned, but if you know all these you have got a pretty good understanding of the subject. The proportions of the different instruments vary in different bands.

Whenever you hear an Army Band in future, go and watch it, and listen carefully to the different instruments. Then, when it stops playing, if you can get a chance to talk to the bandsmen, ask them about their instruments, and try to persuade them to play you a few notes on some of them separately, so that you may recognize their tone better.

QUESTIONS

*(To See Whether You Remember
the Chapter and Understand It)*

1. Mention the Wood instruments in a military band.

2. Describe each of them.

3. Of which Wood instruments are there most? Why do you think this is so?

4. Mention the Brass instruments.

5. Describe each of them.

6. Mention the Percussion instruments.

7. Describe each of them.

THINGS TO DO

1. Go and listen to a band and pick out the various instruments.

2. Walk round and round the bandstand, listening to the tone of each instrument.

3. Then stand a little distance away and try to say which instruments are playing—especially when there comes any bit of solo.

4. Get a Military Band record for your Gramophone, and listen to it carefully, trying to pick out the different instruments.

CHAPTER XV

SULLIVAN

1842-1900

THE bandmaster of the Royal Military College at Sandhurst had a boy who could not be kept out of the room when the band was practising. He knew all the bandsmen, and had picked up from them the way of playing many of their various instruments. Indeed by the time he was eight or nine years old, little Arthur Sullivan was quite an authority on the music of a British military band.

And if you go to hear any one of Sullivan's jolly Comic Operas you will very quickly be reminded of what you have just been told, for it will not be long before you will hear some lovely bit of tune creeping in for Clarinet, or Horn, or some other wind instrument. For what the composer learnt as a tiny fellow he went on adding to in later life, and his orchestration is almost always very effective. You can tell as soon as you hear one of his pieces that he loved orchestral instruments, and especially the 'Wind'.

SIR ARTHUR SULLIVAN

Sullivan as Choir-Boy

When he was twelve years old, young Arthur became a choir-boy—one of Queen Victoria's choir-boys at the Chapel Royal, St. James'. If you are a Londoner, or if you sometimes come to London, you can hear the royal choir by attending the Chapel Royal on Sunday morning. You will find that there is a gallery open to the public, and as you look down at the choir you will see that the boys are dressed in a quite brilliant red uniform. Perhaps amongst the boys you are looking at is one of the great composers of the future, for many of our finest British musicians have been trained in the Chapel Royal. Purcell was one of these—only in his day the choir sang in the chapel of Whitehall Palace, which no longer exists.

Arthur and His First Earnings

Sir George Smart was the organist when Sullivan joined the choir. One day the boy showed him an anthem he had written. Sir George told him to copy out parts for the trebles and altos and tenors and basses and he would see if he could get permission to perform the piece at one of the services. In due course this was done, and after the service the Dean sent for Master Sullivan, and told him he was a clever boy, and if he lived long enough and worked hard enough perhaps some day he would write an Oratorio. Then he asked the clergyman who acted as Master of the Choristers whether Sullivan was a good boy, and when the Master said 'Yes,' he shook hands with him and gave him half a sovereign—'which,' said Sullivan, years after, when he was famous, 'was very satisfactory, and the first money I earned by composition.'

Choir Practice

No wonder Mr. Helmore said that Sullivan was a good boy, for he certainly seems to have been conscientious and hardworking. He had a friend in the choir, Arthur Cellier (who also became an opera composer in later life), and these two boys seem to have been trusted to rehearse the others in the music for the services. Sullivan used to conduct and Cellier to play the accompaniments. Mr. Helmore would say on Saturday morning, 'Now, boys, get the music thoroughly well learnt and then you can go as soon as you like. No need for you to stay in during the afternoon.' Then he would leave them, and the practice would begin. But though they wanted their afternoon's holiday, if they did not feel that they had really got the music well into their heads, they came back after their midday dinner, and went at it again, until they felt sure it was perfect.

It seems strange that the boys should have been left so much to train themselves, but, of course, these Chapel Royal boys are a picked lot, and all really musical by nature.

A Good Memory

Once Sullivan was sent to Oxford to sing the solos in an Oratorio that had been composed by the University Professor of Music, Sir Frederick Ouseley. When he came back he was enthusiastic about a certain march he had heard in this Oratorio, and next time he saw his father, he pressed him to get it for his band. But the Oratorio was not published, so Arthur wrote the whole march out for his father, from memory—a pretty clever thing to do!

The Mendelssohn Scholarship

When Sullivan was fourteen he won a scholarship to the Royal Academy of Music. Admirers of Mendelssohn had subscribed to found a great scholarship in his memory, and Sullivan was the first to win it. He studied at the Academy whilst going on with his duties at the Chapel Royal. His piano teacher was Sterndale Bennett, and his composition teacher, Sir John Goss, organist of St. Paul's Cathedral.

Sullivan was always very grateful to those teachers, and especially to Goss, who, he said, taught him how to write effectively for chorus. In any of Sullivan's operas you will find Vocal Quartets and similar pieces which show by their effective style how thoroughly he knew what was wanted to make vocal writing interesting both to singers and hearers.

Sullivan in Germany

In those days England was nothing like so musical as at present, and any talented young composer was sent to Germany to study. It was part of the scheme of the Mendelssohn Scholarship that its holder should study abroad, so after a time Sullivan was sent to the Leipzig Conservatorium, or School of Music. Here amongst his fellow pupils was a boy from Norway, called Edward Grieg.

Sullivan worked very hard here, but he said there were too many lessons. The fact is that in music, or anything else, there is a sense in which *nobody can teach us anything.* All the best teacher can do is to show us *how to learn,* and it is our work, and not the teacher's, on which our progress chiefly depends. Well, Sullivan found that there were so many music lessons that there was hardly time for proper practice and home study. His composition lessons were given in an interesting place—in the very room where Bach, when he was the great musician of Leipzig, used to compose his music.

Soon the English boy was popular amongst his fellow students of various nationalities, and they made him President of their Music Committee, and appointed him director of an Opera performance they were preparing. In this way he began to get plenty of experience in conducting.

Best of all, at Leipzig he *heard* lots of music, which in London in those days he could hardly have done, for the London musical public was rather conservative then, and liked to have the same few old pieces over and over again.

Back Again

When Sullivan came back, he at once became well known through his music to Shakespeare's *Tempest,* which was performed at the famous orchestral concerts then held at the Crystal Palace. This made such an impression that it was performed on two consecutive Saturdays. Charles Dickens was there and became a great friend of the young musician, and remained such all his life.

Sullivan as Organist

To earn a living Sullivan became an organist at a London church, and also at Covent Garden Theatre, for sometimes in an Opera a little organ playing is required (perhaps in a church scene), and so there is a regular opera-house organist appointed. This chance of being behind the scenes in an opera house, and picking up all sorts of valuable information about opera performance, was valuable.

Once Dickens and Sullivan went to Paris, and Sullivan called on the popular opera composer, Rossini. Sullivan says: 'One morning when I went to see him, he was trying over a small piece of music as I entered.

"Why, what is that?" I exclaimed. He answered me very seriously: "It's my dog's birthday, and I write a little piece for him every year." '

Sullivan's Compositions

Soon Sullivan became very popular as a composer, and very rich, and the works that made him so were his Comic Operas. Generally the words of these were written by Gilbert, and they were always very witty, and had quite a style of their own. Here are the names of some of them (in order of composition):

Cox and Box.
Trial by Fury.
The Sorcerer.
H.M.S. Pinafore.
The Pirates of Penzance.
Patience.
Iolanthe.
Princess Ida.
The Mikado.
Ruddigore.
The Yeomen of the Guard.
The Gondoliers.

Perhaps you have heard some of these. If not, try to do so. The beauty of them lies in their sparkling tunes, which are just as easy to take in and remember and whistle in the street as the latest comic or sentimental song—but usually far better music.

Of course not all the tunes are equally good, but many are perfect. There has always been a great need of good light music, and Sullivan was the very man to compose it.

Mostly, Sullivan's Operas have spoken dialogue interspersed with music.

Sullivan's Rhythms

When Gilbert had written the words of a new Opera, Sullivan would go through them carefully, and begin to set them, song by song. If you look through a book of the words of any of the Gilbert and Sullivan Operas you will find what a variety of word-rhythms Gilbert used, for he was very clever in this way.

Sullivan's first step in setting one of Gilbert's lyrics was to write down the words and put crotchets and quavers under them, all on the same note but in suitable rhythm, and then do the same thing, in other ways, again and again, until at last he felt he had got the very best rhythm possible. Having reached this point he felt ready to make the melody, and this he proceeded to do—but the rhythm came first.

I think if you really look carefully at any of Sullivan's opera songs you will see that the rhythm is one of the chief charms, and if you then hear it with orchestra you will find that the orchestration is another great charm.

Sullivan's Oratorios and Church Music, etc.

Besides his Comic Operas, Sullivan wrote a number of Oratorios, Anthems, and Hymn Tunes. For my own part (you must decide for *yourself* when you get older) I think Sullivan is best in his light music. Shakespeare could write both wonderful tragedies and first-rate light comedies, but not many writers can work equally well in two different styles, as Shakespeare could.

Amongst Sullivan's compositions were also some orchestral works and a great many songs. These also seem to me far inferior to his Comic Operas, but, here again, you must make your own mind up when you are old enough to do so and have heard enough music of different styles and different composers to have formed a standard of judgement of your own.

But whatever decision you come to I think you will agree with me that Sullivan was very great as a comic opera writer, and that the fact he has written such jolly works as *The Mikado* and *The Gondoliers* is quite enough to justify the fame that came to him, that caused Queen Victoria to make him a knight, and that brought the boy who had been born in a small house in a poor part of London into a position of wealth.

There are such a lot of cheap, silly musical plays performed nowadays that it is very cheering to find that people crowd as much as ever they did to hear performances of the Comic Operas of Gilbert and Sullivan. Often you cannot get a seat at all unless you book very early.

QUESTIONS

*(To See Whether You Remember
the Chapter and Understand It)*

1. '*Sullivan had a splendid chance because he was born and brought up in a musical atmosphere.*' Suppose any one asked you what that meant, what facts about Sullivan's early life would you give them to explain it?

2. Where did Sullivan go to study?—two places, please! Mention one of his teachers and one of his fellow pupils.

3. What is your idea about the statement: 'In music, or anything else, there is a sense in which nobody can teach us anything.' It seems worth discussing!

4. Give the names of as many of Sullivan's Comic Operas as you can remember.

5. Who generally wrote the words of his Comic Operas?

6. What do you remember about the rhythms of the poetry and the music?

THINGS TO DO

1. You can buy a great deal of Sullivan's music in the form of Gramophone records. Try to get some, and listen to and learn as many pieces as possible.

2. Some whole Comic Operas are done as Gramophone records. If you can buy or borrow a set of any Opera, get the book of words and give a performance of the whole piece, reading the dialogue in between the musical pieces. You may have to divide this into two or three performances, an Act at a time.

3. You can get the Comic Operas in a piano arrangement (often not difficult), and you will do your piano sight-reading a lot of good, and pick up a great many jolly tunes, by going through an Opera on the piano.

4. Ask your English Teacher to set as a class subject for composition, Arthur Sullivan and His Comic Operas.

The Third Book of the
GREAT MUSICIANS

A Further Course in Appreciation
for Young Readers

by

Percy A. Scholes

YESTERDAY'S CLASSICS

ITHACA, NEW YORK

TO MUSIC TEACHERS

This *Third Book of the Great Musicians* in intention and plan so much resembles its two predecessors that no Preface is needed. But the author would like to take the opportunity of reminding teachers that his three books are meant to be placed *in the hands of the young people themselves,* not to be read to them, or to be read by the teacher and the contents re-told. The whole design of the books, with the abundant illustrations, and attractive 'lay-out' of the type, surely indicates the method of use.

In Class the books should be used much as school 'reading-books', each chapter being read and then (probably at some subsequent lesson) made the subject of discussion and illustrated by musical performance (the Gramophone will often be useful in this).

But besides the Class the author has had in view the individual young student of Piano or Violin, whose lesson does not allow time for 'appreciative' study, and who, without some such opportunity as these books attempt to give him, is often in danger of looking upon music rather narrowly—as a matter of mere 'lessons' and 'practice'. Music is just one of many means of human expression (and one of the best) and an implication of the simple humanity of music is one of the aims of the three *Books of the Great Musicians*.

I have once more to offer my thanks to Mr. Emery Walker. And to Mr. F. Page for assistance in finding illustrations, and to Mr. W. R. Anderson, editor of the monthly journal, *The Music Teacher*, for reading the proofs for me.

The Author

CONTENTS OF BOOK III

BRAHMS

CHAPTER I

BRAHMS

1833-1897

On Having Musical Parents

Do you want to be a composer? If so, I hope your parents are fond of music. Look back over the list of musicians you have read about in the first two volumes of this work, and try to recall which of them inherited their musical talent. Here is the list:

Purcell.	Chopin.
Bach.	Field.
Handel.	Wagner.
Haydn.	Verdi.
Mozart.	Grieg.
Beethoven.	Sullivan.
Schubert.	Elgar.
Mendelssohn.	Macdowell.
Schumann.	Debussy.

If you think it over I believe that you will find that of all these composers there are only five of whom it is not related that one or both of the parents were musical. These five are Handel, Schumann, Wagner, Verdi, and Debussy. The fact that there have been some composers with unmusical parents is of course an encouragement to any of us whose parents are unmusical. If that boy Handel, whose father positively tried to stop his study of music, could yet develop into one of the world's greatest musicians, there is hope for everybody who seems to have been born with a musical brain and is willing to work. But, of course, the young musician who has inherited his gift, and has, moreover, parents who understand what he is striving after, has the better chance.

The Childhood of Brahms

Brahms had that better chance. His father was a musician. But the father himself had had no such chance, since *his* father was not a musician, and had even tried his best to prevent his having anything to do with music. The boy, however, took lessons by stealth, learned to play all the bowed instruments as well as the flute and the horn, and when he was old enough to earn his living became a professional double-bass player—one of the best in Hamburg.

Now a man who has had to struggle in youth generally does his best to make things easier for his children, and Brahms's father, finding his son inherited his talent for music, took care to give him good teachers in piano

2

and composition. The mother, too, was musical, and used to play piano duets with her son.

The young Brahms very soon began to compose, and while still a boy occasionally made a little money by arranging marches and dances to be played by the little bands of the cafés. His father, in summer, used to form a party of six musicians who played in the open air for money, and for this party the boy sometimes composed music. The family, as you have observed already from what I have told you, was only a poor one, and all its members had to work hard. Brahms said that his best songs came into his head when he was brushing boots before dawn.

We nearly lost one of our greatest musicians before the world had heard anything of him, for once in the street a serious accident occurred: the lad fell and a cart went right over his chest. However, he recovered, and grew up a particularly sturdy man. At fifteen he gave a public concert, and this was the beginning of his being recognized as a musician of promise.

The Gipsy Fiddler

A great turning-point in Brahms's life came when he was a youth of twenty. He met the violinist Remenyi, who was a Hungarian, probably with gipsy blood, and who later became famous all over the world by playing his native melodies with great fire. Brahms accompanied this player at some concerts, and then they went on a concert tour together. Once when Beethoven's

'Kreutzer' Sonata was to be played they found the piano was tuned very low, so Brahms transposed its part a semitone higher, which rather impressed Remenyi. The Hungarian dances that Remenyi played attracted Brahms very strongly, and later he himself arranged a good many of these in a most effective way as piano duets; these are very delightful music, and all pianists who love bright, jolly, rhythmic tunes should play them.

Brahms Meets Joachim, Liszt, and Schumann

Up to this time the young Brahms was quite un-known to the leading musicians of the day. But at the concert at which he so cleverly transposed the sonata there was present the great violinist, Joachim, and when the concert was over he came and congratulated the players and offered to give them letters of introduction to Liszt at Weimar and Schumann at Düsseldorf.

They visited both these great musicians and were well received. Schumann especially was delighted with Brahms. He wrote to a publisher, saying that he really must bring out Brahms's compositions, and in a musical paper he wrote an article called *New Roads,* in which he hailed Brahms as a genius of great originality. The Schumanns used to have weekly musical parties, and Brahms played at these, and was accepted by every one as a 'coming' musician of great promise. He played some of Schumann's music in very masterly fashion. When you come to know a good deal of the music of both Schumann and Brahms you will find that it has much in common. There is no doubt that, like Remenyi,

Schumann was one of the great influences in Brahms's life. You already know that Schumann's brain gave way and that he died comparatively young, and his wife, you remember, was a fine pianist who toured Europe making her husband's genius known by her playing. All through Frau Schumann's long widowhood Brahms was her staunch friend. He looked on her almost as a mother, and she on him as a son, and she played his music wherever she went and helped to make it known.

Brahms as Choral Conductor

At twenty-one Brahms had already won such recognition that he had more than one good position opened to him. He accepted that of Director of the Court Concerts and the Choral Society of the Prince of Lippe-Ditmold. This gave him good experience, especially in choral training, and no doubt led to his composing such a great deal of fine choral music as he did now and in after-life. Of his choral works many are frequently heard in English-speaking countries, where they have become very popular.

The First Piano Concerto

When Brahms was twenty-six he brought out his first Pianoforte Concerto. It was performed at one of the Leipzig Gewandhaus Concerts, a very famous series, at which many great works have had their first hearing. There it had no success, but later Clara Schumann played it all over Germany and it became quite popular.

Twenty years later it was played again at the Leipzig concerts and had a triumphant success, but even to this day there are musicians in all parts of the world who do not greatly care for it. Some day you may yourself have a chance of hearing it and of forming your own opinion about it.

Brahms as Pianist and Piano Composer

Brahms himself played this work on its first appearance, and perhaps this was a little against it, for his playing, though in many ways very capable indeed, did not show that he sufficiently considered the nature of the instrument. He was very accurate and very vigorous, and got a big, full tone, but, as Schumann once put it, 'Brahms seemed to turn the piano into a full orchestra.' Many of his piano compositions show this same tendency. They would sound equally well, or almost so, rearranged for other instruments. You will gather better what I mean by this if you think of Chopin's music, which, of all piano music, is perhaps most thoroughly based upon a knowledge of what is effective *on a piano.*

Brahms and the Orchestra

Similarly, when writing for orchestra, Brahms did not get quite the full effect out of his orchestral instruments. If you hear one of his pieces, and then one of (say) Wagner or Elgar, you will feel that these latter composers get, so to speak, many more 'tone-colours' from their orchestral palette than does Brahms from his. Brahms's orchestral works, which include four Symphonies, are very fine indeed, but their scoring (that is, their laying out for the various instruments) is generally rather thick and not so clear and bright as that of most other great Composers. In this he takes somewhat after Schumann. Of both these Composers it has been said, 'He was more a draughtsman than a colourist.'

Brahms at Vienna

When Brahms was about forty he settled in Vienna, which, as you have already learned, has long been a great musical centre. He became conductor of the great choral society there, and got up fine performances of works of Bach, Beethoven, Schumann, and others.

One pleasure in Vienna was listening to the gipsy bands which played in the various public gardens. He used to stop and listen and clap loudly, and once was very delighted when the conductor, seeing him there, suddenly stopped the music, whispered to his men, and then struck up one of Brahms's own compositions. Earlier in this chapter you read something of the composer's love of the gipsy music.

A Lover of Light Music

Brahms was by no means opposed to light, pleasant music if it was good. He used to like to hear the famous dance music of Johann Strauss (Yo-han Strowss— pronounce the 'ow' as in 'cow'), who composed popular waltzes that were played all over Europe and America. When, at a musical party, Strauss's wife was persuading the musicians present to give her their autographs, Brahms wrote for her a few bars of the famous *Blue Danube Waltz* of Strauss and put under it the words, '*Not*, I am sorry to say, by your devoted friend, Johannes Brahms.'

Once, when a friend wrote to him complaining of the rather crude music played by the working men's brass bands and sung by the working men's choirs, he replied saying that he thought these things, though not so good as they might be, were nevertheless the only music then existing in which the working man was able to take part, and hence were to be encouraged.

Brahms's Advice to your Parents

He added something which some of my readers may care to read to their parents. He felt that it was a mistake that all the better-class children should learn the same one instrument, the Piano, and said, 'It is much to be wished that parents should have their children taught other instruments, such as Violin, 'Cello, Horn, Flute, or Clarinet, which would be the means of arousing interest in all kinds of music.'

Brahms's Requiem

One of Brahms's most important works that has not yet been mentioned is his 'German Requiem'. He wrote this after his mother's death, and much of it is very beautiful and touching. Generally speaking, 'Requiem' means a 'Requiem Mass' (i.e. the Roman Catholic service for the dead), but this 'Requiem' is, instead, a setting of texts from the Bible. The 'German Requiem' is constantly sung by choral societies in Britain and in America, and can sooner or later be heard by any of my readers who live in any large town.

Brahms's Death

There are no adventures in Brahms's life, and little to tell about it. In 1897 his dear friend, Schumann's widow, died, and at her funeral he caught cold, fell ill himself, and died at the age of sixty-four. He was buried in Vienna, in the same cemetery as Beethoven and Schubert.

What Brahms Was Like

Brahms was a big, strong, stout man, who dressed carelessly, and loved the open air. He was very athletic, and loved of all things to go on long walking tours or mountain expeditions. At the seaside he used to swim a great deal and liked to dive for coins thrown into the water by his friends. When he was a boy he had a lovely voice, but he spoilt it by using it too much when it was breaking, and so his voice as a man was gruff.

He loved children and was always playing with them. Once in a Swiss city he was seen going through all the streets, with the five-year-old daughter of a friend on his back, and from Italy an American lady wrote to her friends, 'We saw Brahms on the hotel verandah at Domodossola, and what do you think! He was down on all fours, with three children on his back, riding him as a horse.' In the street he constantly stopped to talk to the children, and they would follow him about.

Brahms paid very little attention to other people's praise or blame, and just went on his own way, behaving as he liked and composing as he liked and what he liked. He was often rude to people, and hurt their feelings, especially if they came to him with praise on their lips. Once when he was lying under a tree in a garden a stranger came up and began to flatter him, so Brahms said, 'I think, sir, you must be mistaken. No doubt you are looking for my brother, the composer. Most unfortunately he has just gone out for a walk, but if you will make haste and run along that path through the wood and up the hill, perhaps you will be able to catch him.'

Brahms was always very fond of a joke and did not like very 'starchy' people. Nobody could ever persuade him to come to England, because, as he said, he would have to be always respectably dressed. There is an anecdote about Brahms which illustrates both his kindness of heart and his humour. When he had become a fairly well-to-do man and went to visit his parents at Hamburg, he called the attention of his father, before he left, to his own old copy of Handel's *Saul*. 'Dear father,' he said, 'if things go badly with one the best consolation is always in music. Read carefully in my old *Saul*, and you'll find what you need.' And when the old fellow did look into *Saul* what did he find there?— Bank-notes between the pages!

Brahms and Wagner

Many people who objected to Wagner's music tried to pit that of Brahms against it. They maintained that Wagner's music was very unpleasant, whereas that of Brahms was 'pure' and wholesome. But Brahms himself took no part in this and expressed the greatest admiration for the music of Wagner, although Wagner himself did not care for his. Of course, there is the greatest difference between Wagner's music and that of Brahms. For one thing, Wagner wrote for the stage, while Brahms, on the other hand, never wrote an opera or music drama in his life, as he did not feel drawn to this sort of composition.

Despite the difference in their music both Brahms and Wagner are much indebted to the same inspiration— Beethoven. You have already learned how Beethoven's works excited and inspired Wagner, and now you may learn that they also inspired Brahms. In the first volume of this book you have learned to understand the differences between 'classical' and 'romantic' music. We may say that Beethoven is both classical and romantic, and that Brahms continued his work more on the classical side, and Wagner on the romantic side. Beethoven, as you know, wrote nine Symphonies, and when Brahms wrote his first somebody called it 'Beethoven's Tenth'. Brahms loved Beethoven's works, and could play from memory almost any one of them you cared to ask for.

Like Beethoven, Brahms wrote a good deal of fine chamber music. He also wrote a large number of beautiful songs (more than 200), and a good deal of piano music. In many of his pieces you find several conflicting rhythms going on at the same time. You might look out for this when you hear some of his instrumental music.

Brahms loved Folk Songs and Folk Dances, and a good deal of his music is influenced by these.

QUESTIONS

(To See Whether You Remember the Chapter and Understand It)

1. Without looking back at the beginning of the chapter, write down on a sheet of paper the names of all the musicians you can remember who have been discussed in the two previous volumes of this book. Leave a little space under each name, and then write

under each what you remember as to the parents being musical or otherwise.

2. What do you remember about Beethoven's father and grandfather?

3. Was Brahms born rich?

4. Tell all you remember about that Hungarian violinist whom Brahms met when he was a youth.

5. Do you remember any other great violinist he met?

6. What do you know about Brahms's relations with Schumann?

7. Say what you know (a) about Brahms's Piano Playing style, and Piano Composing style, and (b) about his Orchestration.

8. Where did Brahms settle in middle life?

9. When Brahms heard a good Waltz played by a band in the street did he turn up his nose and say 'What rubbish!' do you suppose? Or do you think he gave the band sixpence? What is *your* idea about 'light music'? Do you like (a) *bad* light music, or (b) *all* light music, or (c) only *good* light music? Have you any idea what makes the difference between good and bad light music? Can you mention any English composer of good light music?

10. What was Brahms's advice to parents?

11. Tell what you know about 'Requiems' in general, and Brahms's Requiem in particular.

12. How old (roughly) was Brahms when he died?

13. Was Brahms a well-dressed man? How did he spend his holidays? Some people did not like him; was he the sort of fellow *you* would have liked? Why? or Why not? (as the case may be).

14. In what way did Brahms continue the work of Beethoven?

THINGS TO DO

(For School and Home)

1. If you have a Gramophone try to get some records of works of Brahms.

2. If you have a Pianola try to get some rolls of his music.

3. If you have neither (or even if you have) try to find some friend who can play you some of Brahms's music, or sing you some of his songs.

4. Look out for the announcement of the performance of any of Brahms's works in your town, and go to hear them. If they are Choral or Orchestral works perhaps you can get in to the rehearsal, so that at the concert you will be hearing the music for a second time, and so understanding it better.

CHAPTER II

CÉSAR FRANCK

1822-1890

IF you had seen César Franck in the streets of Paris probably you would have thought little of him—a short man with grey side-whiskers, and a face making queer grimaces, an overcoat too big and trousers too small. But if you had followed him to the church to which he was hurrying, crept up the dark stairs behind him to the organ gallery, and seen him seated at his fine instrument and surrounded by some of his admiring friends and pupils, you would have had a different idea of him. People who have seen him at those moments, as he prepared the stops of his organ and broke into some wonderful improvization, say that 'he seemed to be surrounded by music as by a halo.' The great musician Liszt once visited him there and came away lost in astonishment and saying that to have heard old Bach himself must have been a similar experience.

Franck's Sincerity

It was not only Franck's skill that so much impressed people who heard him; it was his sincerity, too. We say

15

CÉSAR FRANCK

of a man sometimes, 'he means every word he says,' and people might have said of Franck 'he means every note he plays.' There was in Franck's playing and his composing nothing put in just for effect or to win applause; he did not compose to make money, but to express his true thoughts and feelings, and these were often very deep.

Perhaps you have not yet heard any of Franck's music, but you will some day have the chance, for it is now much performed. If you hear the fine *Symphony* or the *Violin and Piano Sonata,* or the *String Quartet,* or the *Prelude, Choral, and Fugue* for Piano, or the *Prelude, Aria, and Finale* for the same instrument, or any of the *Organ Pieces,* or the great Choral work *The Beatitudes,* I think you will feel the truth of what I have just said. But you must be prepared to study them a little, or to hear them two or three times before making up your mind about them, for great works like this are not to be thoroughly understood the very first time we hear them. If you can get some pianist to play you one of the piano works do so, but, before he begins, get him to go through the work with you, playing you the few chief tunes and showing you how the whole thing is made out of these.

Franck's Early Life

Franck was born at Liège, in Belgium, on December 10, 1822, which was the very day on which Beethoven wrote the last note of what is, perhaps, his greatest work, his Mass in D. This is worth remembering, because, more even than Brahms, Franck was the continuer of Beethoven, carrying further Beethoven's style and his ideas in the Sonata and Symphony just mentioned, and in other works.

Franck's father was a business man, and, seeing his son had musical talent, wished him to turn it to account. When the boy was ten he took him for a tour in Belgium, giving concerts everywhere, and when he was fourteen he took him to Paris to be trained at the great Conservatoire there.

Young Franck at the Conservatoire

When Franck had been a year at the Conservatoire he entered for a competition in piano-playing. He played very brilliantly the set piece he had prepared, and was then given a piece to play at sight. Some queer idea that came into his head prompted him to do a clever yet foolish thing. Instead of just playing the piece as it stood he transposed it three notes lower—and played it perfectly with this added difficulty. The judges said he had broken the rules by doing this, and so they could not give him the prize, but old Cherubini (Ker-oo-*bee*-ny), the head of the Conservatoire, said such a feat ought, after all, not to go unrewarded, so they invented a special distinction for Franck, and conferred on him the 'Grand Prix d'Honneur', a prize which had never been given before and has never been given since.

A year or two later, at an Organ competition at the Conservatoire, Franck did another strange thing.

Amongst other tests, the students had to improvise a Sonata on a 'subject' given them by the examiners, and then a Fugue on another subject, also given. When Franck came to improvise the Fugue, it struck him that the Sonata subject and the Fugue subject would work together, so he brought them both in, and made a long and elaborate composition out of them that surprised the examiners, but compelled them to say again that the regulations were broken. However, they gave him the Second Prize.

Franck Leaves the Conservatoire

About this time Franck's father removed him from the Conservatoire. He wanted him to be a piano 'virtuoso' (that is, a great performer, travelling everywhere and giving recitals) and also to compose piano music that would have a large sale and bring in much money. This, however, did not attract Franck, who did not care for fame, or desire more money than was really necessary to live upon comfortably, and before long this difference of opinion, and one upon another question, drew father and son rather apart.

He Gets Married

The other question was that of Franck's marriage. When he was 26 he fell in love with a young actress and wished to marry her. His father objected, but Franck was not going to give way, and was supported in his intention by a good priest who was fond of him.

This was in 1848, when Paris was in revolution. To get to the church the young couple had to climb over the barricades that the revolutionaries had set up in the streets, but the armed men who were guarding them helped them over and let them pass.

Pupils were scarce just then, for the city was, of course, in a very disturbed state; thus Franck began his married life in some poverty. However, shortly afterwards, the priest who had helped him at the time of his marriage was appointed to a church where there was a fine organ, and he made Franck the organist. This delighted Franck, who was a great lover of the organ, and, as a very devout Christian, was never happier than when taking his part in the church service. Later Franck was appointed to a larger church with a still finer organ, the new basilica of Sainte-Clothilde.

A Disappointment

Every composer has some disappointments, and Franck had more than most. About this time he spent all the time he could spare, for over a year, in writing an Opera called *The Farmer's Man*. Often he sat up almost all night, working at it, and when it was done he was quite worn out and his brain was so tired that he could hardly think. Yet he never got it performed. But note this—years after, when somebody mentioned it, he said he had come to see that it was not worth very much after all, and he should certainly never have allowed it to be printed.

This is what often happens: one works at a thing, expecting to make a great success and then, instead, comes failure. For a time one is cast down, and not till long after does one realize that the failure was a blessing in disguise. But perhaps no good work is ever really wasted, and one realizes in time that though the thing itself failed, one is the better for the effort and for what it taught one. So although Franck never saw the Opera performed, in writing it he had gained strength as a composer, and no doubt afterwards profited by this.

Later Franck had a little greater success as an Opera composer, but Instrumental Music and Choral Music, not Theatre Music, were really the lines in which he was fitted to excel.

A Modest Life

Many other disappointments came to Franck in the course of his life, but where other men would have been cast down he just went quietly on. Largely his time was occupied in going about Paris and giving Piano lessons here and there, or Singing lessons at schools, or Organ lessons at the Conservatoire, or, on Sundays and Saints' Days, in playing at his church. He rose at half-past five and 'worked *for himself*' (as he put it) for two hours. Then he had breakfast and hurried off to do his teaching. By 'working for himself' he meant composing or studying, for, busy as he was, he never dropped composition and study.

Franck as the Friend of Young Composers

In the evening when he got home he would have dinner and then, often, there would gather round him a group of young musicians who wanted his help and advice. There were at that time in Paris some of these young men who felt that the teaching of Composition at the Conservatoire did not give them what they wanted, since it was so largely concerned with writing in the Operatic style, and they were more interested in Instrumental music, in which France had dropped a good deal behind.

These men realized that in Franck they had a man who could guide them and they liked to get his advice, and to bring their compositions to him, for him to suggest to them where these could be improved and strengthened. But Franck was very modest, and would sometimes play *his* music to *them,* and ask what they thought of it, and if they made suggestions that seemed to be sound, he would accept them and put them into practice. Thus there grew up a sort of Franck 'school', as we say—using the word 'school' to mean a set of people more or less influenced by the same ideas and having much the same way of looking at things.

The 'Schola Cantorum'

After Franck's death there sprang out of his teaching a school in the other sense of the word—an institution where music was taught much on the lines of his teaching.

This still exists and is called the 'Schola Cantorum'. Its head is a composer called Vincent d'Indy (*Van*-son *Dan*-dy is as near as I can get the pronunciation, in English spelling). D'Indy has written a fine book about his old master, Franck, and a good deal of what I am telling you now is, of course, what I have learnt from that book.

One thing which they do at this school is to go back to the works of Palestrina and Bach, and others of the greatest writers of the best periods of old-time music, and to learn from them as much as they can. Similarly they study the old Plainsong (the traditional chants of the church). In this way they feel they are laying a solid foundation, and after such training as this their pupils may write in as modern a way as they like but will not be out of touch with the past. For of course the present-day music must be founded on that of past days, and future music, we may be sure, will be to some extent founded on that of the present.

Some of Franck's Sayings

When Franck was talking to some of his pupils he would say, 'Don't try to do a great deal; rather try to do a little *well*.' And when he set them an exercise in composition he expected them to work it in all possible ways, and show him the best working they could make—'Bring me the results of *many* trials, which you can honestly say represent the *very best* you can do.'

Then he would add, 'Don't think you can learn

anything from my corrections of faults of which you were aware—unless before bringing the exercises you had done your level best to correct them yourself.'

All these are sound maxims, and should be applied by all students. It really comes to this—'Don't rely on your teachers to do things for you that you can do yourself. Learn for yourself everything you possibly can do, and then let your teacher's help be *additional to that.*' This applies to Piano practice as much as to Composing, and, indeed, to every possible subject of study.

A Concert That Failed

When Franck was 65 his pupils and friends felt it to be a wrong thing that some of his best works had yet hardly been heard in public. So they got up a subscription to pay for a great concert of his works. A famous Parisian conductor was to direct the first part and Franck the second. But the famous conductor got quite muddled in the middle of one of the pieces, and conducted it at double its proper speed, so that it broke down. And as for Franck, when his turn came, he was so busy thinking of the music he had written that he did not pay enough attention to helping the singers and players, so that he, too, made rather a mess of things. (It often happens that fine composers are poor conductors.)

When the concert was over Franck's pupils gathered round him and said how sorry they felt that things had gone so badly, but he replied, 'No, no, my dear boys; you are really too exacting; for my part I was *quite* satisfied.'

I suppose he heard the music in his mind as he meant it to be, and not as it was really performed. And it was a great treat to the dear old man to hear any sort of performance of his works, since they had up to then been so much neglected.

Franck's Death

When Franck was 68 his beautiful String Quartet was performed, and the audience applauded very heartily. Franck could not believe his ears when he heard the applause, and thought it was all for the performers. But it was applause for him. And he had to go on to the platform and bow, and to be made much of. When he got home he said, 'There, you see, the public is beginning to understand me at last!'

It is pleasant to think that this had at last happened, but success came only just in time, for later in the same year he was knocked down by an omnibus. He seemed to recover, and went about his work as usual, but in a few months he was taken ill and died.

He had written three beautiful Chorales for the organ, and wanted very much to be able to go to the church to try them over, but this was not possible, and they were lying on the bed when the priest came to give him the last comforts of religion.

His was a noble, hard-working, self-sacrificing life.

What Franck's Music Is Like

It is always difficult to describe music in words. Franck's we may say was very fervent, and very pure, and often very tender, and generally mystical. By mystical, what do we mean? It is as difficult to describe mysticism as I just said it was to describe music, but I think I can make you understand if I say that in a piece of Franck's you can generally feel that its composer was not just thinking of the things around him, but in a sort of vision was peering forward into a life beyond what our eyes can see.

QUESTIONS

*(To See Whether You Remember
the Chapter and Understand It)*

1. When and where was Franck born?

2. What great musicians were then alive? Think of four or five, and say whether they were old men nearing the end of their work, or young ones beginning their lives.

3. Where was Franck trained in music?

4. Repeat any anecdotes you can remember of his work as an examination candidate.

5. What traits in Franck's nature came out in his disagreement with his father?

6. What sort of a life did Franck lead in Paris?

7. What did he mean by working *for himself?*

8. How did he influence younger musicians?

9. What is the Schola Cantorum, and who is the head of it?

10. Repeat some of Franck's advice to young composers.

11. Was Franck an old man or a young one when he died?

12. Try to give in words some idea of Franck's music.

THINGS TO DO

1. Of course the chief thing to do is to hear and study some of Franck's music. Try to find a good pianist who can play some of it, and get him (or her) to play you the 'subjects' of a piece before playing the piece as a whole, and to show you how the piece is made out of its subjects.

2. Get a Gramophone record of something of Franck's, e.g. his *Chasseur maudit* (or *Accursed Hunter*). This is published by the Columbia Company, and they give away with it a leaflet telling the story Franck has illustrated in his music.

3. Be on the watch for the announcement of any performance of the great Symphony by Franck. If you see it announced try to get somebody to explain it to you and to play you the 'subjects', before you hear the

performance. Do the same with the Violin and Piano Sonata. Both these are very beautiful works that you are sure to like as soon as you really know them.

4. Older readers might get d'Indy's book on Franck (translated by Mrs. Newmarch and published by John Lane), and read it carefully.

CHAPTER III

RUSSIAN MUSIC

Russia is a big place—twice as big as the whole of Europe, one sixth of the world's land surface! And, of course, so big a country, lying partly in Europe, and partly in Asia, extending from the Arctic Ocean almost to India, and from Central Europe to China, has amongst its inhabitants people of many different nationalities. So when I write a chapter about Russian Music I must narrow down my subject, or it would become not a chapter, but a book. Roughly speaking, then, this chapter will leave out Asiatic Russia altogether, and will discuss, quite simply, the music of European Russia, and even about that will only give a few main facts, such as everybody who cares about music should know.

Russian Folk Music

As you have learnt in *The First Book of the Great Musicians,* all peoples have their Folk Music, and of course the Russians have theirs. Naturally in so vast a country the Folk Music is of many different kinds. If you have heard a few English, Scottish, Irish, and Welsh Folk Songs you can generally, ever after, tell whether any British Folk Song or Folk Dance Tune you may hear comes from England, Scotland, Ireland, or Wales, which shows us at once how people in different countries, or different parts of a country, produce differing styles of Folk Music. And if we have several different styles in these tiny British Isles, of course the Russians, in their vast country, must have still more. Not much has been known of the Russian Folk Music by people in the east of Europe until lately, but Beethoven got hold of some Russian Folk Tunes long ago, and used them in his famous Rasoumovsky String Quartets, so they have not been altogether overlooked.

What the Music Is Like

Since there are so many different styles of Russian Folk Tunes, it is difficult to describe them in a general way, but perhaps we can say with truth that, to us, they generally seem to be either very mournful or very excited and gay. Here is one of the qualities of the Russian character. Russians, as their literature shows, are a very up-and-down people—easily depressed into sadness and just as easily excited into joy.

At various periods the Russian priests have taught that music is a sin, and have tried to banish it, but nobody in any country can get rid of music, because music is a part of human nature, and so Russian Folk Ballads and Folk Dances have gone on, carrying down with them, from generation to generation, the legends of olden days and stories from early Russian history.

Russian Church Music

The orthodox Russian religion is that branch of Christianity which we call the Greek Church. This looks upon Constantinople as its headquarters, as the Roman Catholic Church looks upon Rome, and uses the Greek language in its services as the Roman Catholic Church uses Latin. Like the Roman Catholic Church, the Greek Church has both old Plain Chant melodies that have come down from the early days of Christianity, and also music made for it by skilful composers.

The singing in some of the Russian churches has long had a reputation for great beauty. It is not accompanied by instruments, and one very remarkable thing is that the Russian basses can sing very low notes—far and away lower than any notes our basses can sing.

So far the music we have been talking about is what we may call the real Russian music—the Songs and Dance Tunes that have grown up in the Russian villages, the Church Plain Chant that has grown up in the Eastern Church and come down from the early days of Christianity in Russia, and the composed Church Music. Much of this latter, however, though it is by Russian composers, and written for the Russian churches, has yet been influenced by the style of Church Music in other parts of Europe.

Italian Music in Russia

We now come, however, to music that was not merely influenced by the music of other parts of Europe, but brought complete from them, music that, though performed in Russia, was not in any sense Russian. During the eighteenth century the Imperial Family, who loved splendour of every kind, used to send to Italy for some of the best Italian performers, and used to have performances of Italian Operas at court. As you have already learnt, Italy is the native country of Opera, so it was natural to send there for the musicians to compose and perform it. In this way Italian Opera became popular amongst the aristocracy, both in Petrograd and Moscow.

The First Real Russian Composer

But cultivated Russian musical people began to wish for a real Russian composer, and by and by he came. His name was GLINKA. He was born in 1804. His father was a rich man, and at his country house used to receive many visitors. When he had a big party of these in the house he would send a message to Glinka's uncle, who lived a few miles away, and who kept a private Orchestra for his entertainment. Then the uncle's Orchestra would come over, and little Glinka was in a heaven of joy, and if he was not watched would pick up an instrument and try to join in the music.

GLINKA

His governess taught him the piano and one of the orchestral players taught him the violin. When he went to school at Petrograd he had piano lessons from the famous Irish musician, of whom you have read in *The Second Book of the Great Musicians,* John Field. Then when he was a young man he was sent to Italy for some years, for the good of his health, and there he heard a lot of music, and took regular lessons in composition. At first his compositions imitated those of the Italians, but at last he realized that he was wrong in this, and that as a Russian he would never write really good music by imitating composers of such different national feeling from his own as the Italians. So, after visiting Germany and having some lessons in the technique of composition there, he returned to Russia, where he began to compose music with Russian feeling in it, rather than either Italian or German feeling.

'A Life for the Czar'

The first great work that he wrote was the opera, *A Life for the Czar,* which tells a story from Russian history, the story of a peasant who was forced to act as a guide to an army that was coming to attack that of the Czar, but who led it into the forest, so that the Czar might be saved, although he knew the enemy would kill him when they found that he had tricked them. A good deal of the music of this opera was much in the style of the Russian Folk-Music, rather than in the style of the Italian or German operas. So both in its subject and in its music *A Life for the Czar* may be truly called a national work.

This opera became very popular with patriotic Russians and when, in 1886, the fiftieth year after its composition came to be celebrated, every theatre in Russia made a point of performing it, and so doing honour to its composer—the first really national composer Russia ever had.

Glinka wrote another opera *(Russian and Ludmilla)* and some orchestral music, chamber music, and piano music. There is no need to describe this other music here. For the moment I just want to impress upon your mind the name of Glinka as the first really national composer, and therefore the founder of the Russian 'School' of composition. He died in 1857, so he did not have a very long life. You may sometimes hear his music at concerts, but not very often.

Dargomysky and 'The Five'

Another early Russian composer, born a little later than Glinka, was DARGOMYSKY, and then we come to a group of composers, who worked together in the effort to produce a real 'School' of Russian music. They were always spoken of as THE FIVE. I am going to give their names and dates. You need not learn the dates, but they will be there for you to refer to whenever you want them. The names, however, you ought to learn, so that when you hear any of their music you will be able to listen to it with a little more interest, knowing it to be the work of one of this little band of comrades who set out to bring into existence a body of real Russian music—

BALAKIREF (1836-1910). The leader of the 'School'.

CUI (1835-1918). Partly of French descent.

BORODIN (1834-1887), wrote the Opera,
Prince Igor.

MOUSSORGSKY (1839-1881), wrote the opera
Boris Godounof.

RIMSKY-KORSAKOF (1844-1908), the first Russian
to write a Symphony.

From a glance at that list you will at any rate get into your mind the fact that the famous 'Five' were all born in the eighteen-thirties or eighteen-forties, and that one or two of them lived almost down to your own time. Sometimes instead of 'The Five', these composers are known by the very grand title of 'The Invincible Band'.

They really deserve such a title, for they wrote some very great works, and it was *their* works which, when they began to be performed in Britain in the last years of the nineteenth century and the first years of the twentieth, really proved to British people that Russia was to be looked upon as an important musical country.

QUESTIONS

(To See Whether You Remember the Chapter and Understand It)

1. Roughly, how big is Russia?

2. And what deduction about Folk Music can we draw from this?

3. Tell anything you remember about Russian Church Music.

4. How did Italy come to influence Russia in music?

5. And who first cast off the Italian influence?

6. Whom do we mean by THE FIVE?

7. Give their names, if you can.

THINGS TO DO

1. If you have a Gramophone, and are so magnificently rich that you can afford to buy any records that you want, search the Catalogue and you will find some pieces by Cui, Borodin, Rimsky-Korsakof, and

Moussorgsky (and, perhaps, by the time this is printed, other composers). Get these records and learn to know them thoroughly.

2. Look out for concerts where music by any of the composers mentioned is to be given, and attend them.

3. Ask your English teacher to go through this chapter with the form, and then to set an essay on 'Russian Music'.

TCHAIKOVSKY

CHAPTER IV

TCHAIKOVSKY

1840-1893

I AM giving a whole chapter to Tchaikovsky, not that he is the most important Russian composer, but because at the present time he is the Russian composer whose music you are most likely to hear often, and in whom, therefore, you are most likely to be interested.

Tchaikovsky's Boyhood and Youth

Tchaikovsky does not appear to have been a specially musical boy. He learnt the piano, as other boys do, and when he went to the university he sang in the choral society there. Then when his education was finished he sometimes improvised dance music, for his own pleasure and to please his friends, but did not take music very seriously.

At twenty-one, however, he suddenly 'woke up' to music. He was then a civil servant at Petrograd, but he began to take lessons in composing, and to work hard at musical study generally. After a time he decided to throw up his place in the civil service and go in thoroughly for music, studying at the Conservatory at Petrograd. At first he was poor, for he had now abandoned his means of earning a comfortable living, and as his father had misfortunes he could not afford to help his son very much. Music-teaching, however, brought him in a small income, and this made things a little easier. He did well at the Conservatory, and won a silver medal for a work he composed. When he was twenty-six, the Conservatory of Moscow gave him a post on its staff as a teacher of composition, and then he felt that, though still poor, he was really started in life.

The head of the Petrograd Conservatory was a very famous musician, Anton Rubinstein, the great pianist, of whom you may have heard, and the head of the Moscow Conservatory was his brother, Nicholas Rubinstein. Nicholas believed in Tchaikovsky, and did all he could to help him by bringing his works forward, and getting them performed.

The 'Musician's Temperament'

All his life Tchaikovsky was very 'nervy'. Many musicians are easily excited into joy, and easily depressed into gloom. This comes from their sensitive natures, without which they could not be musicians, and if they suffer from ill health (as Tchaikovsky did), and do not make a steady effort to obtain self-control (as Tchaikovsky probably did not), their nervous temperament gives them a good deal of trouble all through their life. Tchaikovsky was often saddened by not receiving the recognition he felt his work deserved, but when he was about thirty-seven something happened which cheered him and helped him all the rest of his life.

A Generous Friend

A rich woman who loved music had engaged a young violinist to play to her and to organize musical performances in her house. Some of the music they played was the music of Tchaikovsky, of which she was very fond. The violinist used to tell her sometimes about the rather sad life of Tchaikovsky, whose pupil he had been at the Conservatory of Moscow; how he had difficulty in making a living, and could not compose as much as he wished because he had to spend time in giving music-lessons. The lady, who had at one time herself been very poor, wrote to Tchaikovsky and persuaded him to let her help him, and at last offered to allow him a yearly income so that he might be free to compose, and so to give to the world the best that was in him.

After some demur Tchaikovsky accepted this offer, and for a time lived a good deal abroad, in Switzerland and Italy, gradually building up a better state of health, and spending his time in composition. Sometimes, when he returned to Russia, he would spend long periods at one or other of the country houses of this good woman, working quietly and happily.

A curious thing is that Tchaikovsky and his benefactress never met, or at any rate never but in the most passing way—just, perhaps, a 'Good evening' as they saw one another at some concert, and very rarely even that. They corresponded a great deal, however, and Tchaikovsky's letters to this lady are many of them now published and are very interesting as giving an account of his life and showing how he composed his various works, but it seems to have been a point with his benefactress, who was a widow living a very retired life, that her good works should be done at a distance. The name of the good widow, who did almost as much for music as if she had been herself a composer, was Nadejda von Meck.

Success at Last

After years of struggle great success at last came to Tchaikovsky. His compositions, which had at first aroused opposition, became accepted everywhere, and when Nicholas Rubinstein died the authorities of the Moscow Conservatory offered Tchaikovsky his post. But he refused this, for he felt that if he took it he would no longer have time and energy and freedom of mind for his composition.

At last he wrote an Opera which brought him great fame—*Eugen Oniegin.* His health began to improve and his nerves to become stronger as he felt that at last he had made a success of life. Mostly he lived quietly in the country, working hard at his compositions, but sometimes he took tours abroad, conducting his works at great concerts in various cities, and being welcomed everywhere. Several times he came to England and conducted his music at the concerts of the Philharmonic Society in London. He was invited to go to Cambridge to receive an honorary degree of Doctor of Music, and was made much of there. He also went to America and conducted in New York and other cities.

Tchaikovsky's Early Death

Tchaikovsky died far too early—in his fifty-third year. A professor of Russian in one of our English Universities has told me this story. When this professor was a youth he was a musician, and studied in the Conservatory of Budapest. One day a great concert was held at which Tchaikovsky appeared and conducted, and when the concert was over the students carried him shoulder high in triumph back on to the stage which he had left when the music was over.

As they did so, one of the students began to express the joy of the gathering by playing the Tubular Bells, and Tchaikovsky exclaimed with alarm to some of those near him that it was a bad omen, for in Russia when they carry a dead body to the grave the church bells are rung. This, of course, shows what a nervous, fanciful man he was, and the worst is that superstitious ideas of this sort have a way of coming true, because people brood upon them, and so in the end weaken their health.

A little time after, as Tchaikovsky was travelling by train in Russia, he pointed to a village churchyard as the train passed it, and told his friends who were with him, 'I shall be buried there, and as the trains go by people will point out the grave.'

A few days later he drank a glass of unfiltered water, fell ill with cholera, and quickly died. I do not know whether he was buried in that village churchyard. I hope he was, and that as the trains go by the passengers do sometimes point to it and say, 'Tchaikovsky is buried there,' and feel grateful for the music he wrote, which, though it is not amongst the very greatest, has brought pleasure to people in every part of the civilized world, and will do so for a long time to come.

What Tchaikovsky's Music Is Like

Now about Tchaikovsky's music. Some of this you have probably heard, such as, for instance, the *Nutcracker Suite* (often called by the French name of *Casse-noisette*). If you have heard only this piece (or, rather, string of pieces) you will understand what I mean when I say that Tchaikovsky's music is of a kind that anybody can understand at once.

This does not necessarily mean that it is good music or poor music. It means that it is *simple* music—with clear tunes for its 'subjects' or 'themes', with these clearly treated, with harmonies put to them such as do not puzzle one at all, and with orchestration of a kind that any one can enjoy at a first hearing. This Suite is particularly easy to take in as soon as one hears it, because it has no long 'movements', but is just a set of little pieces in which the mind cannot possibly lose its way.

The Symphonies

In Tchaikovsky's bigger pieces, such as his Symphonies, there are the same qualities, but, of course, these bigger pieces express deeper thoughts and are more elaborate in their structure than the little pieces of the *Nutcracker Suite*. In some of their 'movements' you will feel Tchaikovsky's joyousness and in others his depression. Sometimes you will be able to feel what a sensitive and even feverishly excitable temperament he had. The best way to describe Tchaikovsky's music is to say that it is very 'emotional'. The Symphonies most often heard are the Fourth, Fifth, and Sixth. The Sixth has a name—*The Pathetic Symphony*. It is very popular at orchestral concerts in Britain and America.

Other orchestral pieces of Tchaikovsky's are in the form of Tone Poems—pieces in which the composer tries to express in music the emotions connected with some series of incidents, much as a poet might do in words. Thus Tchaikovsky has one tone poem on the subject of *Romeo and Juliet*.

Then there are three Concertos for Piano, and one for Violin, a number of Operas, some dance music for the stage (such as the Ballet, *The Sleeping Princess*), some Chamber Music, and a great number of Piano pieces and Songs.

You can get a good deal of Tchaikovsky's music in the form of Gramophone records.

QUESTIONS

*(To See Whether You Remember
the Chapter and Understand It)*

1. When was Tchaikovsky born?

2. And how long before your time did he die?

3. Was he a clever musical boy, like many of the composers of whom you have read?

4. Where did he study?

5. What sort of a temperament had he?

6. Tell how his early struggles ended.

7. Did Tchaikovsky die young or old?

8. Try if you can give any sort of a general description of Tchaikovsky's musical style.

9. And mention any music of his which you know.

THINGS TO DO

1. If you have a Gramophone, get some of Tchaikovsky's music as records.

2. If you play the Piano fairly well you might get the *Nutcracker Suite (Casse-noisette)* in a piano arrangement.

3. Make a point of hearing Tchaikovsky's music at concerts whenever you can. It is frequently performed.

4. When a week has elapsed from the day you read this chapter, jot down, roughly, on paper, a note of all you can remember of it. Then read the chapter again, and find out what you had forgotten.

CLAVICHORD

VIRGINAL

CHAPTER V

CLAVICHORD— HARPSICHORD—PIANOFORTE

ONE of the words at the head of this chapter you know quite well. The other two words you have surely heard. You ought, if you are a pianist, to know something about Clavichords and Harpsichords, because some of your music was written not for the piano but for one or other of these instruments. And besides, people are now reviving the Clavichord and Harpsichord, and you may any day have a chance of hearing one of them, when you will want to know something about it. Before we go any further you may like to see what these instruments look like. So please study the pictures of them.

Now let me explain the principle. Clavichord, Harpsichord, and Piano are alike in this—they all have wires and they all have keys.

And they are unlike in this—the way the keys bring the sound out of the wires.

Suppose we take a wire and stretch it tight over something, like this—

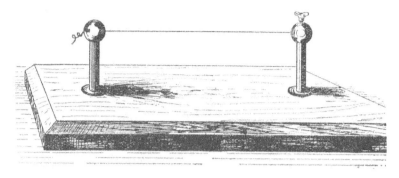

and then begin to consider how music can be got out of it. I suppose there are two main ways—

(*a*) we can *pluck* the wire with our fingers;

(*b*) we can *hammer* it with something.

A fairly common plucked-string instrument is the ZITHER.

A fairly common hammered-string instrument is the DULCIMER.

The Zither

Here is a picture of a Zither—

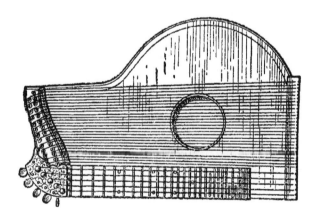

Here the player plucks the strings with his fingers, or with a little piece of metal called a Plectrum. There are a number of strings of different lengths, long strings for the low notes and short strings for the high notes.

The Dulcimer

Now let us look at a Dulcimer—

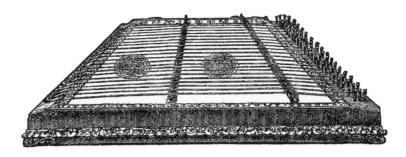

A Dulcimer player knocks the strings with two little hammers (one in each hand). Again, there are long strings for low notes and short strings for high ones.

Now, in a way (I am not speaking very accurately, but only trying to give you a good general idea)—

A **Harpsichord** = a mechanical Zither.

A **Pianoforte** = a mechanical Dulcimer.

What a Harpsichord is Like

The **Harpsichord** is a kind of Keyboard-Zither. Each note of the keyboard has at the farther end of it a little piece of wood called a Jack. And each Jack has in it a Quill. And when the note is pressed down by the player, up goes the Jack and the Quill plucks the string. This diagram will explain it—

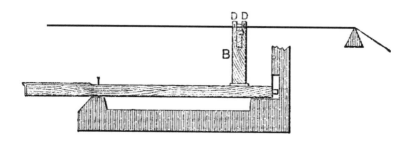

You see there the Key, do you not? And at the back of the Key you see the Jack (*B*). And at the top of the Jack you see the little projecting Quill, just ready to pluck the string. And you can see that if any one pressed down the Key the Jack would rise and the Quill would pluck, and the String would give forth its sound. That explains to you the Harpsichord. It is like a Zither, with a lot of strings of different lengths (long for low, and short for high). But unlike a Zither it has Keys and Jacks.

Some of the later Harpsichords had two or three strings for every note (so as to make a louder sound) and some had two keyboards (like the one in the plate), each with its own set of strings, just as a two-manual Organ has two keyboards, each with its own set of pipes. Some of the two-manual Harpsichords had a number of stops, which varied the sound in different ways (look once more at the plate). A simple Harpsichord, without such contrivances as these was sometimes called the **Virginals**, and sometimes the **Spinet**. Some people say the word 'Virginals' was applied to the instrument because it was played by the Virgin Queen—Elizabeth.

HARPSICHORD

But that explanation won't answer, for it was called the Virginals before she was born. As for the Spinet, the derivation of that word is easy enough—is not the string plucked by a spine?

The Pianoforte

Now about the PIANOFORTE—but I need hardly say much about that at this moment. Go and look at the one in your house and you will find that it is (as I called it) a Mechanical Dulcimer—with all kinds of wonderful modern improvements. Try to find out how it works. Then, later in the chapter, you shall have some pictures to help you.

The Clavichord

But I have not explained the Clavichord! I have left that to the last because it is the most difficult to explain. In the Clavichord we have not a Jack-and-Quill to pluck the strings. And we have not a Hammer. We have something called a Tangent—a piece of metal at the farther end of the key, that strikes the string, and then *stays stretching the string* as long as you leave the key down. Here is a diagram—

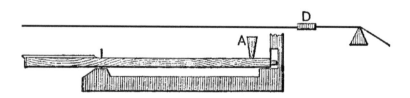

A is the Tangent, D is a bit of felt. When A strikes the string (and stays there, as I just told you) the longer end of the string sounds its note. Why does not the shorter end sound also? Because of that piece of felt, which 'damps' (as we say) that end of the string, or, in other words, checks its vibrations.

Whereas in the Harpsichord and Piano the whole string sounds, in the Clavichord the proper length of string for the note needed is, so to speak, 'cut off' by the Tangent. Sometimes, in early Clavichords, two keys next to one another would share the same string. Then of course the Tangent of the higher key cut off a shorter length than the Tangent of the lower string. For, as we have already learnt, higher notes come from shorter strings and lower notes from longer strings.

Of course, when two keys had only one string you could not play these two keys together.

What These Instruments Sound Like

The **Clavichord** is a very gentle instrument. It is suitable for small rooms, not for big concert-halls. Its sound has a lovely silvery quality. Bach wrote his famous forty-eight Preludes and Fugues for the Clavichord, and on that instrument they sound much more beautiful than on the Pianoforte. There is one special peculiarity about the Clavichord—by slightly moving your finger on the key you can keep a string in vibration, and so prolong the sound. The Clavichord cannot play loudly, but it can make very delicate shades of sound—louder and softer by small degrees.

The **Harpsichord** can, of course, play more loudly than the Clavichord. And if there are two manuals and some stops the player can get a lot of variety. But he cannot prolong the sound as a Clavichord player can, because once a string is plucked it *is* plucked, and there's an end of the matter. Moreover, the player cannot vary the loudness or softness of the sound much, excepting by using the stops, so the Harpsichordist cannot produce delicate *crescendos* and *diminuendos* and neat little accents, as the Clavichordist can.

As for the **Pianoforte**, you know what that sounds like. You cannot prolong the sound of it as you can that of the Clavichord, but (especially by using the sustaining pedal) you can make the sound last a good long while. And you can accent the notes, and make *crescendos* and *diminuendos* just as much as you like. Because this instrument, unlike the Harpsichord, could produce loud or soft notes at the player's will, it was called the 'Piano-Forte' (Italian for 'Soft-Loud'). Some photographs of the 'action' of a modern Piano are given a few pages later. When you have finished reading this chapter you should study them carefully.

Who Used These Instruments, and When

The first of these instruments to be invented was probably the **Clavichord**.

Then came the **Harpsichord**, so now both instruments were living side by side.

Then came the **Pianoforte**, so now there were three.

Then the **Clavichord** died out, so there were only two again.

And then the **Harpsichord** died out, so only the Pianoforte was left.

Nowadays, as I have said, people are reviving the Clavichord and Harpsichord. This is a good thing; they ought never to have been allowed to die!

The keyboard music of our Elizabethan composers (Byrd, Bull, Gibbons, Farnaby) was written for the early, simple Harpsichord, i.e. the **Virginals**.

The keyboard music of Purcell was also written for the Virginals.

The keyboard music of Bach was some of it written for the Clavichord and some of it for the Harpsichord. The Clavichord was Bach's favourite instrument. Some early pianos were shown to him by Frederick the Great, but he would not have them 'at any price' (of course, they were nothing like so good as our pianos to-day).

Handel's keyboard music (do you play the so-called *Harmonious Blacksmith*?) was written for the Harpsichord.

Mozart's keyboard music was also written for the Harpsichord, though possibly he played some of the later pieces on the Pianoforte.

Beethoven's keyboard music was written for the Pianoforte, and so was that of all the composers who followed him, for by this time Harpsichords were dying out, and Clavichords were practically already dead. But Beethoven never heard a Piano with such full loud tone as our Pianos to-day have. His was a gentler instrument than ours.

In Bach's day and Handel's day there was a Harpsichord in the Orchestra, and the conductor, instead of using a stick to direct the players, sat at the Harpsichord and led the band by playing with them.

Queen Elizabeth as a Player on the Virginals

Here is a story told by the Ambassador sent by Queen Mary of Scotland to the court of Queen Elizabeth of England:

> 'After dinner my lord of Hunsdean drew me up to a quiet gallery that I might hear some music (but he said that he durst not avow it), where I might hear the Queen play upon the virginals. After I had hearkened awhile, I took by the tapestry that hung before the door of the chamber, and seeing her back was toward the door, I entered within the chamber, and stood a pretty space hearing her play excellently well. But she left off immediately as soon as she turned about and saw me. She appeared to be surprised to see me, and came forward, seeming to strike me with her hand; alleging she used not to play before men, but when she was solitary, to shun melancholy. She asked how I came there. I answered, as I was walking with my lord of Hunsdean, as we passed by the chamber door, I heard such melody as ravished me, whereby I was drawn in ere I knew how; excusing my fault of homeliness, as being brought up in the court of France, where such freedom was allowed; declaring myself willing to endure what punishment her Majesty should be pleased to inflict upon me for so great an offence. Then she sat down

low upon a cushion, and I on my knees beside her; but with her own hand she gave me a cushion to lay under my knee; which at first I refused, but she compelled me to take it. She then called for my Lady Strafford out of the next chamber; for the Queen was alone. She enquired whether my Queen or she played best. In that I found myself obliged to give her the praise.'

So wrote the Scottish Ambassador at the English court, and if you ask me I think that our vain Virginal-playing Queen had herself given Lord Hunsdean the hint to bring the Ambassador to hear her.

QUESTIONS

*(To See Whether You Remember
the Chapter and Understand It)*

1. Describe how the sound is made in a Harpsichord.

2. Describe how the sound is made in a Pianoforte.

3. Describe how the sound is made in a Clavichord.

4. Which instrument did we call Mechanical Zither, and why?

5. And which did we call a Mechanical Dulcimer, and why?

6. What is a 'Virginal' (or 'Virginals'—the same thing)?

7. What is a Jack? Which instrument has Jacks?

8. What is a Tangent? Which instrument has Tangents?

THE ACTION OF A MODERN PIANO

These photographs show the mechanism of a single note taken out of an upright Piano, and so arranged as to make the movements clear to you.

You will see that a short brass rod has been placed in position to represent the piano string.

You will realize that there are two actions to be brought about by one mechanism—*(a)* the striking of the note, and *(b)* the silencing of it when the time comes for it to cease. This silencing we call 'Damping'.

You will notice, then, that the apparatus includes both a Hammer, to make the string sound, and a 'Damper', to stop its sounding.

When you put a key of the Piano down, the Damper comes away from the String (leaving it free to sound) and the Hammer strikes it (making it sound).

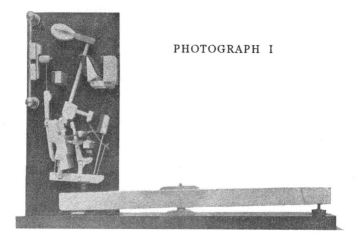

PHOTOGRAPH I

The player is beginning to press down the Key. The Hammer has begun to move forward towards the String. The Damper has not yet raised itself from the String.

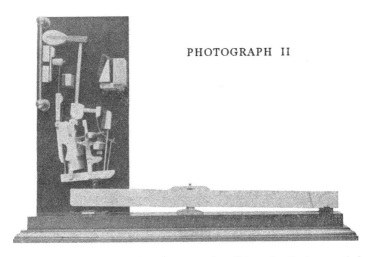

PHOTOGRAPH II

The Hammer is just in the act of striking the String and the Damper is raised from the String (look closely, and compare with Photograph I), and is thus allowing it to sound.

Of course, if the Hammer after striking remained touching the String, it would itself act as a 'Damper', and we should get very little sound. So, immediately after striking, it is made, by an ingenious arrangement, to fall back, out of the way.

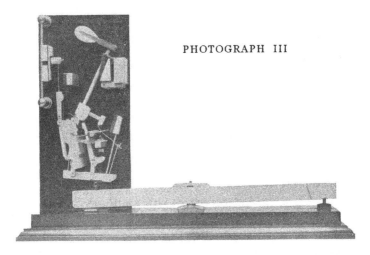

PHOTOGRAPH III

The player has removed his finger from the Key, the Damper has pressed forward and stopped the vibration of the String, and the Hammer has fallen back to its position of rest.

9. If you were giving a recital in a large Hall which would be the worst instrument for your purpose? And which the best?

10. Which was the first of the three instruments to be invented?

11. And which the last?

12. For which instrument did Byrd and Bull and Farnaby write?

13. And for which Bach?

14. And for which Handel?

15. And for which Mozart?

16. And for which Beethoven?

THINGS TO DO

1. There is one thing I never told you in the Chapter—how the Sustaining Pedal (sometimes, but wrongly, called the Loud Pedal) works. Open the front of your Piano and find out for yourself.

2. Why is it wrong to call it the Loud Pedal? Make a few experiments and try to find out. For instance, if it is the 'Loud Pedal' I suppose we could play a loud verse of a hymn with it down the whole time. Do this, listen carefully, and see how you like the effect.

3. Write a little Article for an imaginary musical magazine (or for your own school magazine, if you have one) on 'How the Piano Works'.

In the course of your article mention the predecessors of the Piano, and state the particular characteristics of each. State why the Piano's name in full is '*Pianoforte*'.

4. Write another Article on 'THE DIFFERENCES BETWEEN A PIANO AND AN ORGAN'.

5. For fun—ask the next six people you meet, 'What is the difference between a Piano Pedal and an Organ Pedal?' They are to answer straight away, without any time to think. Tell them it is not a riddle, but just a test of ordinary decent intelligence and observation.

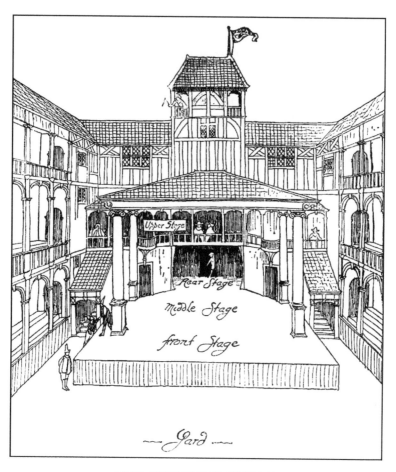

Upper Stage

Rear Stage

Middle Stage

Front Stage

Gard

THE FORTUNE THEATRE

CHAPTER VI

SHAKESPEARE THE MUSICIAN

IF any of the learned Shakespeare writers should take up this book they will smile when they see the title of the present chapter, and say that they wonder how I know something about Shakespeare of which they never heard. So I must tell you how I know it.

Some people think that 'musician' means a man or woman who can play the piano or violin, or sing a song very beautifully, but I think that if any one has a musical ear, so that he *loves* music and understands it, then we may say that that person is a musician. Indeed I know people who have never learnt to sing or play at all, and yet are better musicians than some others who *can* do these things.

Now if there is one thing we can be quite sure about concerning Shakespeare, it is this—he had a musical ear and loved and understood music. I am going to prove that to you, and when you have read my proof you will be able to say with me, 'Yes; Shakespeare *was* a Musician.'

Shakespeare's Word-Music

You can tell that Shakespeare had a musical ear by reading his poetry, for when you do so you find that his words and lines are very musical. In a sense every poet must be a musician, for he has to choose beautiful, sweet-sounding words (that is—musical words), and arrange them so that they sound well with each other, just as the notes of a good tune sound well with each other. And then, too, he has to put them together in rhythm, just as a composer does with the notes of his tunes. If you take a line of the poetry of Shakespeare, or some other poet, you will find that it has accented syllables, just like a piece of music, so that you can divide it by bars if you like, as we do in the case of music. Shakespeare's lines generally have five bars. Just look at any blank verse passage of Shakespeare for a moment, and then try to put the bars in.

Then if you will look closely at any one of Shakespeare's most beautiful passages you will find that he has taken care to bring together sounds that fit one another, just as a musical composer brings together notes that fit. Let me give you just a few examples, and then, if you want, you can find thousands more for yourself. Often the musical effect is got by alliteration—that is the repetition of a letter-sound. For instance:

'pale primrose'

(p's)

'fierce fires'

(f's, r's, and s's)

'curled clouds'

(c's, d's, and l's)

'mischiefs manifold'

(m's and f's)

And you will find that sort of word-music on every page of Shakespeare.

Then we get a line such as:

'I will not struggle, I will stand stone still,'

with its st's and l's and n's;

or this:

'Whatever torment you may put me to,'

with its five t's and three m's;

or:

'Can sleep as soundly as the wretched slave,'

with its s's;

or:

'Then love-devouring death do what he dare,'

with its d's;

or:

'Stand tiptoe on the misty mountain tops,'

with its combination of m's, t's, and p's;

or:

'When the sweet wind did gently kiss the trees,'

with a combination of w's, d's, t's, and of s's, which, besides sounding pleasantly on our ears, seem to give us the very sound of the fluttered leaves;

or:

'Full fathom five thy father lies,'

nearly all f's and th's (two similar sounds), with l's to begin and end it.

Shakespeare's Word Discords

Sometimes Shakespeare seems to have chosen his consonants deliberately to suit the sentiment he wishes to express in his words. For instance there is this passage, where Juliet expresses her dislike of the lark's song, because it brings the unwelcome daybreak, and imagines in her dislike that the song is harsh and unpleasant:

It is the lark that sings so out of tune,
Straining harsh discords and unpleasing sharps.
Some say the lark makes sweet division;
This doth not so, for she divideth us:
Some say the lark and loathed toad change eyes.

There are more than twenty hissing s's in that short passage, and their use by the poet is almost like the use by a composer of the particular instrument, perhaps a harsh one, which he feels will best express the emotion he is at the moment trying to reproduce. This, then, is a sort of verbal orchestration.

Then what a variety of orchestration Shakespeare gets in a passage like this:

> *Strange and several noises*
> *Of roaring, shrieking, howling, jingling chains.*

Every word here reproduces a sound. Hear a really good actor say that, and you will realize that 'roaring' is like a blast of Trombones and Trumpets, 'shrieking' has high, loud Piccolo notes in it, 'howling' has String chromatic passages rising and falling rapidly, 'jingling' has something of Triangle and Cymbals.

Shakespeare's Vowel Music

So far I have been talking chiefly of Shakespeare's consonants. But if we examined his vowels we should find much the same thing. For instance:

> *and rifted Jove's stout oak*
> *With his own bolt.*

Look at those i's and o's.

Set out in musical fashion (Tonic-sol-fa-wise) this would be:

ă |ĭ :ĕ |ō :ow |ō : ‖ :ĭ |ĭ :ō |ō : ‖

or in Staff notation:

ă   ĭ   ĕ   ō   ow   ō   ĭ   ĭ   ō   ō

Say that over in the proper rhythm a few times and you will realize that there is a sort of vowel-rhyming patter in it, which is very agreeable to a musical ear.

Shakespeare's Rhythms

Now another word about rhythms. Many actors (most, I fear) spoil Shakespeare by destroying his rhythm. Very often, in trying to speak the lines expressively, they turn them from poetry into prose. When Shakespeare wants prose he writes prose, and when he sets his lines out as poetry he wants them to be read and recited as poetry. If you want to know how to recite Shakespeare, do as I just suggested—take a few lines of his and set them out with bars, as if they were music.

Let us take the line:

'Methought the billows spoke and told me of it';

set out in the Sol-fa tune notation that would be:

Me - | thought the | bil - lows | spoke and | told me | of it ‖

la | la :la | la la :— | la :la | la :la | la la ‖

or in Staff notation:

Me - | thought the | bil - lows | spoke and | told me | of it ‖

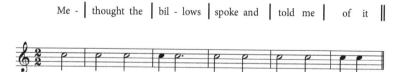

Feel the Rhythm!

The lesson of this is that in reciting Shakespeare (or even in reading it to ourselves silently) we must feel the rhythm. Even a little child's jog-trot way of saying poetry is better than a grown-up person's would-be-clever way of reciting it 'expressively'. Of course it should be expressively recited, but the expression must not be allowed to kill the rhythm. Poetry comes between prose and music. It has words and thoughts, like prose, and it has rhythm and sound like music. And the more we can both grasp the thoughts and feel the rhythms and sound-patterns of Shakespeare the better we shall read and recite him and the more we shall enjoy him.

A great many people when they read Shakespeare lose all the musical side of his work. They are so busy studying his wonderful dramatic plots and his character-painting that they forget that there is also something to study in his use of sounds and his rhythms. If you like you can read a Shakespeare play merely as a tale, and you will get a great deal of pleasure. But if you look upon it as also a sort of Word-Symphony your pleasure will be increased. And as long as you live you can go on finding fresh musical beauties in Shakespeare.

Could Shakespeare Play or Sing?

But besides being a great 'word-musician' (one of the greatest there has ever been) it is quite likely that

Shakespeare was a player and singer. As you know from *The First Book of the Great Musicians*, in the days when he lived Englishmen and Englishwomen were famous for their playing of various instruments, and almost all of them could sing.

People were so musical that in a barber's shop there was often an instrument called a cittern (a kind of lute or guitar) hanging on the wall for any customer who was waiting his turn to be shaved to play upon, just as nowadays there are newspapers for him to read. So that shows that people *must* have been very musical in those days, doesn't it?

Some of the Instruments

There were other instruments, too, that people were very fond of (though they did not play these in barbers' shops), such as:

1. *The Virginals*: Something like a small grand piano in shape, and with a keyboard like a piano. Described in Chapter V.

2. *Viols*: A family of stringed instruments (little and big), something like our Violins, Violas, Violoncellos, and Double-basses.

3. *Lutes*: Another family of stringed instruments, but plucked, not bowed—something like the Mandoline of to-day, but better.

4. *Recorders*: A family of Flutes, blown at the end (not the side)—like tin whistles made of wood and very much glorified.

OLD ENGLISH INSTRUMENTS

TOP ROW: *Modern Bow and old Bow (showing difference in shape), Tenor Viol, Treble Viol, Small Treble Viol, Recorder, 'Cornet', Tabor Pipe*

MIDDLE ROW: *Queen Elizabeth's Virginal*

BOTTOM ROW: *Viol da Gamba, two Lutes*

Shakespeare mentions all these instruments in his plays. In addition to instrumental playing, people were very fond of singing, and loved Madrigals (a sort of part-songs) and Rounds and Catches (like 'Three blind mice', which has come down to us from Shakespeare's day). This Choral Music has been spoken of in *The First Book*.

Shakespeare's Musical Plays

Now I come to something *very* important—the actual music that Shakespeare put into his plays. There is one point about this that even the learned Shakespeare writers have never discovered, but you and I, as musicians, can see it quite well if we look through the plays. *When Shakespeare wants to make us feel very awe-struck he uses music.*

You know that there are lots of ghosts and witches and fairies in the plays, don't you? Well, almost always when these strange, supernatural creatures appear there is music—sometimes singing and sometimes instruments. Get your English teacher to look through the plays with you, and you will find that this is so.

And then, too, when Shakespeare makes his characters fall in love, which, as you will some day find (but not too soon, I hope), is a very awe-inspiring, though happy, state to be in, he has music. When he represents anything that seems miraculous, such as people who seem to be dead restored to life, he has music again. And when real, actual death takes place (and this is the most awe-inspiring experience of all, isn't it?) then he often has music, too, so that one may be made to realize how solemn it all is, and feel touched by the sadness of it.

SHAKESPEARE'S DRAMATIC USE OF MUSIC

Some Illustrations of the Foregoing Chapter

Here are a few examples of Shakespeare's use of music. I have chosen them so that if you are reading any particular play of Shakespeare's you may find here a hint as to the purpose of the music in it. You need not read all that follows. It is just put into this book for you to refer to whenever you find it of interest to do so. Indeed this list of examples is perhaps more for the use of your English literature teacher than of yourself. If you are reading a Shakespeare play that is mentioned here, show this list to your teacher, and ask him or her to explain it.

Shakespeare's Fairies and Their Music

A Midsummer-Night's Dream. (1) Here we have the scene of a fairy queen and her court at their good-night revels—a picture in gossamer. Titania calls to her attendant fairies to sing her to sleep, and they join in the lovely song, 'You spotted snakes', with its soothing 'Lullaby' refrain.

(2) The fairy king and queen, Oberon and Titania, dance to music 'such as charmeth sleep', whilst the

spell is removed from the mortals who have passed so strange and disturbing a night in the 'Wood near Athens'.

(3) The play ends in the glimmering firelight, the happy lovers now retired to their several rooms receiving a blessing of song and dance as the fairies trip from room to room.

Music and Witchcraft

The witches of *Macbeth* have their own grim music. (1) Hecate, the Queen of the Witches, is summoned in music ('*Music and a Song within: "Come Away"*'). The use of music behind the scenes, mysterious music from we know not whither, is plainly Shakespeare's way of impressing us with a sense of weirdness and mystery.

(2) When the cavern and cauldron scene is reached, shortly after, we find music again; at Hecate's command the witches sing ('*Music and a Song: "Black Spirits"*'). Macbeth appears, and for him they conjure up the three apparitions, each with thunder. At last the cauldron sinks—to music (the rough, coarse tone of early seventeenth-century hautboys is the music Shakespeare calls for in his directions). Then the witches dance to music— and vanish.

Ghostly Music

Cymbeline. Posthumus is in prison. He sleeps, and 'Solemn music' is heard. Then pass before the dreamer in procession, his father and mother, with musicians walking before them and after them followed by his brothers, 'with wounds, as they died in the wars'. Once again, Shakespeare has contrived to awaken in his audience a sense of the uncanny, and, again, largely by music.

Antony and Cleopatra. It is night. Four soldiers are on guard before the palace. Suddenly, as they talk in undertones of the battle of the morrow, music is heard, coming from nowhere (Shakespeare's directions are *'Music of hautboys as under the stage'*). Awestruck, the sentinels speculate as to its meaning. The music moves away, and they follow it. Here again (this time acting on a hint from Plutarch) the dramatist has used music to produce an impressive effect; into our minds, by the music and the anxious conversation of the soldiers about it is brought the strained feeling of the eve of battle.

Julius Caesar. Brutus is in his tent. The great quarrel with Cassius has just occurred, and the moving reconciliation has followed. The friends have now parted for the night, and Brutus feels the need of calm. He asks his boy, 'Where is thy instrument?' The sleepy boy plays, and drops asleep as he does so. Quieted in mind Brutus takes up a book to read, when Caesar's ghost enters. Here, again, music has tuned the minds of the audience and prepared them for great happenings. A stage ghost, unheralded by music, is little likely to be convincing to an audience, though once, in Hamlet, Shakespeare has achieved ghostly conviction by other than musical means.

The Winter's Tale. The King has, he believes, killed his Queen. Long years after, when he has become repentant and mourns his ill-doing, he is invited to see a statue of the murdered Queen. Then, as he gazes, the word is given, music strikes on his ear, and to it the statue comes slowly to life, steps down from its pedestal and embraces him—no statue, indeed, but his actual wife, long hidden from him by some who loved her. It is to music that an apparent miracle takes place— without music perhaps to most of us no miracle but a commonplace conjuring trick. Music and the sense of mystery are once more associated.

Henry VIII. A case like that of Posthumus, already quoted, is the one of poor, ill-used Queen Katharine. 'Take thy lute, wench,' she says, 'my soul grows sad with troubles. Sing and disperse 'em.' Then comes the lovely song, 'Orpheus with his lute'. Later in the play the Queen again calls for musical comfort, and this time, in vision, 'spirits of peace' appear to her. The audience is brought to realize that the Queen is already in touch with that spiritual kingdom to which she is so soon to pass. (Not all of this play is by Shakespeare himself, but, musically, his principles are followed.)

Music and the Act of Choice

The Merchant of Venice. Bassanio's choice, on which his life's happiness and that of the woman he loves depend, is made to music (*'Music whilst Bassanio comments on the caskets to himself'*). For the previous suitors Shakespeare provided no music, but here, in the case of Bassanio, is a choice on which turns the whole plot of the play, and the dramatist uses a musical means to bring the solemnity of it home to us. The point cannot be laboured here, but is there not something of the supernatural about the act of choosing; do we not feel a sense of mystery when pondering a great decision?

Music as Medicine

You are not likely to read *Pericles* just at present, as it is not a play of much interest to younger people. But when you are older you will probably do so and then you may be interested to refer to what follows:

(1) Thaisa, wife of Pericles, travelling with him by sea, gives birth to a child during a storm, and, as is thought, dies. Her body is hastily placed in a large chest and cast over into the sea. The chest floats ashore, and is carried to Cerimon, a lord of the place, by his servants. The body is discovered, and Cerimon announces that life is not extinct. He calls for fire, clothes, and appliances and—for music. To the sound of the viol the Queen is restored to conscious life. Dramatically the case is interesting. The use of drugs would have been prosaic and commonplace; extraordinary means are used for the performance of what is almost a miracle, and the attention and awe of the audience are secured.

(2) Heartbroken at the loss of his wife, Pericles soon suffers another loss—his daughter, the babe born on shipboard, being carried away by pirates. Years after,

distraught by sorrow, he comes to Mytilene, lying speechless in a pavilion on the deck of his ship. The Governor of the place comes off to see him, and to the attendants proposes, as a cure, the music of a maid famous for such in Mytilene. She is sent for. No immediate cure is effected, but the music was not without effect, for, on her speaking to the stricken prince, he replies. A gradual recovery takes place, and Pericles recognizes in the music-maid his lost daughter. Then mysterious music in the air steals into his ears and ours; to it he drops into a calm slumber, during which, to music, Diana appears to him and proclaims to him the impending recovery of his wife. The plot of *Pericles* is, in fact, the separation of a family by storm and violence and its re-union by music. There is very slight exaggeration in this statement.

King Lear. Cordelia sits in the camp beside her poor old mad father. He sleeps, 'soft music playing'; the latter provided by the doctor's orders as a means of restoring shattered nerves and shaken mental powers. Lear wakes, bewildered and hardly able to realize he is still on earth. Gradually he collects his mental forces and recovery is evident. (Compare the prescription of Saul's servants, in *his* madness.)

Music as a Sign of Madness

Snatches of song, abrupt and disorganized, are with Shakespeare one of the symptoms of madness, as ordered organized music is its cure. Lear 'singing aloud; Crowned with rank fumiter and furrow weeds', and Hamlet's Ophelia, again with song and flowers, are cases in point.

Those of Shakespeare's characters who feign a lack of wit, his clowns and fools, show the same sign of irresponsibility—the clown in *Twelfth Night* visiting Malvolio in prison, Edgar in *King Lear* 'disguised as a Madman', and calling himself Poor Tom, are amongst the examples.

Petruchio, in *The Taming of the Shrew*, pretends to be a man of uncontrolled impulse, so that he may subdue his violent wife—and it is part of his pretence that he sings mad snatches of wild melody.

As to the state of drunkenness, surely akin to that of madness, the references to this in the above must suffice for the moment.

Love and Music

Romeo calls on Juliet—'If the measure of thy joy be heaped like mine . . . then sweeten with thy breath the neighbour air, and let rich music's tongue unfold the imagined happiness'. The Duke in *Twelfth Night*, in whom music is 'the food of love', is, however, Shakespeare's greatest instance of the lover who needs music. Cleopatra, in *Antony and Cleopatra*, calls for 'some music, moody food of us that trade in love', and even when she goes a-fishing has her 'music playing far off'. Don Adriano, in *Love's Labour's Lost*, is another musical lover ('Sing, boy; my spirit grows heavy in love', and, later, 'Warble, child; make passionate my sense of hearing '). Speed, in *Two Gentlemen of Verona*, speaks of one of the signs of love—'To relish a love-song like a robin-redbreast'. Claudio in *Much Ado about Nothing*, having become a lover, becomes a devotee of the tabor and pipe.

The love-serenades in *Two Gentlemen of Verona*, and *Cymbeline*, and elsewhere, and the many references to such in other plays must pass with mere allusion.

In *The Merchant of Venice*, Shakespeare has cunningly used music and moonlight (and romantic conversation about both of them) to bring our hearts into tune with those of the three newly and happily married couples.

Music and Death

Music is heard to prepare us for the death of Richard II, and Henry IV ('Let there be no noise made, my gentle friends; unless some dull and favourable hand will whisper music to my weary spirit'). King John sings as he lies a-dying. Desdemona chants her sad songs as the shadow of impending death creeps over the stage. Claudio, in *Much Ado*, sings at the grave of his betrothed.

Hamlet and *Coriolanus* end with dead marches. So does *King Lear*. In these plays, the spirit of tragedy reaches its culmination in music. But the most touching instance of the connexion of music and death is in the harping and singing over the body of Imogen, in *Cymbeline* ('Fear no more the heat of the sun').

Music in 'The Tempest'

The unfolding of the plot in *The Tempest* almost turns on music. Yet many otherwise excellent critical essays have been written on the play, without so much as a mention of music.

In *The Tempest* every one is musical—the human beings, the fairy-sprite, Ariel, and the man-devil, Caliban. Music, throughout the play, is the means by which the actions of mortals are directed. To treat this subject at all adequately would mean at least two pages. Read *The Tempest* for yourself, marking the instances where music is heard or spoken of, and then consider why Shakespeare made of this a musical play.

QUESTIONS

*(To See Whether You Remember
the Chapter and Understand It)*

1. What is a musician?

2. Are you one?

3. Do you, or do you not, agree with me that Shakespeare was a *Word-Musician*?

4. And (in either case) why?

5. Why do we think Shakespeare may have been a player or singer (or both)?

6. Mention a few of the instruments Shakespeare must often have heard.

7. Why did Shakespeare use so much music in his plays?

THINGS TO DO

1. Turn to your favourite passage of Shakespeare and see whether there is any 'Consonant Music' in it.

2. And whether there is any 'Vowel Music'.

3. Pick up one or two of the best lines and say them over a good many times until you feel sure you've seized the rhythm.

4. Then write down this music rhythmically (in either Staff notation or Sol-fa *la's*), and write the words under the music.

5. If you are reading a Shakespeare play at school, go through it and make a list of any references to music.

6. Then write a little essay on 'Shakespeare's Use of Music in *The Tempest*' (or whatever the play may be).

7. If there is a musical part of this play, that can be acted conveniently, act it with some of your school friends.

8. There is one sort of music in Shakespeare that the chapter never mentions. What is it? . . . *Quite right!* The ceremonial music—Trumpets when great personages enter, Hautboys and other instruments when soldiers march, etc. Now see if you can find a few examples of that.

CHAPTER VII

MORE ABOUT BRITISH MUSIC

IF you look back over the two parts of *The Book of the Great Musicians* that came before this one you will find that I have hardly seemed to be quite fair to British Music. The only chapters, so far, on British Composers have been:

1. 'English Music in the Days of Drake and Shakespeare'.

2. 'Henry Purcell—the Greatest British Composer'.

3. 'The Inventor of the Nocturne—John Field'.

4. 'Edward Elgar'.

Let us set out in centuries all the British names so far mentioned:

SIXTEENTH CENTURY
Tallis, Byrd, Bull, Gibbons, Farnaby, Dowland, and others (nearly all these lived on into the next century).

SEVENTEENTH CENTURY
Henry Purcell.

EIGHTEENTH CENTURY
    Field (lived into the next century).

NINETEENTH CENTURY
    Elgar (still alive in next century).
    Sullivan.

A Comparison with Germany

Now suppose we make a list of the great German and Austrian Composers who were living and working during the eighteenth and nineteenth centuries:

EIGHTEENTH CENTURY
    Bach (born previous century).
    Handel (born previous century).
    Haydn (lived into next century).
    Mozart.
    Beethoven (lived into next century).
    Schubert (lived into next century).
    Weber (lived into next century).

NINETEENTH CENTURY
    Mendelssohn.
    Schumann.
    Wagner.
    Brahms.

I could have made a longer list of German Composers if I had wished, but I thought it best only to include the very greatest, yet even so you will at once get the idea that during the eighteenth and nineteenth centuries Germany went far ahead of Britain in music, and this idea, I am sorry to say, is true.

How It Happened

Why did this happen? Different people give different reasons.

1. Some say it was because at the beginning of the century Handel came to this country, and was so great a composer that people did not wish to listen to our British composers unless they imitated Handel (and imitation is always a weak thing and never results in much).

2. Others say it was because the British were so busy fighting and exploring and trading that they had not time for music. But this does not seem to be a very good reason, for we were very actively fighting and exploring and trading in the sixteenth century, yet we had plenty of fine composers then.

3. Still others say it was because in Germany and Austria there were a great many different centres at which fine music was going on, whereas in Britain there was really not much going on except in London.

You can form your own ideas, but for myself I think there is something in 1 and 3, and, perhaps, especially in 3.

Centres of Musical Activity

I must explain to you a little this idea about the number of centres in Germany and Austria. The chief places where music was cultivated in the seventeenth and eighteenth centuries were the Courts of monarchs. A King would have his private Orchestra, and often his private Opera House, and generally his Organist and Choir to carry out the music in the Royal Chapel, and lots of other music of different sorts.

For instance, Henry VIII and Queen Elizabeth had fine Royal Chapel choirs, and (as you have learnt) encouraged Masques (which are something like Operas), and also stimulated the playing of the Virginals and the composing of music for them by having about their Courts good players and composers who could provide them with entertainment. And Charles II, James II, and William and Mary continued this cultivation of music to some extent, their chief musician being, as you know, Purcell. But there were in Britain only two Courts in early times, and after the Stuarts came to the English throne only one, whereas what we now call Germany was then a number of separate small states, each with its own King, or Duke, or Elector to rule it, and, thus, each with its own Court, which generally had a Royal Choir for its Chapel, a Royal Orchestra, a Royal String Quartet, and a Royal Opera Company.

The Development of Instrumental Music

Now the time had come in the history of music when the great thing needed was the development of Instrumental Music and of the Opera. The eighteenth century is especially the century of the invention and perfection of the Sonata and the Symphony. But how could people in Britain compose Symphonies, when they had no decent orchestras except in London? You see what I mean: almost every Court in the German countries was a centre of musical enthusiasm and culture, and the British had only one centre, whereas these lands had a great many. So I think they can be forgiven.

What of To-day?

Nowadays, of course, things are rather different. Many towns have their Orchestras, and there are good Choral Societies everywhere, and public concerts, and good education in music. The British still concentrate their music too much in London, but nevertheless we may fairly say that the old conditions have disappeared, because in this and all countries fine music is no longer dependent on Courts and Kings, but has come right down to the people at large. And a very good thing too—since it gives us all a chance! And, of course, in America the same thing has happened.

Naturally, from Purcell to the present day there

have been English composers at work. But until recently they have not been great enough men to rank with those on the Continent.

This is just a short chapter to explain to you how it came about that Britain, which often took the lead so long as music was a matter of Choral Singing and Virginal Playing, fell behind when it became a matter of Opera performance and Orchestral Concerts. In a few short chapters which follow I shall tell you a little about some of the best of the British composers during this rather dull period, and also about some of the best during our own more vigorous days.

QUESTIONS

*(To See Whether You Remember
the Chapter and Understand It)*

1. Mention all the British composers you can remember whose names have so far come into these three *Books of the Great Musicians*.

2. Give as clear an idea as you can of when they lived.

3. Mention all the German and Austrian composers discussed in the three parts of this book.

4. Give as clear an idea as you can of when they lived.

5. What are the three reasons sometimes given for Britain's falling behind?

6. Which do you yourself think are most likely to be true?

7. Why should a King or a Court have so much influence on music?

8. Tell anything you can about British monarchs and music.

9. What do we mean if we say 'Music is now a democratic art'? Is it true?

10. Is it wholly true?

11. Is it as true as it might be?

12. Have you any suggestions for making it more true?

THINGS TO DO

Think of some for yourself. I can't think of any except this—You might get up a good school concert called 'An Afternoon of British Music'. The programme would be something like this:

1. A piece or two of Elizabethan keyboard music, e.g. something of Farnaby (published by Novello).

2. A piece or two of Purcell's keyboard music (published by Chester).

3. A Purcell Song, by one of the Singing Classes.

4. One movement, or two movements, from Purcell's Violin Sonata (published both by Schott and by Curwen).

5. Another Purcell Song by another of the Singing Classes.

6. If you have a School Orchestra, one or two of Purcell's little pieces arranged for Strings (published by Novello).

7. An Arne Song by one of the Singing Classes (read about Arne in the next chapter).

8. A Field Nocturne by the best pianist in the school.

9. A Sullivan Song by one of the masters or mistresses or by some local singer who wants to help you (let it be a song from one of the Comic Operas—don't have *The Sailor's Grave* or *The Lost Chord*, which are very poor Sullivan).

10. Something of Elgar's if you can manage it.

11. To end the concert, *Elgar's Land of Hope and Glory* by the whole school, or Arne's *Rule, Britannia* (but don't let them sing 'Britannia rules the waves—which is wrong!), and then *God save the King.*

Another plan would be to get up a subscription to buy British records for the school Gramophone and then give a Gramophone Concert of Madrigals, Purcell, Arne, and Elgar. Or you could have *both* concerts with a month or so between them, perhaps raising money by the first in order to get the records to give the second—which might then be free.

I have just thought of another thing to do (I am assuming now that I am speaking to British readers; American readers are not so likely to want to do this). Write to the British Music Society, 3 Berners Street, W., and ask the Secretary how to form a School Branch of the Society.

CHAPTER VIII

ARNE, THE COMPOSER OF 'RULE, BRITANNIA'

1710-1778

THERE is at least one eighteenth-century British composer about whom you ought to know something; especially as you have certainly heard and probably sung some of his songs—Thomas Augustine Arne.

Arne was an Eton boy who made himself a nuisance to his school-fellows by practising on an old cracked flute, so that years after, when old Dr. Burney, who was writing his great *History of Music*, asked several of them to tell him about Arne's schooldays that was what they told him, and he duly put it into his 'History':

> 'I have been assured by several of his school-fellows that his love for music operated on him too powerfully, even while he was at Eton, for his own peace or that of his companions; for with a miserable cracked common flute, he used to torment them night and day, when not obliged to attend school.'

How the Boy Arne Went to the Opera

Then Burney asked Arne himself to tell him about his early life, and he told him how after he had left Eton he used to get into the Opera House without paying.

His father was an upholsterer and had a shop not very far from the Opera House. Now, in those days, whilst the masters and mistresses were in the stalls and boxes of the theatre, their servants, who had to wait for them either to drive them home again or to attend them on foot with torches, were allowed to sit in the gallery. So young Arne used to borrow the livery of a footman, put it on, walk boldly in at the gallery door and spend the evening enjoying the music.

You may be sure his father did not know of this, for he intended him to be a lawyer and did not encourage him to study music.

How He Practised the Harpsichord

You remember, from the first volume, how little Handel got over his difficulty by taking a harpsichord up to the garret and practising quietly at night, when the family was asleep. Well, Arne, as a youth, tried the same trick.

Perhaps Arne learnt this trick from Handel, for Handel was born twenty-five years before Arne, came to England in the very year of Arne's birth, and all through Arne's earlier life was the most popular composer in

THOMAS ARNE

England. No doubt Handel sometimes talked of his boyish escapades and the tales might come to Arne's ears. Handel, you remember, was found out, his harpsichord being heard one night by the family. Arne was more wary. He used to put a handkerchief over the strings in such a way as to muffle the sound.

Arne as a Lawyer

The part of London where Arne's father lived was (and is still) crowded with lawyer's offices, and Arne was sent to one of these to serve his 'articles', or apprenticeship.

Soon after the 'articles' were served, Mr. Arne, senior, had occasion one evening to call on a customer of his. He heard music and was told a private concert was being held, and was invited to go upstairs and become one of the audience. When he walked into the room what was his surprise to find that the leading violinist was his own son! 'Who taught you to play the fiddle?' he must have asked, and then young Tom had to confess that all the time he had been studying law he had been studying the fiddle too, taking lessons from a famous London fiddler of those days, called Festing.

Arne Teaches His Sister and Brother

The father saw that his boy was meant by nature to be a musician and not a lawyer, so he forgave him, and allowed him to practise music openly at home in future, and also to give lessons to his sister, who seemed to have a pretty good voice. So good, indeed, was her voice, and so well did he teach her that she was soon able to appear in public at the Opera House, and then, finding her a great success as an opera singer, Arne wrote an opera called *Rosamund* specially for her. His little brother appeared in this too, so it looks as though the father had quite got over any objection to his family taking part in music.

The opera was performed ten times, the last time for the benefit of the composer, who probably made a nice little sum of money that night. He was now twenty-three.

This success had to be followed up, of course, so Arne wrote another opera, on Tom Thumb, with his young brother in the part of the hero.

Arne Composes 'Rule, Britannia!'

Arne was now becoming quite well known and soon he was asked by many theatre managers to compose music for them. When he was thirty a great musical performance was to be given in the garden of the country house of the Prince of Wales, at Cliveden in Buckinghamshire. Arne was asked to write the music for a masque called *Alfred*, and did so. The song which ended the masque was one which soon became very well known—*Rule, Britannia!*

What are the next words after 'Rule, Britannia'? 'Britannia rules the waves.' There, I knew you'd say that.

And of course you're wrong, for if the poet were about to make the statement, 'Britannia rules the waves', he would not, just before this, tell her to do that very thing. The first bar of the chorus (from which the title of the song has been taken) is really 'Rule, Britannia! Britannia, *rule* the waves!' (imperative mood, not indicative).

Wagner, years after this song was written, heard it and said 'the first eight notes contain the whole character of the British people.'

Other Arne Songs

Other songs which have helped to make Arne famous are some that he wrote for a performance of Shakespeare's *As You Like It*:

1. 'Under the greenwood tree.'

2. 'Blow, blow, thou winter wind.'

3. 'When daisies pied.'

Later, for Shakespeare's *The Tempest*, he wrote another very beautiful song, which is often heard to-day:

4. 'Where the bee sucks.'

It is chiefly by his songs that we remember Arne to-day, for his Operas and Oratorios are forgotten. But the songs have such good *tunes* that they will, I should think, never die. A really good simple tune is one of the finest gifts to his countrymen a composer can leave behind him when he dies.

Besides solo vocal and choral music Arne wrote some harpsichord and violin music that is still worth playing.

Women in Oratorios

Now I have told you just enough about Arne to make you feel interested when you hear any of his music, and so to make you listen to it more carefully, which is what I meant to do. There is just one thing further I will tell you.

If you hear a Choral Society singing an Oratorio to-day, who sings the Treble and Alto parts? Ladies, of course! Well, until Arne thought of giving the ladies a chance to take part in Choral Singing (in his Oratorio *Judith*, in 1773) nobody had ever done so. They used, up to his day, to have boy Sopranos and men Altos, and no women at all. So all Handel's Oratorios were originally sung (except for some of the solo parts) entirely by boys and men.

The Influence of Folk Song

There is another thing I ought to tell you, or rather to which I ought to draw your attention. Arne's best songs are very *English* in melody. English Folk Song has had its influence on Arne, as you can feel. Now remember this:

1. Those Elizabethan composers I talked of in the first volume used a lot of English Folk Songs in their keyboard music—often making a long piece by taking a Folk Song and then writing Variations upon it.

2. Purcell's songs have often got the English Folk Song style about them.

3. Arne's songs have this too.

4. Sullivan's songs, in his comic operas, are often 'influenced' by English Folk Song.

5. Some composers to-day, like Vaughan Williams, have the English Folk Song influence in their music.

So you see that the Folk Songs of which we read in the very first chapter of *The First Book of the Great Musicians* have always had an influence upon English composers.

'Folk Music' and 'Art Music'

In another book I have put it this way—Folk Music is like the Wild Rose, which just grows up nobody knows how, and without any watering, or pruning, or tending of any kind. 'Art' Music (that is, real 'Composed' Music) is like the Garden Rose, which centuries of clever gardening have developed out of the Wild Rose.

And all the time that the Garden Rose has been developing the Wild Rose has gone on flourishing. And the two to-day still grow side by side   one on one side of the garden wall, and one on the other side.

In Purcell's and Arne's songs you see the Wild Rose gradually turning into the Garden Rose, but still not so very much unlike the Wild Rose. In some music to-day you see the Garden Rose so much developed that at first you are in danger of forgetting that it ever came from the Wild Rose. But so it was, and if you think about it for a moment you will see that every bit of 'Composed' Music is really the development of the Folk Music from which the first composers got their ideas about composition.

QUESTIONS

*(To See Whether You Remember
the Chapter and Understand It)*

1. When was Arne born?

2. When did he die?

3. Where did he go to school?

4. For what profession was he trained when he left school?

5. And how did he manage to escape from it?

6. What do you know of *(a)* Arne's Father, *(b)* his Sister, (c) his Brother?

7. Which branch of Arne's composition is best remembered to-day?

8. Mention any pieces by Arne.

9. What did Wagner say about *Rule, Britannia*?

10. What do you think about this saying?

11. What change in Oratorio performance did Arne bring about?

12. Repeat any ideas about Folk Song which you have got out of this Chapter.

THINGS TO DO

1. Get your singing-class teacher to teach you some Arne songs.

2. Persuade your Form to give a half-hour Form Concert of Music by Arne, and to admit the rest of the school.

3. Look through the Gramophone Record Catalogue for any pieces by Arne, and persuade your parents that it would add to the family happiness to have the ready means of performing such good tunes.

4. Ask your English Teacher to set as a subject for composition *The Life and Works of Arne*. And your French teacher to set you a brief French composition:

'*Comment Arne assistait à l'Opéra sans payer*', or

'*Comment le jeune Arne devint musicien en dépit de son père*'.

(If you want to know the French for 'upholsterer', it is '*tapissier*'; 'harpsichord' is '*clavecin*'; 'to muffle' is *assourdir*—and now you're ready to start!)

CHAPTER IX

STERNDALE BENNETT

1816-1875

THE proverb says 'Give a dog a bad name and you may as well hang him.' The idea is, I suppose, that once you make people think that the dog is useless or vicious they will go on thinking so, and by and by he will think so himself, and then will probably actually become so, and so, in the end, deserve his fate.

In the same way, if there is a boy at school who is always being told he's a worthless scamp he will probably become more and more worthless all the time, whereas if he got a bit of encouragement now and again, when his better side came out, he would probably develop that better side, and in time become as good a scholar and as well behaved a one as his companions.

Of course we must not push this idea too far, but there is something in it. On the whole it is better to encourage than to blame.

The Depressed Britons

Now at the beginning of the nineteenth century the British composers did not get a great deal of encouragement. During the preceding century Germany (as we have seen in the last chapter but one) had had Bach and Handel, Haydn and Mozart, and now it had Beethoven and Weber and others. And Britain had no musical giants of that size. So British people came to have a poor idea of their own composers, and not to give them much encouragement to work hard and become greater, until soon there was an idea that Britain was not a music-producing country, although, if people had only stopped to think, they would have remembered the Elizabethans, and Purcell, and would have seen that even Arne, although not a great composer, was, on the whole, a quite good one.

How Mendelssohn Found a British Composer

The way a change of thought came about is rather interesting. There was a student at the Royal Academy of Music who was a good violinist and pianist and composer. Now one day Mendelssohn, who was visiting England, was invited to be present at a Students' Concert at the Academy. When he had heard this student play a Concerto of his own he said, 'I want to have a good look at that boy.' So they brought the boy and he was introduced, and Mendelssohn said, 'You must come to

WILLIAM STERNDALE BENNETT, AGED ABOUT 16

Germany.' The boy replied, 'If I come to Germany may I come as your pupil?' but Mendelssohn said 'No, no, you must come as my friend.'

This boy was William Sterndale Bennett, and he was then seventeen. He went to Germany a few years later, and Mendelssohn, Schumann, and other musicians there made much of him. So, when he came back, people in England thought more of him and listened more readily to his music, and put it into concert programmes. Germany was considered the great musical country then, and if the young composer was praised there the English people were prepared to believe in him.

The Turn of the Tide

So Sterndale Bennett got his chance. I may as well say at once that his life is a little disappointing to read because the promise of his youth was never *quite* fulfilled. He wrote a lot of fine things and then, in middle life, got so tied up with teaching work, on which in those days every musician in England had to depend for a living, that he stopped composing. But before he did so he had done one splendid thing—given the British people a bit of faith in their own composers. Bennett is the tide mark in British music. Before him the tide was always going out: after him it began to flow in again and to rise higher and higher, until now it has risen very high indeed (or so it seems to those of us to-day who are watching it).

A North Country Musical Family

Sterndale Bennett belonged to a North Country musical family. He was born at Sheffield, where his father was an Organist, and his grandfather a Singer and a player on the Oboe. When William was three his father died, and his grandfather, who was then living in Cambridge as a member of the choir of King's College, adopted him, brought him up, and when he was eight had him admitted as a choir-boy.

How Sterndale Bennett Went to London

When the boy was ten, as he seemed very gifted in music, he was sent to London to try if he could win a place in the new Royal Academy of Music. In those days the Academy was very different from what it is now. Small boys were accepted as students. They lived at the Academy itself, and they wore a uniform.

The examiners tested Bennett and were so pleased with him that they decided he should be admitted without paying any fees at all, which was a very unusual concession. His grandparents had expected that, even if successful, he would come back to Cambridge for a time, and had only given him the things necessary for one night, but he was told to start his residence at the Academy at once and sent to join the other boys who were already students.

The Boys' Ear-Test

One of the Professors went to another one and said, 'Come and see the funny little fellow who has just come into the house!' They went to the room where the boys were, and there was little Bennett being put through another examination, this time by the boys. They had put him in a corner of the room and were striking on the piano handfuls of notes, and asking him to name them, and he could do it correctly every time.

I think the boys liked this new companion all the better for being small, for they were able to let him down out of the window in a basket at night to go and buy good things to eat.

Bennett Becomes a 'Grand–Pupil' of Mozart and Beethoven

Bennett had a beautiful alto voice, and sometimes Mr. Attwood, the organist of St. Paul's, would send for him to sing in the choir. Attwood had been a pupil of Mozart, and Potter, who was Bennett's teacher, had been a pupil of Beethoven. So no doubt he would hear tales of these great composers. Later in his life he made Mozart's music his special study, and advised every one who wished to compose clearly to do the same.

At this time he did not often see his grandparents in Cambridge, and could not even write to them very often, for in those days postage was very costly, and was paid by the person who received the letter, and

Bennett's grandfather could not afford the fees that were charged. You will realize, if you think for a few minutes, that very few of the great musicians you have read about in *The First Book of the Great Musicians* or *The Second Book of the Great Musicians* came of well-to-do families, and some of them, as you see, were really poor in their boyhood. Bennett's main instrument at the Academy was the Violin, but after a time he was allowed to give more attention to the Piano. One fact that will surprise you is this—all the practice pianos of the Academy were in one room, and a number of pupils would practise together, all playing their different pieces at the same time. A retired sergeant was always in the room to see they did not neglect their work, and he must have suffered, poor man! But he used always to go and stand by Bennett's piano and listen to him, and perhaps he trained himself to keep the sounds of the others out of his head.

Bennett as Organist

When Bennett was eighteen, and already an accomplished musician who had been praised by Mendelssohn, there was a vacancy for an organist at a church at Wandsworth, and he decided to try for it. In those days the parishioners used to vote for their organist, and when they met there was a show of hands, and it was seen that Bennett had lost. But those who were in favour of his being given the post demanded a poll. This was held. The polling booth was open all day, just as in a Parliamentary Election nowadays, and when at night they counted the votes they found that Bennett had a majority of 67. So he got the post, and with it £30 a year as salary. But he was still very poor, and sometimes, in going to Wandsworth, had no money to pay the toll at the bridge over the river and would leave with the bridge-keeper his gloves, or some other little thing, instead of money. Soon, however, he began to get some pupils near London, and to make a little money in this way too. He still lived at the Academy, however, and was considered to be a student there.

Some Pianoforte Music

Possibly some of the readers of this book play Bennett's three pieces, *The Lake, The Mill Stream*, and *The Fountain*. These were written whilst he was still at the Academy, and when he was about twenty. His own playing of these became famous. Then he went to Germany (as I have already related). Soon after this, Schumann heard him play them and said that his playing of *The Fountain* created an effect 'almost magical'.

I ought to tell you how it was that he was able to accept Mendelssohn's invitation to go to Germany. The great piano firm of Broadwood (which, of course, still exists) came forward and said that if he would like to go they would pay the expense of the visit. That was generous and very wise expenditure; it is always a good thing for a young musician to travel and hear music in other countries and meet musicians of other nationalities.

Bennett went several times to Germany and enjoyed his association there with Mendelssohn and Schumann. Here is a funny Canon he wrote one night, after his Concert Overture *The Naiads* had been played at a great concert in Leipzig. Schumann and he and some friends had retired, after the concert, to an old inn, and there Bennett wrote this, and perhaps the others sang it (I have translated the words into English for you. The original is to be found in Sterndale Bennett's Life, by his son, published in 1907 by the Cambridge University Press):

A DESCRIPTION OF SCHUMANN

How they sang the treble part of this I do not know—unless there were some boys or ladies present. *You* can sing it, in a pretty effective sort of way, with *all* treble voices, if you like, but if you do so I should advise you to tell those who sing the upper stave to end on B (as shown in brackets), instead of on A.

Bennett's Later Years

Right through all three parts of this book I am telling you more about the youth of the musicians than about their later life, because I think that will interest you most, and now, having told you about Bennett's youth at some length, I must pass more quickly over his later years.

Bennett had to teach, and to do it all day and every day. This is the sort of life he led in his middle years. He gave his first lesson at seven or eight o'clock in the morning, and with short breaks for meals went on giving lessons until ten or eleven o'clock at night. A few of his lessons he gave at home, but most of them he gave at schools or at the houses of pupils, and he had a horse carriage with books and music to study as he went along, and often food for his meals. One day every week he was awakened at four o'clock by the policeman, so that he could catch the early train to Brighton, and there he worked hard all day, teaching piano in a school, not getting home again until eleven o'clock at night. Yet he kept cheerful with all this hard work, and really loved his teaching, taking the greatest pains with all his many pupils. The pupils said that he took as much interest in every piece he taught them as though it were a new piece he had never seen before. But of course this 'grind' checked his composition, and at last quite stopped it.

What Bennett Did for Bach

Although he was so busy, Bennett found time to do an excellent piece of work in showing the London musicians the beauties of Bach's music, which was still very little known in Britain. He founded a Bach Society, and gave the first performance in this country of the great *St. Matthew Passion*.

Honours Come

Of course, people realized what a good musician and fine man Bennett was, and honours of one sort and another came to him.

He was appointed Professor of Music at Cambridge University, and did a very good work there (he did not need to live at Cambridge, but only to visit it occasionally).

For ten years he was conductor of the Philharmonic Society in London—a very important appointment.

And he was made Principal of his old school, the Royal Academy of Music.

And at last Queen Victoria gave him a knighthood, and he became Sir William Sterndale Bennett.

But he did not earn very much money. For his Cambridge Professorship there was, for a long time, no stipend, and from the Royal Academy he would not take much, as it was short of funds, so for years he received for all his hard and valuable work there only about £20 a year! Bennett was a very self-denying man, and did not mind how hard he worked, or how little he received for his work, if he felt that what he was doing was for the good of music.

His Death

Bennett died comparatively young—at the age of fifty-nine. He was buried in Westminster Abbey, and there you can see his tombstone in the North Choir Aisle. Whilst you are in the Abbey, look, too, for the memorial of Purcell. Sullivan and Arne, two other British musicians who have chapters to themselves in this book, are buried respectively in St. Paul's Cathedral and St. Paul's Church, Covent Garden.

Bennett's Compositions

Besides a fair amount of piano music, Bennett wrote several Concert Overtures (*The Naiads, The Wood Nymphs, Paradise and the Peri*), a Symphony, some Piano Concertos and Orchestral works, a sacred Cantata (*The Woman of Samaria*), and a few songs. Hear any of this music that you can, and remember that in composing it Sterndale Bennett did us another great service in showing that an Englishman may be a fine musician.

The style of Bennett's music is, as you would expect, something like that of Mendelssohn. It is elegant and charming, not strong and forceful. But the composer's own individuality comes out in it, too. Schumann spoke of Bennett in his earlier days as 'a thorough Englishman, a glorious artist, and a beautiful and poetic soul.'

QUESTIONS

*(To See Whether You Remember
the Chapter and Understand It)*

1. Why did Bennett never quite fulfil his early promise?

2. Where did his family come from?

3. Was it a musical family?

4. What was Bennett's first musical position?

5. How did he come to be a Londoner?

6. Tell anything you remember about life at the Royal Academy of Music in its early days.

7. Of whom was Bennett a 'grand-pupil'?

8. Who was the great German musician who 'discovered' Bennett?

9. How did Bennett manage to get to Germany?

10. Why was it important in those days that a young musician should go there?

11. And why is it now nothing like so important?

12. What effect had Bennett's recognition in Germany upon his recognition at home?

13. What great musician was still insufficiently appreciated here in Bennett's day?

14. And what did Bennett do to remedy this?

15. What honour came at last to Bennett?

16. Mention some of his compositions—all you can recall.

17. Is his music to be described as 'powerful'?

18. What (roughly) were Bennett's dates of birth and death?

THINGS TO DO

Find a pianist who knows some of Bennett's music and make him or her play it to you. Thus try to get an idea of what his style is like.

CHAPTER X

PARRY

1848-1918

No doubt some of the readers of this book have sung school songs by Parry, or, perhaps, played some of his piano pieces, and will be glad to know something about him.

Like Arne, more than a century earlier, Hubert Parry was an Eton boy. His father was a well-to-do man in Gloucestershire, a good amateur painter and the author of books on art and other subjects.

Hubert had begun to compose chants and hymn-tunes when he was eight, and a little later he had heard the great organist Samuel Sebastian Wesley play, which had increased his already great enthusiasm for music.

A School-Boy Musician

Whilst at Eton he spent a good deal of time at music, and when his voice broke it soon settled again, into a good baritone. He became quite famous amongst his school-fellows for his singing and playing and composing. When he was nineteen, and whilst still at school, he took his Bachelor of Music degree at Oxford University. He then left Eton for Oxford, and took his B.A. degree after the usual three years of study, and then went to London, where he went into business in the City. But he felt he must be a musician, not a business man, so after three years he left office work and began to spend his time in music.

The Beginnings of a Reputation

When he was about thirty-two Parry's name began to be known to people as that of a talented composer. A Piano Concerto of his was played at the famous Crystal Palace Concerts, and various choral works were sung at the Gloucester Festival. The first of these choral works was one which is still sung, a setting of Milton's poem, 'At a Solemn Musick', called by Parry (from its opening words) *Blest Pair of Sirens*. This is for eight unaccompanied sets of voices, which are wonderfully combined, so that the effect is very thrilling. Hear it, if you can!

Later, Parry wrote a good many Oratorios, some Orchestral Music, some Chamber Music, a large number of Songs, and some Piano Pieces. In all these things there are interesting passages and much fine music, but few of them have become popular, and some are already falling out of use. They have dignity and sometimes humour, and are very well composed, but in some cases lack real life, perhaps because their composer did not give himself enough time for composition, but occupied himself in so many other ways. What were these ways?

Parry's Busy Life

Well, first of all, when he was thirty-five, Parry was appointed assistant to Sir John Stainer, the Professor of Music at Oxford University, and when he was fifty-two he succeeded Stainer and himself became Professor. Meantime, when he was forty-six, he had become Director of the Royal College of Music, a very important

SIR HUBERT PARRY

ON BOARD THE 'WANDERER'

position, and one that took much time, for he wished to do his duties very thoroughly. Then he took to writing books, good ones, which you should some day read, such as:

Studies of Great Composers. This is meant for young people.

The Evolution of the Art of Music. This is too difficult for you at present, but you should read it when you grow older.

The Seventeenth Century. A volume in the great Oxford History of Music.

Style in Music. A very fine book, too little read.

John Sebastian Bach. (Parry was a great Bach enthusiast.)

A Summary of Musical History. This is only a good 'cram' book, suitable for people who are going in for musical examinations, or who want to get hold of the dates of the history of music as a basis for their further reading.

Queen Victoria made Parry a Knight and King Edward VII made him a Baronet. Parry well deserved these national honours, and everybody was glad when he got them, for every one admired the splendid work he was doing, especially as head of the Royal College of Music.

Parry and His Students

Parry's influence on the College students was very great. He was always very sympathetic with all of them, and by his support and example encouraged them to work hard and to aim at the highest possible.

He hated any sort of shams, and liked people to be thoroughly genuine.

Bad music he detested, for he felt it really did harm to people's characters to listen to what was cheap and base.

He was interested in the whole of life and not merely in music, and tried to make his students widen their lives in all possible ways. He had no patience with a musician who was *only* a musician; he wanted musicians to be broad-minded, well-educated, thinking men and women.

He believed in plenty of sport and was a good athlete as a young man, and a great yachtsman and swimmer in later life.

Parry was one of the most good-humoured, cheerful, friendly men one could ever meet, and to shake his hand and have a word or two of conversation with him always cheered one up and made one feel 'ready for anything.'

Some of Parry's Sayings

Here are a few paragraphs taken from the Addresses he used to give to the Royal College students at the opening of each term's work.

I

'The happiest people are those who have the widest outlook.'

II

'There is nothing better for musicians than to cultivate literary tastes, poetry, history, even philosophy.'

III

'An enormous waste of life comes about from our not taking our opportunities to see into things that come in our way. People take to spending their lives in such unprofitable futilities as card-playing, and even worse, because they have not had energy enough to look sensibly at the things that happen round them every day.'

IV

'A specialist is liable to see all life out of one window and not to know what it looks like out of another window. He may know his own subject all right, but when he comes across a man who is equally engrossed in another special subject, the two are mutually unintelligible.'

V

But though Parry wanted musicians to take an interest in other subjects than music, he did not approve of their dabbling first in one subject and then in another:

'Mere dissipation of energy is completely futile. It is deplorable when a man has so little power of coherence and concentration that at one moment he is studying geology, the next painting in water-colours, and the next listening eagerly to the theories of a fad doctor, and the next practising a mouth-organ, and the next studying the pedigrees of race-horses.'

VI

Can you see what Parry meant when he said:

'It is better to be a rebel than a slave'?

VII

'On the whole there is something even more chivalrous and fine about loyalty to an enemy and a rival than to people who merely engage our personal interest and regard. Such loyalty means readiness to admit and welcome whatever is well and honestly done, wherever we come across it, especially in rivals and adversaries if we have any.'

VIII

'The beauty of order is that there is so much more room for things. If you have twenty letters by post of a morning, and open them and throw them all down helter-skelter on the table, they look perfectly awful—it looks as if it would be best to put them in the waste-paper basket at once, and not try to answer them. But if you put them in a few piles, in accordance with the nature of their contents, they look ever so much smaller, and you don't despair of answering them all. Now one of your first objects in life is to get as much into it as you can. When you get old enough to look back, you will get a bit worried not to have done some things that were worth doing, and it is always well to remember we each have a little spell to get things done, and we do not get the chance to get them done again. The older you get, the shorter you will find your one chance; and the only way to pack life as full as it will hold is to put its contents into some sort of order. But there is no order that does for every one, and every one has to find the order that suits his disposition best—and that is where the room comes for your impulses and queernesses.'

IX

'Most of us are capable of being idiots at times. You will remember the familiar saying that "people who do not make mistakes do not make anything." You cannot have personal initiative without risk of making mistakes; and you cannot get things done without personal initiative.'

X

'If people make mistakes, that is useful too. For those who have any sense at all can learn as much from making mistakes as from anything else they make or mar.'

XI

'The man who is too greedy for appreciation too often produces not the best he might do if he were perfectly sincere, but the thing which will get him credit with a lot of people who are incapable of really judging whether what he does is good or bad. The poor thing thirsts for sympathy, and would sacrifice everything— his happiness and cleanliness of mind and his general well-being and his good relations with really intelligent friends, and all that really makes life worth living—to get it. And the result is that the appreciation he gets is less worth having every day he lives. For as he goes on adapting his achievements to those who have no understanding, he goes on making them stupider day by day, and his own work becomes worse and worse as it follows their increasing dullness; and he ends by being little better than a crazy egotist, who has lost the capacity to do things well and lives only to heal his excitable dupes pouring hysterical flatteries into his ears. The craving stupidly gratified becomes a kind of disease, and the pretence of great achievement a mockery.'

XII

'A man establishes his definite identity by making consistent and sensible use of such qualities and aptitudes and impulses as he has. He cannot alter them or pick and choose what he will have, any more than he can pick and choose his parents. But he can direct them.'

QUESTIONS

*(To See Whether You Remember
the Chapter and Understand It)*

1. When was Parry born?

2. When did he die?

3. Mention any facts about his school life.

4. What did he do when he left school?

5. Give the name of a great choral work of his.

6. What important educational positions did he hold?

7. So far as you can make out from what I have told you, what sort of a fellow *was* Parry?

8. Was he the sort you would have liked to know?

THINGS TO DO

1. Get Parry's set of British Tunes arranged for Piano Duet and practise them with a friend. They are pretty easy. (Published by Augener.)

2. Or, if you are a fairly good player, get his *Shulebrede Tunes* and practise those. (Same publishers.)

3. Ask the conductor of your local Choral Society when he is going to perform *Blest Pair of Sirens,* and promise to buy a ticket when he does so if he'll let you come to one or two rehearsals as well as the proper performance—so that you can get to know the music well.

4. Get your English teacher to set as a subject for an essay one of the Parry sayings quoted in this chapter.

A LITTLE DICTIONARY OF

BRITISH COMPOSERS

OF

OUR OWN TIMES

As I did not want to make the three parts of this book too big for you to read, the only chapters on British Composers of our own day and recent times that I have included in them are those on Sullivan (Second Book), Parry (Third Book), and Elgar (First Book). But there are many others about whom you will from time to time wish to know something, especially if you chance to hear one of their works, or, perhaps, to have one given you to learn for your Piano lesson, or to practise in your school Singing Class or Choral Society.

The list I have made below is not for reading, but for reference. Of course you can read it through if you like, and if you do, so much the better, but the idea is that this is a sort of short Biographical Dictionary to which you can turn whenever you want to know whether a modern British Composer in whose music you are interested is living or dead, or old or young, and when you want to know something about his life and what music he has written.

RALPH VAUGHAN WILLIAMS

But we have hundreds of composers, and to pick amongst them those I should include in my list has been difficult. However, in the end I think I have been able to decide on a choice that includes all the best British Composers of our own day whose work you are likely to come across. But of course a list like this will be always getting out of date, and so in every edition of this book that comes out (if other editions are called for) there will have to be changes and additions.

AUSTIN, Ernest. Born in London in 1874. On leaving school he became a business man, and only took up composition as a profession when he was over thirty. He is almost self-taught in music. His compositions include some Orchestral pieces and Choral music, a good deal of Chamber Music, a big 'narrative-poem' in twelve parts, for the Organ, called *The Pilgrim's Progress*, Songs and a great deal of Piano music, much of it especially composed for children's playing. (Frederic Austin, the singer and composer, is his brother.)

BAINTON, Edgar L. Born in 1880, and trained at the Royal College of Music. Bainton is Principal of the Conservatoire of Music at Newcastle-on-Tyne, and conductor of the Philharmonic Orchestra in that city. He has written many Orchestral works, Piano pieces, Choral works, Songs and Part Songs (many of these especially for school use), etc. During the war he was one of the little band of English musicians who were interned at Ruhleben, and who busied themselves in all kinds of musical activities there.

BANTOCK, Granville. Born in London, 1868. His father was a well-known surgeon. Granville was trained as a chemical engineer, but neglected his engineering work and gave much of his time to music. The Principal of the College where he was studying pointed this out to the father and persuaded him that the boy was meant by nature to be a musician. He was then sent to the Royal Academy of Music, where he did *not* neglect music for chemical engineering, but worked hard at his proper studies for four years, composing a great deal of music whilst still a student there.

On leaving the Academy Bantock started a musical paper, called the *New Quarterly Musical Review*, which lived for three years. Meanwhile he did a good deal of work as conductor of touring theatrical companies, including one engagement that took him round the world. In San Francisco he went one night to see the Chinese quarters, and was chased by rowdies who shot at him with revolvers, but he escaped them. When he came home he brought with him an ape, a parrot, and other animals and birds. Soon after his return he married a poetess, and he has set to music many of her poems. Then he became conductor of the band at the Tower, New Brighton, near Liverpool.

All this time he was composing all sorts of music. He conducted a Choral Society at this time, and so got experience which helped him in writing very fine pieces of Choral music in later life. When he was thirty-two Bantock was appointed Principal of the great School of Music at Birmingham, and this position he still holds. He is also Professor of Music at Birmingham University.

GRANVILLE BANTOCK

Bantock has written

1. A great many SONGS.

2. A great many PART SONGS.

3. Some TWO-PART SONGS and UNISON SONGS, for children.

4. A good many arrangements for Chorus of old FOLK-SONGS.

5. CHORAL MUSIC on a big scale, such as *Omar Khayyam* (Chorus and Orchestra), and *Vanity of Vanities* (for Chorus alone), and *Atalanta in Calydon* (Chorus alone).

6. ORCHESTRAL MUSIC, such as *Fifine at the Fair, The Pierrot of the Minute, Old English Suite,* and the great *Hebridean Symphony,* the chief musical 'subjects' of which are Hebridean Folk-tunes.

A good many of Bantock's songs and other pieces are Oriental or Scottish in their subjects.

Bantock has also edited a good deal of Elizabethan choral and instrumental music. Readers who can play the piano decently should get the keyboard works of (1) Bull, (2) Byrd, (3) Farnaby, as edited by him and published by Novello (especially get Farnaby).

BAX, Arnold, was born in London in 1883. He studied at the Royal College of Music. He has written:

1. Much ORCHESTRAL MUSIC, such as *The Garden of Fand* and *November Woods.*

2. Some good *Chamber Music.*

3. A number of Piano Pieces, including two Sonatas and many short and attractive things.

4. A very large number of SONGS.

BLISS, Arthur. Born in London in 1891. Educated at Rugby and Cambridge. A very original sort of composer who goes his own way and composes in new styles to please himself. His music includes a *Piano Quintet*, music for theatre performances of Shakespeare's *The Tempest*, some Songs, a *Rhapsody* for Tenor and Mezzo-Soprano voices, with Flute, Oboe, and String Quartet, *Rout*, a rowdy, jolly piece for Mezzo-Soprano voice, Flute, Clarinet, String Quartet, Double Bass, Harp, Side Drum, and Glockenspiel. A *Concerto* for Tenor voice, Piano, Strings, and Percussion. *Conversations* for Violin, Viola, 'Cello, Flute, Bass Flute, Oboe, Cor Anglais, and Piano (not all used at one time; one of the pieces is an unaccompanied solo for Cor Anglais: the names of the different 'Conversations' are 'The Committee', 'In the Wood', 'At the Ball', 'Soliloquy', and 'In the Tube at Oxford Circus'); *A Colour Symphony*.

You will notice in that list the unusual combinations of instruments sometimes used. This is characteristic of the composer, and so is the use of the voice *as an instrument amongst other instruments*, and without words.

BOUGHTON, Rutland. Born in 1878. He studied music at the Royal College of Music, and then went to teach singing in the Birmingham School of Music of which Bantock is Principal.

A friend of Boughton's, named Reginald Buckley, wrote the poems for a great 'cycle' of Music Dramas, on the subject of King Arthur, and Boughton started to set these to music. He then went and settled in Glastonbury (where King Arthur is supposed to have lived), and every year held musical festivals, at which he gradually brought out some of these music dramas. He hoped to build a special theatre there for the purpose, but the war spoilt all the plans and he has not yet succeeded.

Now he lives at Bristol, where he carries on his Festival School, but Festivals are still held at Glastonbury in summer time. One of his ideas is that the young people of Glastonbury shall take as much part as possible in the singing and acting and dancing of these dramas about the legends of their own district, and in the other music dramas and performances of various kinds which he gives there.

Boughton's works include:

1. STAGE WORKS—*The Immortal Hour* (this has proved very popular and has been a great deal performed in various parts of the country), *The Birth of Arthur, The Round Table, Bethlehem* (a Christmas 'Nativity Play'), *Alcestis.*

2. SONGS.

3. A little CHAMBER MUSIC, PIANO MUSIC, etc.

4. Some PART SONGS (Boughton was the first to think of the good idea of arranging British Folk-songs with Choral Variations).

BOWEN, York. Born in London, 1884. Studied for seven years at the Royal Academy of Music. His works include Orchestral Music, Chamber Music, Songs, and a large number of Piano pieces.

BRIDGE, Frank. Born at Brighton in 1879. Studied at the Royal College of Music. He is a very fine Viola player and takes part in a great deal of Chamber Music playing.

His music includes:

ORCHESTRAL WORKS. A Suite, *The Sea*, and a *Lament* for String Orchestra (to commemorate a little girl who was drowned in the *Lusitania*) with many other pieces.

CHAMBER MUSIC. A great many Quartets, etc. The pieces that would be most enjoyed by younger listeners are *An Irish Melody* (an arrangement for String Quartet of the famous and beautiful 'Londonderry Air') and three books of *Miniatures*, for Piano and Violin and 'Cello (easy to play; published by Goodwin & Tabb).

PIANO PIECES. A great many short pieces (published by Augener and Rogers).

VIOLIN PIECES. A number (published by Augener and Rogers).

SONGS. A good many, including a number of School songs (published by Rogers).

CARSE, Adam. Born at Newcastle-on-Tyne in 1878, and trained at the Royal Academy of Music. He has written two Symphonies and many other Orchestral works, several Cantatas, many Songs, a good deal of Piano Music and Violin Music (some of it especially for young people), and books of studies for the Violin and other things. The name on some of his music appears as A. von Ahn Carse. I mention the fact lest you should think this to be another composer.

COLERIDGE-TAYLOR, Samuel. Born in London, 1875; died 1912. Coleridge-Taylor's father was a West African negro, who came to England, was trained as a doctor of medicine, and practised here. He married an English girl. When Samuel was a few years old, his father, who had been unsuccessful as a doctor in England, went back to West Africa, and the mother and child had no money to live on.

But the people with whom they lodged (at Croydon, near London) were very kind to them, and so they managed to live, in a very simple way indeed, they and the kind man and woman who supported them having only three rooms amongst them.

When Samuel was five years old the man gave him a small-sized violin, and this was a great delight to him. He had a few cheap lessons in violin playing, and learnt to play easy things. One day the conductor of the Croydon Orchestra, looking out of the window, saw a curly-haired black boy playing marbles in the street, and holding in one hand a little fiddle. He went out and persuaded him to come in and play some simple violin duets with him, and was so pleased with his playing that he said he would give him music lessons for nothing, and for seven years he did so. When Coleridge-Taylor could play well enough his teacher made him play at a concert; there were ferns and plants along the front of the platform, and the boy was so small that they had

SAMUEL COLERIDGE-TAYLOR

to put a box for him to stand on or the audience would not have been able to see him.

At school Coleridge-Taylor's nickname was 'Coaley'. His teacher was very keen on singing, and taught the boys to read well at sight. He used to make 'Coaley' stand on a table and play an accompaniment to the school songs.

At the Presbyterian Church in Croydon at that time a Colonel Walters was the choirmaster, and his brother was the organist. Colonel Walters used to look out for the boys who could sing and the headmaster of the school told him of 'Coaley', who was then admitted to the choir and soon became solo boy. Colonel Walters was very good to him, and used to ask him to come to his house to learn more about music.

Colonel Walters had faith in him and believed he would some day be a great musician, and so when his schooldays were over he sent him to study at the Royal College of Music. Here he studied Violin, Piano, and Composition. His chief teacher of Composition was Stanford. By and by he gained a scholarship at the College. He was still very poor, and one of the things that the writer of his biography remembers is 'a large circular patch on his trousers.'

When Coleridge-Taylor was about twenty, the negro American poet, Paul Lawrence Dunbar (of whom you may read something when you are older) came to England, and Coleridge-Taylor and he gave some recitals together, Dunbar reciting his poems and Coleridge-Taylor having some of his compositions performed. Coleridge-Taylor was proud of being a negro, and the negroes in America (a very musical race) were proud of him. He went to America in later years to perform some of his music, and I have been told by people there that the negroes followed him about so closely that the white people could hardly get near him.

The first real recognition that Coleridge-Taylor got as a composer came through Elgar, who had been asked to compose a short orchestral piece for the Gloucester Festival. He wrote and told the Committee that he was too busy to do this and begged them to let Coleridge-Taylor do it instead, because, he said, 'he is by far the cleverest fellow amongst the young men.' The work Coleridge-Taylor wrote for Gloucester is the *Ballad in A Minor*. It was very much praised in all the papers and brought his name into notice for the first time.

Soon after this Coleridge-Taylor's choral-orchestral work *Hiawatha's Wedding-Feast* (a setting of parts of Longfellow's well-known poem) was performed at a College Concert. This was a very great success. Sullivan, then a dying man, was present, and praised the work highly. From this moment Coleridge-Taylor was famous, and here I may leave my account of his life, of which you may read a fuller account, if you wish, in the book *Samuel Coleridge-Taylor*, by W. C. Berwick Sayers (Cassell), which is out of print but can be seen in libraries.

Coleridge-Taylor died very young—at thirty-seven. He left a widow and two children, and the negro musical people of America, who were so proud of him, with help from a few other people, bought the house in which

Coleridge-Taylor had been living and gave it to them.

Coleridge-Taylor's chief works are:

CANTATAS. *Hiawatha's Wedding-Feast; The Death of Minnehaha; Hiawatha's Departure* (all these three are settings of parts of Longfellow's poem); *A Tale of Old Japan.*

ORCHESTRAL WORKS. A Symphony, a Violin Concerto, *Four Characteristic Waltzes,* and many other things.

CHAMBER MUSIC.

VIOLIN MUSIC.

SONGS.

PART SONGS.

ORGAN MUSIC.

PIANO PIECES (these include *Twenty-Four Negro Melodies, transcribed for Piano Solo*).

DALE, Benjamin. Born in London, 1885. He studied at the Royal Academy of Music, and is now a Professor of that institution. During the war he was interned by the Germans at Ruhleben. He has not published a great deal of music. Some of his pieces are for the Viola, an instrument usually neglected by composers; these include an *Introduction and Andante for Six Violas*—surely the only piece ever written for such a combination. His *Piano Sonata in D Minor* is a long and fine work which attracted a great deal of attention in 1905 when it appeared. (Readers for whom this is too difficult, and who possess a Piano-player, can make acquaintance with it as a piano-player roll.)

DAVIES, (Sir) H. Walford. Born at Oswestry in 1869. When he was twelve, Sir H. Walford Davies became a choir-boy at St. George's Chapel in Windsor Castle, and when his voice broke he became assistant to the organist, Sir Walter Parratt. Then he won a scholarship at the Royal College of Music, and at the same time that he was carrying on his studies there he held various positions as organist in London churches.

When Sir Henry was twenty-nine he obtained a very important position—that of organist of the Temple Church. This is the old church of the Knights Templar, between the Strand and the Embankment, a famous old building that is now the church of the lawyers, who since the order of the Knights Templar was destroyed in the early fourteenth century have occupied their London headquarters. The music at the Temple Church is by many people thought to be the best Church music in England—and, therefore, probably in the world. For one thing the boys are beautifully trained, and when the Psalms are sung you can follow every word, even if you have no book. There are many special musical services in the Temple Church, and when they are held the church is always crowded.

Besides holding this post Sir H. Walford Davies also holds that of Professor of Music in the University of Wales. He is a rather unusual sort of professor, for he does not merely give lectures to students in the University and hold examinations, but visits all parts of Wales in his car, trying to make the country more musical by showing schoolmasters how to do better music teaching, by getting up concerts and so forth.

During the war Sir H. Walford Davies was a major in the Air Force, and his duties were to teach airmen how to keep themselves happy with singing and other music.

Sir H. Walford Davies's works include the Cantata *Everyman* and other fine choral pieces, a *Peter Pan* String Quartet, a good many *Nursery Rhymes* skilfully and humorously arranged for Vocal Quartet, a Children's Cantata, *Humpty Dumpy*, *A Solemn Melody* for Organ and Orchestra (you can get this as a Gramophone record), a number of Songs (some of them very popular, such as *The Jocund Dance* and *When Childher Play*). And he has edited a good book of songs for us all to sing when we gather together—*The Fellowship Song Book* (Curwen).

DELIUS, Frederick. Born at Bradford in 1863. His parents were German. When he was nineteen or twenty he went to Florida and became an orange-planter. As a keen musician, however, he spent all his spare time in studying music. After some time he left America and went to Germany to study at the great Leipzig School of Music (or 'Conservatory'). After this he lived mostly in France and spent his time in composing pieces which gradually made his name well known. Once he wrote some music for a Norwegian play, and when the play was performed in Christiania a man in the audience, who did not like the way he had brought the Norwegian National Anthem into his music, fired several revolver shots at him, but, fortunately, missed him.

Some of Delius's chief works are these:

OPERAS. *Koanga, A Village Romeo and Juliet, Fennimore and Gerda.*

ORCHESTRAL PIECES. *Paris, Brigg Fair, On Hearing the First Cuckoo in Spring* (this is a very favourite piece), *Summer Night on the River,* a *Piano Concerto,* a *Violin Concerto,* a *Double Concerto for Violin and 'Cello, Appalachia* (this ends with a chorus).

CHORAL PIECES. *Sea Drift, A Mass of Life, a Requiem,* and *The Song of the High Hills.*

There are also some pieces of Chamber Music and some Songs.

DUNHILL, Thomas. Born in London, 1877. He was trained at the Royal College of Music, and then became an assistant music-master at Eton. He is now a Professor at the Royal College of Music. Some years ago he gave a great many concerts in order to make known the works of the younger British composers.

Dunhill's works include some Orchestral Music and a good deal of Chamber Music, some Piano pieces (including a good many easy ones, specially written for children), a large number of Songs (including songs for school singing classes), and a very useful book about Chamber Music.

FARJEON, Harry. Born (of British parents) in New Jersey (U.S.A.) in 1878. His father was a well-known novelist. Farjeon was trained at the Royal Academy of Music. He has composed a great deal of music of all kinds, including Singing Games for Children (Augener), much Piano music (some of it for children), Songs, Orchestral pieces, etc.

GARDINER, H. Balfour. Born in London, 1877. He was educated at Charterhouse School and Oxford, and then went to Germany to study music. Afterwards he became a music master at Winchester College, but has now retired from work of this sort and lives quietly in the country. Being a well-to-do and generous man he has frequently held concerts specially in order that the younger British composers should have a chance of performing their Orchestral works.

Balfour Gardiner has written a good deal of attractive Orchestral Music (you can get his jolly *Shepherd Fennel's Dance* as a Gramophone record), some Songs and a good many Part Songs, and very popular and good Piano pieces, such as the *Preludes* and a *Noël* (with a Christmas tune in it).

GERMAN, Edward. Born at Whitchurch in Shropshire in 1862. When he was a youth he got up a village band, which used to perform at concerts in the countryside around where he lived. He also taught himself to play the Violin. Then he went to study at the Royal Academy of Music, and after this he played the Violin in Orchestras in theatres and concert-halls for a time. Then he was made musical director of a London theatre, and began composing music for some of the plays. The music he wrote for Shakespeare's 'Henry VIII' made him very popular (you can get some of it for Piano or for Gramophone). His light opera *Merrie England* was a great success; he has also written a good many other light operas, as well as Symphonies and Suites and a *Welsh Rhapsody*, Songs and Part Songs.

Nearly all his music is light and pleasing rather than serious and solemn.

GOOSSENS, Eugene. Born in London in 1893. His grandfather was a Belgian and also called Eugene; he was a well-known opera conductor. His father is also called Eugene, and is also a well-known opera conductor. Eugene III studied at the Bruges Conservatory of Music, at the Liverpool College of Music, and at the Royal College of Music. He became a very good violinist and played for some years in the Queen's Hall Orchestra. Then he took up conducting and became assistant conductor to Sir Thomas Beecham. In 1921 he founded an Orchestra of his own, which is sometimes heard in London. He is also one of the conductors of the National Opera Company. Goossens's works include some very good Chamber Music, some Songs and Piano pieces, and some Orchestral pieces. His later music is very modern in style.

GRAINGER, Percy Aldridge. Born in Melbourne in Australia in 1882. His mother was his first teacher, but he afterwards travelled in Germany and had lessons from some famous pianists there. When he was eighteen he came to England and played at many concerts. In Norway he became a very great friend of Grieg, who, when he was dying, asked the Committee of the Leeds Festival to let Grainger play the Grieg Concerto, as he was himself too ill to be able to keep his promise to do so: Grieg died a few weeks before the Festival took place. Grieg's interest in Norwegian Folk-tunes made Grainger interested in British Folk-tunes, and he has written some very jolly pieces made out of such tunes. For instance there is a String Quartet called *Molly on the Shore*, which is made out of Irish Reels, and a piece (to be had either for Orchestra or Piano) called *Shepherd's Hey*, made out of English Folk-dance tunes, and there are some Part Songs which are 'arrangements' of Folk-songs. During the war Grainger became a citizen of the United States.

HOLBROOKE, Joseph. Born in London in 1878. He was trained at the Royal Academy of Music. He has written some Music Dramas, a good many works for Chorus and Orchestra, a great deal of Orchestral Music (you can get his *Three Blind Mice* as a very effective Gramophone record), a lot of Chamber Music, and many Songs, Part Songs, and Piano pieces. The list of his compositions is, indeed, enormous.

HOLST, Gustav. Born in Cheltenham in 1874. (His original name was 'von Holst', but he dropped the 'von' when he went out during the war to do musical work amongst the soldiers in Salonica and Constantinople. He is not German by descent, as people have thought, but one of his four great-grandfathers, a long time ago, came to England from the Baltic provinces of Russia.)

Holst's father was a Pianist and Organist. He sent his son to the Royal College of Music, where he became a pupil of Stanford. On leaving the College, Holst joined the Carl Rosa Opera Company as a trombonist and also as a sort of sub-conductor; then he joined the Scottish

GUSTAV HOLST

Orchestra, and afterwards he became Musical Director at Morley College (a College for working men and women, just a little south of the Thames at Waterloo Bridge). Here he does splendid work conducting a Choir and Orchestra and teaching the students to compose. All his pupils there like him very much because he throws himself heartily into the work and makes them work heartily too. He has made Morley College a notable centre for the study and performance of the works of Byrd and Purcell. He is also Music Master at the great St. Paul's School for Girls, at Hammersmith, and a Professor of Composition at the Royal College of Music.

Holst's works include:

OPERAS, such as *Savitri* and *The Perfect Fool*.

ORCHESTRAL PIECES, especially *The Planets*, which has been performed in many parts of the world.

CHORAL MUSIC, such as the *Hymn of Jesus* and *Ode to Death*.

MILITARY BAND MUSIC. Most people neglect the military band, but Holst does not, and this is a good thing, for far more people hear Military Band Music than hear Orchestral Music, and the music written for such bands ought, therefore, always to be good.

SONGS AND PART SONGS—quite a lot (some of the later solo songs have accompaniment for a Violin only, which is a new idea).

HOWELLS, Herbert. Born at Lydney in Gloucestershire, 1892. Studied at the Royal College of Music, of which he is now a Professor. His works include a Piano Concerto, a piece for Orchestra and Chorus, *Sine Nomine*, Orchestral pieces, *Lady Audrey's Suite* for String Quartet, and other Chamber Music, and some Piano and Organ pieces.

IRELAND, John. Born at Bowdon, Cheshire, in 1879. His father was editor of the *Manchester Examiner*. He was trained at the Royal College of Music. His works include a fine (and very difficult) Piano Sonata and many smaller pieces, such as *The Island Spell* (one of a set of pieces called 'Decorations'), *Chelsea Reach, Ragamuffin,* and *Soho Forenoons,* a good deal of Chamber Music, Orchestral pieces, *The Forgotten Rite,* and *Rhapsody*, and a good many Songs, including some for school use (Year Book Press, Curwen, Stainer & Bell).

MACKENZIE, (Sir) Alexander Campbell. Born at Edinburgh in 1847, into a very musical family; his great-grandfather played in a Militia Band, his grandfather was a Violinist, and so was his father, who was leader of the Orchestra in an Edinburgh theatre.

When the future Sir Alexander was only ten he was sent to Germany to study music. Here he learnt to play the Violin and to compose, and played in an orchestra. When he came back, at the age of fifteen, he had forgotten his native language and had to learn it again. He then won a scholarship at the Royal Academy of Music, where he stayed until he was eighteen. Meantime he earned some money and got further experience by playing in various theatre orchestras in London. When he left the Academy he was quickly recognized as a fine Solo Violinist. He settled for a time in Scotland and

SIR ALEXANDER MACKENZIE

conducted a Choral Society, acted as Precentor in an Edinburgh church, gave concerts, and composed.

By and by Mackenzie felt he was working too hard at these activities and not composing enough, so he went and settled in Italy (at Florence). There he stayed ten years, though of course he often visited London and performed there, or superintended the performance there of his compositions. When he was forty-one he was appointed Principal of the Royal Academy of Music, his own old school, and there, at the time this book is written, he still remains.

His works include:

OPERAS. *The Cricket on the Hearth*, and five or six more.

ORATORIOS AND CANTATAS. *The Rose of Sharon* and a dozen more.

ORCHESTRAL PIECES. *Britannia Overture* (you can get this as a Gramophone record), *London Day by Day* Suite, a *Violin Concerto*, a *Piano Concerto* and a very large number of other pieces.

SONGS AND PART SONGS. A great many (including some school songs).

PIANO PIECES AND VIOLIN PIECES. A fair number.

McEWEN, John B. Born at Harwich in Roxburgh-shire in 1868. He is a Professor at the Royal Academy of Music. His works include Symphonies, three or four Overtures (including *Grey Galloway*) and some Suites and Scottish Dances, a Concerto for Violin and another for Piano, a number of Cantatas, Chamber Music (a little of which you can get in the form of Gramophone records), Songs and Piano Music, and some theoretical books.

O'NEILL, Norman. Born in London, 1875. He has written many Orchestral pieces (and, especially, 'incidental music' for plays), Songs, Piano pieces, etc.

QUILTER, Roger. Born at Brighton, 1877. Educated at Eton, and musically trained in Germany. His Orchestral compositions include a very jolly *Children's Overture*, on nursery rhyme tunes (this can be got as Piano solo or duet, published by Rogers, or as a Gramophone record). He has also written very many Songs, and some Piano music and Violin music.

ROOTHAM, Cyril Bradley. Born in 1875 at Bristol, where his father was a very well-known musician. Educated at Clifton and at Cambridge, and trained in music at the Royal College of Music. He is a Doctor of Music, and is organist of St. John's College, Cambridge, and conductor of the University Musical Society. His music includes an Opera, *The Two Sisters*, many Orchestral and Choral pieces, Chamber Music, Songs, Part Songs, etc.

ROWLEY, Alec. Born in London in 1892. He has composed a great deal of Piano Music (much of it especially for children), and Organ Music, and some Songs (some for school use), and has edited some Old English Harpsichord Music, so that it may be played by Piano pupils.

SCOTT, Cyril. Born at Oxton in Cheshire in 1879. He was educated in Germany. His compositions include much Orchestral and Chamber Music, a very large number of Songs and much Piano Music, some of it suitable for moderately advanced piano pupils (Elkin). He has also published a volume of Poems and a book called *The Philosophy of Modernism in its Connection with Music.*

SHAW, Geoffrey Turton. Born in London, 1879. He was a choir-boy of St. Paul's Cathedral. He has composed a good deal of Church Music, and many School Songs, and is co-editor, with his brother Martin (see below), of several volumes of the *Motherland Song Book*. He is Inspector of Music to the Board of Education.

SHAW, Martin. Born in London, 1876. He studied at the Royal College of Music, and then held various positions as Organist and also as a theatrical conductor. He is now in charge of the music at St. Martin's Church, Trafalgar Square, and at the Guildhouse, Eccleston Square. He has composed various musical plays, such as *The Cockyolly Bird* and *Brer Rabbit and Mr. Fox*, and written the music for the children's Shakespeare plays, *The Pedlar* (from 'The Winter's Tale') and *The Fools and the Fairies* (from 'A Midsummer-Night's Dream'). He is the compiler and editor of *Songs of Britain*. His brother is Mr. Geoffrey Shaw, above mentioned.

SMYTH, (Dame) Ethel. Born at Sidcup, 1858; daughter of an artillery General. She studied music in Germany, and her earlier compositions were all performed there. She was a friend of Brahms. For some time her works were very little heard in her own country,

DAME ETHEL SMYTH

but now they are rather more frequently performed. She has written a number of Operas, which have been performed at various German Opera Houses and at the great Metropolitan Opera House in New York and at Covent Garden Opera House in London. Her comic opera *The Boatswain's Mate*, which is founded on a short story by W. W. Jacobs, has often been performed in England.

In 1910 Durham University made Miss Smyth a Doctor of Music, as a recognition of her work; in 1911 she was imprisoned for two months as a Women's Suffrage agitator; during the war she did radio work in France, and in 1920 the King, in recognition of her musical work, conferred on her the feminine equivalent of knighthood, so that she is now known as Dame Ethel Smyth. She has written a large and very interesting two-volume book about her life, called *Impressions that Remained*; and another shorter book, called *Streaks of Life*.

SOMERVELL, Arthur. Born at Windermere, 1863. He was educated at Uppingham and King's College, Cambridge, and trained in music in Berlin and at the Royal College of Music. Dr. Somervell has composed a large number of Orchestral and Choral works, Operettas, Songs, Part Songs, Piano pieces, etc., and also written many educational works. He is H.M. Chief Inspector of Music in Schools and Training Colleges, and has been the means of securing greater attention for British Folk-songs in British schools.

SIR CHARLES VILLIERS STANFORD

STANFORD, (Sir) Charles Villiers. Born at Dublin in 1852. His father was a good amateur singer and encouraged his musical bent.

At eight years old Charles composed a march, which a year or two later was performed in the pantomime, 'Puss in Boots,' at Dublin. When he was eighteen he went to Cambridge as a 'choral scholar' at Queen's College, that is to say, he had a scholarship given him in return for his services as a singer in the college choir. Later he was made organist of Trinity College, Cambridge, and from there he took his degree with Classical Honours. He became conductor of the Cambridge University Musical Society.

Then for a time he went to Germany to study, and when he came back he composed the music to one of Tennyson's plays, which was performed at the Lyceum Theatre in London. After this he composed a great many symphonies and choral works, which were given at the great Festivals and at Concerts in London. When he was thirty-five he was appointed Professor of Music at Cambridge University, and later he also became Professor of Composition at the Royal College of Music. King Edward knighted him in 1901.

Sir Charles Stanford's works include:

OPERAS. *Shamus O' Brien, The Critic, The Travelling Companion,* and six others.

CHORAL MUSIC. T*he Revenge, Phaudrig Crohoore, Requiem, The Last Post, Songs of the Sea, Songs of the Fleet,* and a great many other works.

ORCHESTRAL WORKS. Seven Symphonies, five Irish Rhapsodies, eight Concertos, and many other works.

CHAMBER MUSIC. Many Trios, Quartets, and Quintets.

SONGS AND PART SONGS, PIANO PIECES, VIOLIN PIECES, ORGAN PIECES, etc.

BOOKS. A very fine volume on Composition and two or three volumes of Reminiscences, etc.

As might be expected, much of Sir Charles Stanford's music has a flavour of Irish Folk-music; also, he has edited volumes of Irish Folk-songs.

SWINSTEAD, Felix. Born in London in 1889. Trained at the Royal Academy of Music. Swinstead has written a great many Piano pieces (some of them especially for young players) and also some Songs and Orchestral pieces.

WALKER, Ernest. Born at Bombay in 1870 and educated at Balliol College, Oxford, where since 1900 he has been Director of Music. Here he conducts a remarkable series of concerts on Sunday evenings in term time, to which members of the University may come, and he also helps to carry on the University Musical Club and Union, which holds weekly concerts. He is a Doctor of Music of Oxford University, has been 'Choragus' of the University, and is now University Lecturer in Harmony. He is also an Inspector in Music for the Girls' Public Day School Trust. His compositions include Songs, Choral Music, Chamber Music, etc.

WALLACE, William. Born at Greenock in 1860. His father was a surgeon and he became one too. Then he came to London, and studied for a short time at the Royal Academy of Music. During the war he served as an army doctor, and he still takes a great interest in hospital work. He has composed a number of fine Orchestral works, including a Symphonic Poem on William Wallace (his ancestor), and another, *Villon* (this can be obtained as a Pianola roll). He has also written many Songs, some of which, such as *Son of Mine* and the *Freebooters' Songs*, have become popular. He has also written two learned books on the working of the mind of the musician. They are called *The Threshold of Music* and *The Musical Faculty.*

WHITTAKER, William Gillies. Born at Newcastle-on-Tyne in 1876. At first he was a schoolmaster, and this taught him how to train children; then he was placed in charge of the music at Armstrong College, Newcastle, and there he had to train teachers. He also conducted several Choral Societies, and learnt to train amateur singers, and was Organist at various churches at various times. He now conducts the Bach Choir at Newcastle. He has composed a number of Songs, and arranged in a very effective way for choral singing many North Country Folk-songs, and he has compiled and edited a fine collection of Northumbrian Folk-songs, for use in schools and elsewhere. He has also published a very useful book for young pianists called *Time Studies* (Curwen). He is a Doctor of Music of Durham University.

WILLIAMS, Ralph Vaughan. Born at Down Ampney in Gloucestershire in 1872. He was educated at Cheltenham and Cambridge and trained in music at the Royal College of Music, and in Germany and France. He also pursued his musical studies amongst the village people of England, collecting their Folk-songs. This made him very fond of the 'Modes' (or old scales in which many of the Folk-songs are composed), and so his music is very often 'Modal', that is to say, it is often in one or other of these old scales. Dr. Vaughan Williams is a Professor of Composition at the Royal College of Music, and Conductor of the London Bach Choir. At the beginning of the war he enlisted as a private in the R.A.M.C. and served to the end of the war in various fields.

His works include:

OPERA. *Hugh the Drover* (Ballad Opera, i.e. an opera made out of old folk-tunes, interspersed with spoken dialogue).

ORCHESTRAL PIECES. *A London Symphony* (in this the composer gives us the spirit of London in various aspects); *Pastoral Symphony* (in this he gives us the spirit of the country as he feels it); Suite, *The Wasps; Fantasia on a Theme of Thomas Tallis* (for Strings alone), three *Norfolk Rhapsodies* and other works.

WORKS FOR CHORUS AND ORCHESTRA. *A Sea Symphony; Five Mystical Songs; Fantasia on Christmas Carols; Toward the Unknown Region.*

SONGS. A good many, including some Song Cycles (that is songs meant to be performed as sets); one of these is *On Wenlock Edge*. (Dr. Vaughan Williams has also edited and published books of Folk-songs and Sea Songs. One book of Folk-songs is arranged specially for schools; it is published by Novello.)

PART SONGS. A good many (and also some Folk-songs arranged for Men's Voices).

CHAMBER MUSIC. A String Quartet and a String Quintet.

ORGAN PIECES. Three Preludes founded on Welsh Hymns and Melodies. Dr. Vaughan Williams has written an interesting pamphlet on *Folk-songs* (Joseph Williams), has edited some of Purcell's music, and has also edited *The English Hymnal*.

WILLIAMS, John Gerrard. Born at Catford in 1888. Gerrard Williams was trained as an architect, but preferred music. He has written two String Quartets and some other Chamber Music, a number of Songs and Part Songs, a little Orchestral Music, and some Piano Music. When he gave up Architecture he at once started composing very actively indeed, and became well known in an unusually short time.